OUR BHOYS HAVE WON THE CUP!

30 Times Scottish Cup Winners

OUR BHOYS HAVE WON THE CUP!

30 TIMES SCOTTISH CUP WINNERS

David Potter

Foreword by Paul McStay

JOHN DONALD PUBLISHERS LTD
EDINBURGH

ISBN 0 85976 454 0

A catalogue record of this book is available from the British Library.

The author and the publishers are indebted
to *The Sunday Post* (D.C. Thomson & Co. Ltd., Dundee)
for permission to reproduce the illustrations on pages 86, 99, 105,
114, 124, 130, 141, 143, 148, 165, 179, 185, 190 and 192

Phototypeset by WestKey Ltd, Falmouth, Cornwall.
Printed in Great Britain by Bell & Bain Ltd., Glasgow.

FOREWORD

It gives me great pleasure to write the foreword to the book *Our Bhoys Have Won The Cup*. I, of course, was privileged to receive the Scottish Cup on May 27th 1995 from H.R.H. the Duchess of Kent on behalf of our club, and it was a proud moment for myself and my family. To have won the Scottish Cup 30 times (more than anyone else) is a magnificent achievement, and I am delighted that my family have been involved in so many of the Celtic successes in this tournament.

I fully intend that this will not be the last time that I shall lift the trophy, and I feel that, with the players we now have, there will be a great deal more silverware to come our way. Celtic is all about pride and history, and it is up to us all, players and supporters, to do his or her bit to maintain the proud traditions of our club in the Scottish Cup and other tournaments as well.

In the meantime, enjoy the book, and I trust that the author will very soon be drafting the 31st chapter of this ongoing story.

Paul McStay

ACKNOWLEDGEMENTS

My grateful thanks go

To all who have encouraged me, in particular three Celticologists called Eugene McBride, Tom Campbell and George Sheridan whose fanzine *The Celt* has been a constant source of wonder.

To Andrew Smith of *The Celtic View* for photographs and other help

To my family who have indulged me in my passion

and

To my late father, Angus Potter, who fed me McGrory with my porridge, Gallagher with my tatties and McInally with my pudding, and on whose heart was written 'Celtic' in such large letters that there was little room for rancour or hatred of anyone else.

Portraits of former Celtic Greats on the front cover:
Top left, Jimmy McStay; *Bottom left*, Jimmy McGrory; *Top right*, James Young; *Bottom right*, James Quinn.

CONTENTS

—1—
MORE THAN FOOTBALL AT STAKE
1892

These were heady days in the East End of Glasgow in 1892. The infant Celtic team, not yet four years old, was here to stay in a big way. The Glasgow Cup had been won the last two years, great crowds were being attracted to see the team.

The Irish had been arriving in Glasgow since the 1840's. The big Potato Famine was in 1846, and the callous indifference of Westminster had forced thousands away to the new world or to Liverpool and Glasgow. Those who arrived in Glasgow did not immediately find a land flowing with milk and honey, but there were jobs because of the Industrial Revolution, and life was marginally more tolerable than back home.

But, thanks to the vision of men like John Glass, Willie Maley and James Kelly, who built the great Celtic Football Club, the Irish in Glasgow had a focus for their aspirations.

In early 1892 a new stadium was being built. It would be the best in the world, a symbol of Irish Life in Scotland, and it would be the rallying point of the Glasgow Irishmen. So ran the rhetoric, but the reality was that the club was being forced out of its existing home by the same sort of evil landlords that had caused them to leave their native land in the first place. Fortunately a site became available very close to the first Celtic Park, and there was no great uprooting. New Celtic Park would still be in the Irish heartland of Glasgow's East End.

On the playing side, the club were doing well. As well as the retaining of the Glasgow Cup (a brilliant thrashing of hapless Clyde in torrential rain at Cathkin Park to the tune of 7-1), the club were now in the Final of the Scottish Cup. The Scottish Cup had been in existence for almost 20 years and was rightly considered to be the 'Blue Riband' of the Scottish football scene. A victory in this competition (they had already reached the Final in 1889) would clearly signify that the Celtic were here to stay.

Yet there were other issues at stake as well. The opponents would be Queen's Park, snooty, aristocratic, amateur, gentlemanly Queen's Park whose players also indulged in pursuits like cricket and rowing. Queen's had disdained to join the Scottish League, founded in 1890, on the grounds that it would open the door to professionalism, something that polite Victorian genteel society looked on with horror. (They still found it hard to accept those whose livelihoods were earned by trade and commerce!)

The whole issue of professionalism is not entirely dissimilar to recent Rugby Union and Olympic Games controversies on the same issue. Everyone knows that it goes on, but the authorites pretend that it doesn't. Professionalism wasn't officially legalised until 1893, but Celtic did not make any great pretence about it. How else could they lure James Kelly from Renton and Sandy McMahon from Hibernian, thereby incidentally ruining both these clubs? They would even argue that this was at least in part what Celtic were about—to give these talented young Irishmen (albeit second generation) a good living.

There was also the issue of social class. In the 1860's and 1870's, football was very much a bourgeois pursuit. Rangers, for example, were founded in 1873, reputedly, by young men from a Rowing club. Yet in the 1880's with Britain's Industrial Revolution now well developed and the population urbanised, the game was spreading down the social scale. All you really need for the game is a ball, and as Saturday was slowly being recognised as a half day by reluctant employers, the working class were taking to the game in droves, so much so that Brother Walfrid and his friends saw football as the obvious way to feed their poor at the famous meeting in November 1887.

There were thus many issues at stake at Ibrox Park on March 12th 1892 when the 19th Scottish Cup Final took place. Queen's Park had won 9 of the previous 18 Cups, so it was the established team against the upstarts.

Glasgow had endured a heavy fall of snow off and on for three days previous to the game, but March always brings swift thaws and there was no further snow falling on that Saturday. Yet there was still some snow about and the pitch was slippy and hazardous.

Throwing snowballs was also a way in which the crowd could amuse themselves, and it was a huge crowd. Some think that it was as high as 40,000, a huge crowd for the 1890's and there is certainly a great deal of evidence that Scotland considered this to be the match of the century. Thirteen special trains and many ordinary ones arrived at

Ibrox Stadium disgorging passengers, and from mid-day onwards, onlookers were amazed at the trek of the Irish from their own part of the city to the slightly more prosperous shipbuilding heartlands of Govan.

The game was scheduled to start at 4.00 p.m., but the ground was packed by 2.00 p.m and by 3.00 p.m the gates had to be closed, leaving thousands of disappointed fans outside. 100 policemen (4 on horseback) under Captain Hamilton were not enough for this massive support, all of them apparently shouting for Celtic, but they did their best, and it must be said that the crowd, although huge and clearly too large even for magnificent Ibrox Park, were well behaved and sober.

The crowd had already encroached onto the playing area more than once by the time that the teams ran out. Celtic came out first to a tremendous cheer and unfurling of banners, as distinct from the polite applause that greeted Queen's Park. The teams were;

Celtic: Cullen; Reynolds, Doyle; Maley, Kelly, Dowds; McCallum, Brady, Madden, McMahon, Campbell.

Queen's Park: Baird; Sillars, Smellie; Gillespie, Robertson, Stewart; Gullilland, Waddell, Hamilton, Lambie, Sellar.

The referee was Mr George Sneddon, who was also the President of the S.F.A. That this was the cream of Scottish football was proved by the fact that everyone on the Queen's Park side either were Internationalists or would become so in the near future and that Celtic had seven in that category.

But good football would not be on show that day, for the footing was treacherous as the thaw had been a rapid one, and even the mighty Celtic left wing of McMahon and Campbell were finding things difficult. A more serious problem was caused by the crowd because serious crushing was leading to frequent stoppages as the crowd surged forward breaking the ropes and the flimsy barriers that attempted to contain them.

After one prolonged stoppage in the first half, both linesmen (each side provided one linesman in these days, rather like in modern junior and amateur football) and captains approached Mr.Sneddon and said that they thought it was all so unfair that a replay might be a better idea. Mr Sneddon agreed, but could not make a definitive decision there. Accordingly the game proceeded.

By the second half, conditions had clearly improved and the crowd had become more settled thanks to the sterling efforts of the Glasgow

Police. Willie Maley who played in the game gives us an account of the only goal of the game which occurred on the hour mark.

Madden contributed to this success by shooting strongly. Baird with a great leap stopped the shot but fell, and the ball going out to Campbell, the outside left had no difficulty in scoring.

Queen's Park then apparently equalized, but Mr Sneddon had already blown for offside.

Full time came to great rejoicing among the Celtic ranks. 'The heavens were rent with shouts of accalamation that greeted the performance' says the *Scottish Referee*, but it was all in vain, for the S.F.A. were to meet and decide on a replay. It is perhaps a blessing that the crowd, in the absence of a public address system and any other way of conveying information, went home rejoicing, convinced that their Celtic had won the Cup, for although they had been very well behaved, they might have turned nasty if thwarted.

The game was to be replayed at Ibrox on April 9th to allow Rangers time to make more ground improvements. The price of admission was to be increased to deter such a large crowd. Cynically, Celtic went along with that idea, although it would be their supporters who would be more likely to be penalised by the move.

That the East End was now on a high was proved by the events at New Celtic Park a week later. The ground was as yet unready for play, but the Committee invited the Irish politician Michael Davitt to plant a few shamrocks on the centre spot. A crowd of 10,000 were present to see this ceremony (Davitt constantly referring to the team as 'the Keltic') and then they all trooped across to old Celtic Park to watch Davitt take the first kick in the League game against Clyde. Presumably the Irishman was somewhat unimpressed by the subsequent game for it was a dull 0-0 draw. He might have seen a better game in Belfast that day where Scotland were beating Ireland 3-2.

But more evidence of Celtic's incipient hegemony in the Scottish game came on April 2nd when three Celts were chosen to play for Scotland against England. (Curiously Dowds who had played against Ireland and who did not have a bad game according to the Press was dropped) James Kelly was of course an established International, but first caps were given to Dan Doyle and Sandy McMahon. Dan was played out of position at right back, rather than left, and Scotland went down 4-1 to a fast English team.

On April 9th, 23,000, about half the previous attendance rolled up

4

Top row: Jerry Reynolds, Joe Cullen, Dan Doyle. Second row: W. Maley, J. Kelly, P. Gallagher. Third row: N. McCallum, Alex Brady, J. Madden, Alex McMahon, J. Campbell.

to Ibrox to see the replayed Cup Final. The decision to double the admission charges was rescinded the day before but not made sufficiently public to attract the crowd. The basic charge would be 1/- but admisssion to some parts of the ground would cost more. Effectively this meant that Queen's Park's middle class support would be in the Stands and Pavilion and the Celtic fans would be standing. It was an early form of crowd segregation. Girls were seen collecting money for the East End Weavers Strike Fund to the disapproval, one feels, of those who were keen on Victorian values.

Both teams were compelled to make changes for the Replay. Queen's Park lost the services of Bob Smellie, their left back, drafted left winger Sellar to the defence and brought James Lambie into the left wing position. James Lambie however played under the pseudonym of Scott, presumably to distinguish himself from his brother William Lambie who was playing at inside left. Celtic had to drop Johnnie Madden, who had been struggling against an injury in the first game, put utility man Peter Dowds in the centre and at left half introduced the hard working Paddy Gallagher who seems to have been a Victorian Peter Grant in his love for the green and white vertical striped jersey.

The crowd was comfortable this time, and the ground conditions were better although there was a strong wind. Queen's played with the wind and at half time led by a well taken Waddell goal. But thereupon began one of the greatest Celtic traditions of them all - the ability to fight back in a Scottish Cup Final.

The wind was now behind them in the second half and the mighty left wing of McMahon and Campbell roared into action. Within five minutes Johnnie Campbell had equalized in a goalmouth scramble, then immediately afterwards took a delightful through pass from Sandy McMahon to put Celts in the lead and unleash an orgy of celebration behind the goals. Maley then describes Celtic's third goal.

McMahon, indulging in one of those mazy runs - head down, arms outstretched - simply walking through the amateurs' defence to register the third goal.

The amateurs were indeed bewildered by all this, conceded an own goal to make it four and then lost a fifth when Sandy McMahon rose like a bird to the first of the many Celtic Scottish Cup Final headers, setting a precedent for McGrory and McNeill.

The cup would be presented by the referee and S.F.A. President Mr Sneddon in the Alexandra Hotel, Bath Street following a dignified banquet attended by both teams. But by this time, news had been relayed all over Scotland with Celtic strongholds like Coatbridge, Leith and Dundee holding street parties, but the greatest celebrations took place in the East End itself. 'Our bhoys have won the Cup' was the cry and the *Scottish Referee* says

Bands! You ought to have seen them. They perambulated all the district until well on in the evening, and with the aid of a liberal use of party music helped to make things hum along merrily. Truly the East End was a perfect turmoil until the very early hours of the Sunday, and many of the crowd won't be able to get over the rejoicing racket for days to come.

In the midst of all the sore heads and feelings of crapulence the next morning, however, there was something else. It was self belief, self respect and a new confidence in the Irish ability to settle in Scotland and make life a success. From now on their football team would be their banner; they would revel in its success and cry in its failure; there would be no real need for violence or criminality to win recognition. Their bhoys had indeed won the Cup.

Nor was this the end of it this season. Celtic finished second to Dumbarton in the League, only defeats by Leith Athletic and Dumbarton themselves in the month of April preventing them from winning their first ever Championship, and then on June 1st Celtic defeated Rangers 2-0 thanks to two Johnny Campbell goals to win the Glasgow Charity Cup.

—2—

CELTS TWO TOO GOOD
1899

The phenomenal success of Celtic in the first ten years of their existence guaranteed them support, stability and finance. By 1899, they had won the Scottish League and the Glasgow Cup four times each, and the Glasgow Charity Cup five times. They had transformed the Scottish scene, and although there was still a certain amount of prejudice against the green and white vertical stripes in the ranks of the Scottish establishment, most people were being won over to respect, at least, the brand of exciting attacking football that had been their hallmark. Proof of this can be seen in the amount of Junior and Juvenile 'Celtic' teams that were springing up all over Scotland.

Yet there seemed to be a bit of a jinx as regards the game's ultimate award - the Scottish Cup. They had lost in the Final of 1893 and 1894, gone down to the infant Dundee team at Carolina Port in 1895 and had disappointed thereafter with one particular result threatening to become an albatross around the neck, and this was the fiasco at Dunterlie Park, Barrhead on January 9th 1897 when Celtic went down to lowly Arthurlie, a result that was still being cast up to Celtic fans after the Second World War.

There were some strange happenings to explain it all. McArthur the goalkeeper was injured, as indeed was goalscorer Sandy McMahon. Curiously, the famous Dan Doyle, the Internationalist left back, simply did not turn up. Nor did Patrick Gilhooly, the talented winger. Meechan, Battles and Divers were all serving a club suspension for refusing to play in an earlier game against Hibs in view of Press criticism, and it was a makeshift Celtic team who took the field, the club being forced to include goalkeeper Joe Cullen and forward James Blessington who were in disgrace, having each been fined 3 guineas for creating a disturbance in Dunlop Street on New Year's Day.

In addition Dunterlie Park itself was a little less than perfect. It was commonly known as 'The Humph' and James Handley in 'The Celtic Story' describes it thus

In addition to a variety of heights and hollows the ground rose to such a hump at one corner that a player taking a corner kick had much the same view of the goalmouth as a person leaning from a second-storey window would have of the scene below.

Dunterlie Park is no longer with us for us to check it out, but anyone who has visited the ground of the famous Carlton Cricket Club at Grange Loan, Edinburgh, will get some idea of what Handley means. There may be however, one suspects, an element of exaggeration in all this to excuse Celtic's dreadful performance, but Arthurlie carved their own piece of Scottish Cup history by beating Celtic 4-2.

The consequences were swift and far-reaching. The energetic Willie Maley was appointed Secretary (and *de facto* manager) from April 3rd 1897 and players were bought from England. Johnnie Campbell the hero of 1892 returned, having been 'pining for home' from Aston Villa who also supplied James Welford. From Everton came Davie Storrier and John (Jack) Bell. In the meantime those who had disgraced the cause at Barrhead were gradually being replaced, and by season 1898-99 Celtic had a fine team once again. The League had been won for the fourth time in 1898, but it was the return of the Scottish Cup that the faithful were seeking with ever more alacrity.

Season 1898-9 got off to a bad start for Celtic, and the month of September saw some of the worst performances in the short history of the team. This effectively ruled out any realistic chance of winning the League, but by the time that the Scottish Cup came round after the New Year, the team had rallied and the imports from English teams were beginning to prove their value.

Both full backs did something remarkably rare in Scottish football. They both played cricket in the summer. Left back Davie Storrier starred for his native Arbroath almost until his death in 1910, but more famous was right back Jim Welford. Bald and very Victorian looking with a moustache, Jim often gave the impression of being slow and cumbersome, yet he was fit and quick to the tackle. In 1895 he had won with Aston Villa the F.A.Cup then had a season playing First Class Cricket with Warwickshire, the highlight being a sparkling innings of 118 against Leicestershire in May. When he died in 1945, he was considered important enough to rate a mention in *Wisden*, which annoyingly however does not mention his Celtic career nor his remarkable achievement of being, until very recently, the only Englishman to have won both an F.A. Cup winner's medal and a Scottish one.

Jim must have felt at home on February 18th 1899 in the Quarter

Final of the Scottish Cup when 'bad light stopped play'. Such a thing is a common source of frustration to a cricketer but is almost unknown in football, except when floodlights fail. It was a dull day at Hampden and the game possibly should have kicked off a little earlier than 3.30, but Celtic were comfortably leading 4-2 over Queen's Park when the referee abandoned the game with only a few minutes remaining.

The suspicion of the spectators was nothing to do with the referee being pro- Queen's Park or anti- Celtic. A large crowd had paid the inordinate amount of 1/- (5p) and felt that both clubs fancied another big gate. Fortunately the demonstration and the protest did not lead to violence, but this is certainly a recurring theme in 1890's football—that Celtic's vast following could always be exploited, and of course the 1909 Scottish Cup Final would see these feelings brought to their logical conclusion.

Celtic did not make any great effort to claim the tie, and 35,000 turned up next week at Celtic Park, an illogical choice of venue, for this game was not a Replay. Celtic won 2-1 with Sandy McMahon scoring both goals. Sandy, commonly known as 'The Duke' after a French politician, was a great Celtic hero. Clumsy and ungainly looking, he still had a delicate touch and in the opinion of Willie Maley was a better header of the ball than even McGrory.

Having then disposed of Port Glasgow in the Semi Final, the stage was set for the second ever Cup Final between Celtic and Rangers (Rangers had won the first one in 1894) at Hampden Park on April 22nd 1899. 25,000 turned up, a large crowd by the standards of the day, but less than those who had been at the Celtic v. Queen's Park Quarter Final. Rangers, although steadily growing in popularity had still not reached mega star status. There was also of course the fact that admission charges at Hampden Park tended to be higher than anywhere else.

The teams were:

Celtic: McArthur, Welford, Storrier; Battles, Marshall, King; Hodge, Campbell, Divers, McMahon, Bell.

Rangers: Dickie; N.Smith, Crawford; Gibson, Neill, Mitchell; Campbell, McPherson, Hamilton, Miller, A.Smith.

The weather was fine, a nice, dry spring day and the referee Mr Tom Robertson of Queen's Park had few problems in the first half which was somewhat dull with Celtic's half backs of Barnie Battles, Harry Marshall (called the 'Portobello boat man' because of his nautical interests) and Alick King being outstanding, crushing any Rangers

The successful 1899 team.

Back row: Friel (trainer), Campbell, Hodge, McMahon, Divers, King, W. Maley (secretary/manager). Middle row: Bell, Marshall, Storrier, Welford, Battles. Front row: McArthur, Orr.

attack at birth and only fine goalkeeping by Dickie keeping McMahon, Divers and Campbell at bay.

The second half was similarly stalemated until a crude challenge by Nick Smith of Rangers on Celtic's left winger Jack Bell in the 55th minute left Bell a passenger and led to Smith being spoken to very firmly by Mr Robertson who was seen to gesticulate in the direction of the pavilion. Bell hobbled bravely, but clearly wanted to come off. Manager Maley however indicated that he should stay on for nuisance value if nothing else.

Celtic now briefly gained the ascendancy, and in fact scored. Mr Robertson had however already blown for a free kick, which Celtic took quickly, broke up field and forced a corner. Rangers were still arguing with the referee when the corner came over from right winger Johnny Hodge and 'The Duke' rose majestically to head home and put Celtic one up in the 67th minute.

From then on, Celtic with Welford and Battles in inspiring form took command, and Bell's limping up the wing, his knee now heavily bandaged, was hardly noticed, such was the dominance of Celtic. Bell would yet however play a decisive role. Time was running out when the ball spun off a Rangers player and landed at the feet of the now almost immobile Bell. Bell immediately booted the ball with his one serviceable foot and sent it over to the other wing where Johnny Hodge was standing on his own. The Rangers players claimed 'Offside', but Mr Robertson did not agree and Hodge ran on and scored.

There was now no way back for Rangers, and Celtic were presented with the Scottish Cup after the game in the pavilion. The Board were so delighted that each player was given £20 each, a phenomenal amount for 1899.It was not the end of the story for Celtic either that season for they beat Rangers later by the same score in the Glasgow Charity Cup Final. Rangers however did have the consolation of having won their first ever Scottish League Championship.

The intense rivalry between Celtic and Rangers had not yet in 1899 reached the fever pitch that it would become in the twentieth century, but Rangers, whose early history from 1873 had not been particularly outstanding, were gradually emerging as the challengers to Celtic, now that professionalism was killing off Queen's Park as the main force in the land.

— 3 —

AMATEURISM BLOWN AWAY
1900

Historians will argue whether the New Century begins on January 1st 2000 or January 1st 2001. Those of us who are not interested in pedantry will stifle many yawns as the subject begins in the next few years to dominate the Readers' Letters columns of many newspapers. It will be of no solace at all for us to know that similar arguments raged on *vis à vis* 1900 and 1901, and I dare say 1800 and 1801. Be that as it may, Celtic won the Scottish Cup in 1900, and it would be nice to think that the year 2000 would contain a similarly happy event.

In early 1900 it was now openly being asked how long Queen Victoria could stay as Queen. Born in 1819 and Queen since 1837, there were very few people who could remember anyone else on the throne. Her remarkable era as monarch (she did not die until January 22nd 1901) is often described quite blandly in history books and by superficial politicians as a time of progress at home and expansion overseas. It is not the function of this book to discuss these hypotheses, other than to say that the infant mortality rate in Glasgow in 1900 would disgrace many of to-day's Third World countries, and that news of casualties from the Boer War in South Africa was beginning to cause a great deal of concern, not least among the Glasgow Irish population.

Joining the Army did often seem to offer a way out of the misery and filth of the Glasgow slums. Images in recruiting posters portrayed fit young men, happily serving Queen and Country and impressing the girls on their return home with their steady income. To be fair, there was an element of truth in all this. Good reliable food, healthy outdoor exercise and a structure of discipline could and did work wonders with the undernourished. What the recruiting sergeant did not tell them however was that the Boers of South Africa (the grandparents of the Afrikaaners whose odious apartheid system would prevail until very recently) were determined at any cost to maintain their lands in the Transvaal and the Orange Free State. Although the might of the British Empire would eventually grind them down, the cost would be horrendous in British lives.

13

If you did not take the Queen's shilling and stayed back home, you still had football.

If we accept that the New Century began on 1st January 1900, then Celtic opened the New Century with a win over Rangers 3-2 at Celtic Park. This was in fact the last game of the Scottish League season, and was not enough to win Celtic the League. Too many draws early on, and some consistent play from a fine Rangers team had sent the Championship to Ibrox.

Following the New Year, we had something called the Inter City League, an expansion on what used to be called the Glasgow League and now incorporating Hearts and Hibs. This competition lasted only one year, generated little interest or crowd pulling, and has deservedly been relegated to the footnotes by most historians, although we are pleased to mention that Celtic did win it. What really mattered was the Scottish Cup.

Celtic of course had won it the previous year, but their line up had undergone a few changes since that 2-0 win over Rangers last April. There was however a determination to retain the trophy, and the early rounds saw little opposition from Bo'ness, Port Glasgow and Kilmarnock. The Semi Final however was a different matter - Rangers at Ibrox!

The 1890's had seen the gradual emergence of Rangers. Like Celtic, they had built a fine stadium and were clearly ambitious. Not yet identified with Orangeism and religious intolerance, it would be a few years yet before their rivalry with Celtic would be described as the 'Old Firm' (a sly reference to the ability of football teams to make money and produce commercial wealth), but nevertheless, Rangers were slowly taking over from Queen's Park as Glasgow's real challengers to the Irishmen of Celtic Park. Unlike the genteel Corinthian amateurs of the wealthy South Side, the West of Glasgow, like the East, had its vast slums and heavy industry - fertile ground for football players and supporters. Rangers may have had their middle class roots, but by the turn of the century they had embraced professionalism and had given Govan a team to be proud of.

The first Semi Final drew over 30,000 to Ibrox to see an even 2-2 draw with Celtic needing a Johnny Campbell penalty to stay in the tie. A similar crowd came to Celtic Park to see the replay, but on this occasion Celtic chose to turn on the style and Sandy McMahon scored twice and Hodge and Bell once each as Celtic ran out 4-0 winners, delighting their supporters by some fine play. This put Celtic into the Final at Ibrox on April 14th against Queen's Park.

Queen's Park had by now had their day. Their refusal to turn professional, while laudable and admirable in some ways, meant that they could only count upon players with a comfortable income who were becoming proportionately less as football made more and more inroads into the working classes. More damaging perhaps had been their snobby refusal to join the Scottish League (it would be next season 1900 - 1901 before they first took part in League football) which meant that they lacked the competitive edge which others had. On the other hand, one has to admire their ideals when considered against the backdrop of modern professionalism with all its excesses and ludicrous demands, and to their credit they have, to date, remained amateur with the Latin motto 'ludere causa ludendi' -'to play for the sake of playing'. They are usually in the lower reaches of the Leagues, but on three occasions in recent years (1965, 1967 and 1986) they have given Celtic a very good game in Scottish Cup ties.

In 1900, although slowly slipping from pre-eminence, they still retained many fine players. They still produced many Internationalists for the Scotland team, including notably 'Toffee Bob', better known to anyone who walks down Scottish High Streets as R.S.McColl. He was a typical Queen's Park player in the sense that his business allowed him the financial security to play the game as an amateur. He would later turn professional and play for Newcastle United and Rangers, but returned to his beloved Hampden to be re-instated as an amateur while his confectionery business expanded, helped no doubt by the mighty name of R.S.McColl.

No doubt many youngsters would buy McColl's toffees the week before the 1900 Scottish Cup Final, for on April 7th at Celtic Park, Toffee Bob became one of the very few Scotsmen to win eternal glory by scoring a hat-trick against England in a fine 4-1 victory over the auld enemy. The joy of the many Celtic fans in the crowd was tempered by the thought that he might repeat the feat the following week, but Celtic's centre half 'Beef' Marshall who watched the game from the Celtic Park Stand was determined to stop him, and made jokes about sticking to him like toffee etc.

Ibrox Stadium had recently been rebuilt and was the only obvious choice for the Scottish Cup Final. A crowd of 17,000 appeared on a fine brisk dry but rather too windy day. The wind was a strong westerly one, and as Ibrox would not have its impressive stands for another 80 years, there was little at the Broomloan Road end of the ground to act as a windbreak. History does not record who won the toss for ends, but certainly it was Celtic who played with the wind in the first half. The referee was Mr J.Walker of Kilmarnock and the teams were:

Celtic: McArthur, Storrier, Battles; Russell, Marshall, Orr; Hodge, Campbell, Divers, McMahon, Bell.

Queen's Park: Gourley; D.Stewart, Swan; Irons, Christie, Templeton; W.Stewart, Wilson, McColl, Kennedy, Hay.

From the start it was obvious that the wind was going to be a spoiler, and each team's tactics were to use the aerial route with the wind and the short passing game, allied with the punt into touch when against it. To everyone's surprise it was Queens who scored first in ten minutes. Centre half Christie got the ball half way inside Celtic's half and with everyone expecting a pass, took advantage of a lull in the wind to boot in the general direction of Celtic's goal, deceiving Dan McArthur and putting his team one up.

This was the signal for prolonged and sustained Celtic pressure which penned the Amateurs back in their own third of the field for all the remainder of the first half and produced three goals. McMahon scored in the 22nd minute with a shot from the wing which took advantage of the wind, the same McMahon then headed across goal some five minutes later for Divers to head in just on the line (some sources give the goal to McMahon) and then just before half time Celtic's pressure paid off yet again when outside left Jack Bell was on hand to score after 'much hustle and bustle in the goalmouth'.

Celts thus turned round 3-1 up, but the Amateurs were confident that Toffee Bob, with the benefit of the wind (now so strong that some newspapers refer to this game as the 'Hurricane Final') would destroy Celtic the same way as he had destroyed England the previous week. It did not look likely as Celtic went further ahead in the early minutes of the second half. Playing sensibly against the wind, McMahon and Campbell with a quick passing movement, released Divers who dashed up the field with the ball at his feet and rounded Gourley.

4-1 seemed all over, and already the Celtic fans were beginning to celebrate. Yet Queens pressed hard and scored a good goal through Wilson. Celtic's defence however was now coping well with the hurricane and Queens were making the fatal mistake of over-kicking the ball past their attackers and out of play for a goal kick. Henry Marshall never let McColl out of his sight, and Celtic's only hiccup came very late in the game when Barney Battles rose with Kennedy to clear a high ball and had the misfortune to head into his own goal.

The remaining minutes saw some frantic pressure from the Hampden side, but Celtic with Marshall immense, Storrier tackling

16

ferociously and Dan McArthur making many people ask the question why he had not been in the goal for Scotland last week, held out to win the coveted trophy for the third time.

Mr Walker's final whistle released intense joy among the windswept terracings and sporting congratulations from the Amateurs, who, sadly, have never again appeared in a Scottish Cup Final.

The wind played havoc with the banners on the triumphal march home. (The new Underground was expensive and inspired a genuine terror in those who had never travelled in it). Songs like 'The Wearing o' The Green', 'Slievenamon' and 'Father Murphy' resounded through Glasgow's West End, causing curiosity, interest but, as yet, no great resentment among the inhabitants. The wives and children of the East End anxiously awaiting the return of their menfolk and news of the result would have heard the Irish music wafting on the favourable wind and correctly deduced that for the third time 'Our bhoys have won the Cup'

As it was a holiday weekend, the carnival atmosphere continued until Monday when there was even more reason to celebrate. Rangers came to Celtic Park for an Inter City League game, and Celtic won 2-1. The New Century did indeed seem to be getting off to a good start.

— 4 —

THE MIGHTY QUINN 1904

The late balmy days of the 1960's saw a youngster appear on the Celtic Park scene by the name of Jimmy Quinn. Much was expected of him, for our grandfathers had waxed lyrical about his grandfather of the same name, Jimmy Quinn. Sadly the young man, although not really a failure, never quite made it at Celtic Park to the same extent as the original Jimmy Quinn did.

Round about the same time a pop group lead by Manfred Mann brought out a single called 'The Mighty Quinn'. It was about a famous Eskimo, but whenever that record was played at Scottish grounds, the Celtic fans would take it over and claim it as their own, such was the legend and mystique associated with this mighty man of sixty years ago:

Come on without, come on within,
You'll not see nothing like the mighty Quinn.

Tom Campbell, that fine Celtic historian, tells of the time when, as a very young boy, he was walking along Queen Street, Glasgow with his grandfather, and a man with a pipe passed him. His awestruck grandfather then asked if the great man would shake young Tom's hand. It took the grandfather some time to recover from this ordeal, for young Tom had shaken hands with 'the greatest centre forward that ever kicked a ba'.'

There are other stories about him as well—the Scots granny who reminisced about the sight of Jimmy Quinn coming off a train carrying the team's hamper with a clay pipe in his mouth 'just like an ordinary fella'; the crusty old Latin teacher who rebuked a pupil for mispronouncing the Latin word 'quin' (it should be like 'queen') by saying 'No! No! Quinn was a footballer'; the other Latin teacher of a generation later who stopped his minibus tour of Roman Scotland in Croy so that they could all see where *he* was born, the BBC Sports commentator who introduced boxer Pat Clinton 'from Croy, birthplace of Jimmy Quinn'. Who then was this man, and how did he earn his fame?

18

He was born in Croy in 1878, and was by all accounts a self-effac-ingly shy youth when Maley eventually persuaded him to join Celtic in January 1901. He played for Smithston Albion just across the road from his home near Croy Station. He was very reluctant to turn professional, but Maley was determined, being so impressed by his power and physique. His first games were mainly on the left wing, (he would play in that position in the Scottish Cup final defeats of 1901 and 1902) and it was only by chance that he found himself in the centre forward position in the Scottish Cup Final of 1904.

Celtic's centre at the time was Alec Bennett, himself to become one of the Celtic immortals in the next few years. But Alec had a problem —and that was that he was a self-confessed Rangers fan. There would of course in future years be quite a few Ibrox minded Celts - Willie Wallace, Kenny Dalglish, Dixie Deans immediately spring to mind, but the problem was an acute one in 1904 for Bennett, for Rangers also admired him and were very keen on signing him.

In the circumstances, it was felt that it might be an idea to drop Bennett for the Scottish Cup Final between these two teams. Stories were circulated that he had flu or was injured, but in fact Maley felt that his commitment to the cause might be less than total. Enter then Jimmy Quinn as centre. It was not his first outing in that spot (in fact he had played there a fortnight before in a 2-1 defeat at Hearts) but he had never yet been a great success, either at centre forward or left wing.

1904 had been a strange year for both Celtic and Rangers. Neither had really challenged strongly for the League which had been won by Third Lanark for the first and only time. Celtic had been in the doldrums, and in circumstances which would be repeated in the early sixties, everyone was waiting for the new Celtic team to take off.

The policy of buying established stars from England had now been discontinued in favour of a youth policy. Players were brought from the junior ranks or in the case of Jimmy Young, for example, from lesser English teams like Bristol Rovers. As would be the case in the 1960's, the youth policy was not instantly successful, there were many failures and disappointments, and even the most talented of players took some time to blend and mature, but when it did happen, the world was never the same again.

The path to the Final had not been easy—three games were required to dispose of a determined Dundee, and the Semi Final victory over Third Lanark had been tight. But the club was delighted to be at Hampden, and it was of course the first Final to be played at the new

19

Hampden. Outdone by the magnificence of Celtic Park for a while, Queen's Park, possibly realising that their chances of keeping up with Celtic and Rangers on the field had gone given that these two were now wealthy professional outfits, had decided that they could carve a niche for themselves in hosting Internationals and Cup Finals, and thus they built this superb Hampden Park. Shrewdly the price of admission was kept down to 6d (2p approximately) and thus 64,323 appeared for the game betweens Glasgow's giants on April 16th 1904.

The teams were:

Celtic:Adams; McLeod, Orr; Young, Loney, Hay; Muir, McMenemy, Quinn, Somers and Hamilton.

Rangers: Watson, N.Smith, Drummond; Henderson, Stark, Robertson; Walker, Speedie, Mackie, Donnachie and A.Smith.

The referee was Tom Robertson of Queen's Park. As Rangers had had to rest the injured Hamilton, their famous centre forward, much interest focussed on the two inexperienced centres. This was the first Scottish Cup Final in which Celtic wore the famous green and white hoops, for the change had been made from stripes to hoops at the start of the season, and it was round about now that the term 'Old Firm' began to be applied to Celtic and Rangers.

It was a fine dry day with only a minimum of wind. Over the years Hampden would develop a reputation for attracting a match-spoiling wind. That could not be said of to-day's game. Celtic started briskly against the slight breeze, and soon their young team were beginning to impress with the left wing pairing of Peter Somers and Davie Hamilton looking good. Wing halves Young and Hay were looking sound, and Loney was commanding, particularly in the air.

It was however Rangers who went ahead, and it was a disaster for goalkeeper Davie Adams. Davie was born in the Angus village of Oathlaw and had joined Celtic from Dunipace Juniors. After a struggle to prove himself, he was now looking a worthy successor to Dan McArthur, but disaster struck in ten minutes. A break down the left by Alex Smith beating McLeod and Young, then a cross to the unmarked Finlay Speedie. Speedie's header was a poor one, straight at Adams but the nervous 20-year-old goalkeeper collided with a post and the ball squeezed through to give Rangers the lead.

This goal was still being debated among the Celtic support when, as often happens with the loss of concentration in a defence, Rangers scored again a minute later. Again it was Smith and Speedie. Smith won a corner kick, took it himself and with the Celtic defence flat-footed, the ball came to Speedie who lashed home through a ruck of players. The Rangers fans who arrived late had missed it all, the Celtic fans just could not believe it. Finlay Speedie, who had scored for Scotland in last year's game against England and was now unaccountably out of International contention, had scored twice. It was as if he were making a point that he should have been playing in last week's International at Celtic Park which England won 1-0. The same man would go on to win the Military Medal for gallantry with the Argyll and Sutherland Highlanders in the First World War.

But the great thing about a young, fit team is that they never say die. This team certainly did not, and had the talent to back up their determination. Even before Quinn scored a great individual goal in the 37th minute, the Rangers defence were showing signs of strain against the speed of Muir, the wiles of McMenemy, the subtlety of Somers, all backed up by the mighty wing halves Young and Hay. Quinn's first goal was an early example of a typical Quinn goal. It was a head down charge, forcing his way through the tough tackles and the shot for goal at exactly the right moment. His shoulders have been compared to those of a stevedore or a bison, and he needed every ounce of strength to counteract the harsh tackling of Stark. Accounts vary as to how many Rangers men he charged through - four or five according to the newspapers, and 'aboot 20'if you listened to my grandfather.

Celtic's tails were up, and it was no surprise that they equalized before half time. Bobby Muir, who would only play one season for Celtic (he joined Notts County only 4 days after this game) had his moment of glory when he waltzed past Drummond and Robertson and crossed for Quinn to hammer home from about 10 yards.

Half time came almost immediately and Celtic went in, level and full of confidence.Adams was still apologetic for his mistake, and had to be told by the stentorian Sunny Jim Young, 'Davy, f—-in' shut up aboot it! We'll win as lang as it disnae happen again!' Quinn sat in a corner of the dressing room, silent and brooding, as if giving himself hypnotherapy for more goals.

The Celtic fans were now in good voice. The breeze had now strengthened a little, and Celtic's youngsters had the advantage, but heroic saves by Watson in the Rangers goal at the King's Park End of the ground denied Celtic time and time again, as even full backs McLeod and Orr were seen joining the attack. McLeod who would lose his life in Flanders in 1917 was a fine example of an attacking full back that day as he strove to give Celtic the extra goal that would win the day.

This state of affairs continued until ten minutes from time, when a left wing combination of Willie Orr and James Hay released Quinn. It was to be the Croy man's supreme moment, as he charged for goal avoiding Stark, shaking off Drummond and only a ferocious challenge from Nick Smith knocking him off his stride. It was only momentary, however, for he recovered, and now well inside the area, slipped the ball past the advancing Watson. The heavens seemed to open to applaud such brilliance, and the Celtic supporters went mad. So did the players, as they embraced the hero. Jimmy however, his face set like that of a man possessed, walked grimly up the field, telling everyone that there were still ten minutes to play out.

He need not have worried, however, for Rangers were a spent force. Any further attempts at goalscoring were from Celtic, although Watson was still on top form. Mr Robertson blew his whistle, and Celtic had won the Scottish Cup for the fourth time.

Rangers would have to wait another 24 years before they would win the trophy again, and it was a defeat from which they never recovered for many years. Similarly, nothing would now stop Celtic for the rest of the decade, and the following week the point was proved when the miner boy from Croy scored 5 against a luckless Kilmarnock.

Pat Woods and Tom Campbell in 'The Glory and The Dream' describe the 1965 Scottish Cup triumph and the supporters' reaction as

.. a tumultuous welcome to the future and the instinctive realisation by all Celtic's support that the young men had grown up and that nothing, now nor in the years to come, would withstand their collective spirit.

These sentiments could apply equally well to the glorious young men of 1904.

Three men's emotions need to be examined. One was the luckless, but now relieved Davie Adams who might have been vilified for ever, (like cricketer Fred Tate who played one horrendous Test Match two years previously in 1902,) but who would now become arguably one of the greatest Celtic goalkeepers of them all, denied a Scotland cap only because of lack of practice in view of the excellent outplay in front of him. Stories would abound of him and his successor Charlie Shaw going home for their tea in the middle of a game or courting the actress at the Kings Theatre between the matinee and evening performances and no-body noticing his absence from the Celtic Park goal.

Alec Bennett's feelings are harder to imagine. One way or another as a deposed Celt or a dyed in the wool Bluenose, he would not have enjoyed the events of April 16th 1904. Yet, to his credit, he soon swallowed his differences with Celtic and with his ex-partner at Rutherglen Glencairn, Jimmy McMenemy formed the most devastating right wing in Celtic's history. He would eventually join Rangers in 1908, but his best years were with Celtic.

As for the hero of the hour, there would be no boasting, no tantrums, no desire to leave for England. He reputedly kept his medals in a biscuit tin in his Croy home, and occasionally gave one away to a deserving youngster. He probably did genuinely dislike the adulation given to him, for he remained a shy man. International Caps of course came his way, his most famous one being the game in Dublin in March 1908 when he scored 4 of Scotland's 5 goals. He was Celtic's trainer for a time, but most of his working life after he retired from football in 1915 was down the pit. He died in his beloved Croy in November 1945. Even though we are now almost a century away from the *floruit* of the great man, there can be little doubt that the name Quinn continues to exercise a fascination over us all.

— 5 —

ONE UP FOR THE WEST
1907

There were changes happening in Britain in 1907. The Liberals were now in power, and supported by a small but ever growing Labour Party were beginning to address themselves to some of the evils that had afflicted Great Britain thanks to the rapid industrialization of the past 100 years. School meals, Old Age Pensions and Labour Exchanges were now making an appearance to much bewilderment and shaking of the head of the Victorian establishment.

New issues like 'Votes for Women' were beginning to appear to vie for newspaper space with the perpetual problems of Ireland and South Africa. On the football field however Newcastle United were in their heyday in England, and in Scotland there was little to stop the mighty Celtic.

The Scottish League was won very comfortably with only two reverses.One was at Ibrox on New Year's Day 1907 and the other was at the hands of Third Lanark at Cathkin Park in mid March. The team played superb football throughout the season, and the Scottish Cup seemed also to be within the grasp of this splendid side who could with some justification claim to be the best in the world.

Yet there were a few hiccups en route to the Final. Morton and Hibs both took Celtic to three games before the issue was settled. Against that, there was a comprehensive 3-0 win over Rangers at Ibrox Park, and the feeling that when this side were on song there was very little that could stop them. Hearts would be the opponents in the Cup Final.

The Tynecastle men were also a fine side in 1907. They had won the Scottish Cup the previous year, had had one or two near misses in the Scottish League, and Celtic men had vivid memories of Hearts' Scottish Cup victory over them in 1901. They had many fine players, a Scotland defender in centre half Charlie Thomson and a superstar in Bobby Walker, an almost automatic choice for Scotland in the Edwardian era. He was an inside forward of the highest calibre, and it was often felt that as long as Walker was in the team, no matter the

24

circumstances of who the opponents were or how many the team were trailing by, the Hearts were always in with a chance. Dubbed the King of Hearts by the adoring Gorgie fans, Walker, although himself a shy, retiring fellow, attracted fans wherever he went and was one of the few people, and probably the only football player who was instantly recognised in Edwardian Edinburgh. For Hearts historians, the Edwardian years are often described as 'the Walker era' He is of course not to be confused with Tommy Walker who played and managed the club in later years..

But Celtic fans claimed that they now had an inside forward to rival Bobby Walker. This was James McMenemy. It was the fashion in Victorian and Edwardian times, then as now, to nickname footballing heroes. Willie Groves, for example, had been 'Darling Willie'; Jimmy McLaren was the 'Auld Gineral' and Sandy McMahon was 'The Duke'. Military metaphors were continued when McMenemy was called 'Napoleon'

At first sight this appears to be a strange nickname. After all, it was less than 100 years since Britain had finally defeated Bonaparte. But France was now no threat, and the British always had nourished an admiration for the little Corsican with his tactical awareness, coolness under pressure and general cleverness. This was also the reason, presumably, why Celtic fans gave the name 'Napoleon' to the genius from Rutherglen Glencairn. He was crafty with a particular ability to release Bennett (with whom he had an almost telepathic understanding) or Quinn with a defence-splitting inch-perfect pass, and he could shoot ferociously, and head a ball as well. At 5 feet 7 inches and 11 stone 7lbs, he lacked height and physique. He had no taste for the fierce tackling of the day, but this was seldom a problem for he had a great degree of speed and ability to avoid the physical challenge. Noticeably, whenever McMenemy had a poor game, Celtic tended to under-perform.

At outside left, Celtic had that charismatic soldier of fortune Bobby Templeton. A brilliant player and a great personality, Bobby had had the misfortune to be indirectly responsible for the 1902 Ibrox Disaster.It was the Scotland v.England game and Bobby's first International. His mazy run down the left wing had caused the crowd in the rickety and ill-constructed West Stand to rise and strain to see. The pressure was too much for the wooden structure, it collapsed and 25 people were killed with many more injured.

He had already played for Aston Villa, Newcastle and Arsenal before he joined Celtic. He would not last long at Celtic Park, being rather too full of the joys of life for the liking of Willie Maley, and would move on to Kilmarnock (from where he hailed) and Fulham, but those who saw him, albeit briefly, in the hoops considered him to be one of the best. Celtic had reached the 1907 Cup Final thanks to his demolition of Hibs in the Semi Final.

He is famous for his entering a lion's cage and tweaking its tail for a bet. He was a Kilmarnock player by this time, and he did it one Saturday night in August 1908 after Killie had been hammered 5-1 by Celtic at Celtic Park.It seemed to be a characteristic of Bobby - brilliant, dashing and courageous but also foolhardy and irresponsible. His greatest moment as a Celt however would come on April 20th 1907.

There was a great deal at stake that day. Hearts' supporters, although not entirely free from sectarianism as a result of being the city rivals to the avowedly Irish Hibs (the Latin word for Ireland is *Hibernia*). There was not therefore any great religious issue at stake, but there were other factors.

Traditional Edinburgh v.Glasgow rivalry was one thing. Even in the early days, genteel Edinburgh disliked Glasgow, and vibrant Glasgow, proudly the 'second city' of the Empire, looked upon Edinburgh as a quaint, irrelevant medieval relic with castles, palaces, kings, queens and rugby. Edinburgh was determined on the football fields to show itself the equal of Glasgow. Hearts had won the Cup four times (indeed they were last year's holders and had put Celtic out at the Quarter Final stage) and so had the emerging Celtic.Celtic were winning the League, and it would be nice to balance things up between the two cities.

There was also the fascinating chance for everyone to see who was the best inside right in Scotland. Walker was of course the sitting tenant in the Scotland team, having played honourably in the 1-1 draw at St.James Park, Newcastle a fortnight previously, but the claims of McMenemy were becoming hard to ignore, for it had been 'Napoleon' who had won the League for Celtic with his promptings of Bennett and Quinn. He had been outstanding in the only time the teams had met so far that season - a 3-0 win for Celtic at Celtic Park in the middle of September.

The Hearts fans who travelled through by the special trains that fine spring morning were disturbed by rumours of injuries to their star players. It had been a confusing season for the Tynecastle men with transfers out and in, and the team really needed to settle. In the event three men were injured - left half Dickson, the creative Peddie and centre half Charlie Thomson. Thomson was the most serious problem, for he had the advantage, physically at least over Quinn. He was a good three inches taller and a stone heavier, so it was felt that he would have come out best in any barging competition.

The crowd was given as 55,000 on a pleasant day at Hampden, but they were all a little nonplussed when the kick-off was inexplicably delayed by quarter of an hour. It was felt that it was perhaps to allow for the late arrival of an Edinburgh train carrying fans, but the real reason was somewhat more crucial to the day's events. It was the late arrival of Hearts goalkeeper Allan. Presumably, he had been caught up in the late arrival of a train, or perhaps even in 1907 his motorised transport had let him down, but his tardiness was never explained, nor does he seem to have been in any way punished for it. It is difficult to imagine it happening to-day, however!

The teams were:
Celtic: Adams, McLeod, Orr; Young, McNair, Hay; Bennett, McMenemy, Quinn, Somers, Templeton
Hearts: Allan, Reid, Collins; Philip, McLaren, Henderson; Bauchope, Walker, Axford, Yates, Wombwell.

Contemporary reports indicate that the game was bright and breezy, like the conditions. In spite of their handicap, the understrength Hearts gave as good as they got, but making little headway against Celtic's fine defence, marshalled by Alec McNair who had filled the centre half role admirably since the injury to Willie Loney. McNair would of course settle down at right back in years to come, but he was a very versatile and dependable character, coping admirably, as he had all season, with everything that the opposition threw at him.

By the same token, Celtic's forwards were not doing at all well against Hearts' makeshift defence. McLaren, who had played at right half in last season's Cup Final, had an excellent first half, not allowing the menace of Quinn to develop. Those who were interested in the Walker v. McMenemy competition would have little to go on, for although both were playing adequately, neither had as yet taken a grip on proceedings and both teams were quite happy to settle for a 0-0 scoreline at half- time.

The game turned on a disputed penalty. No-one quite seemed to know what happened, other than that 'there was a clash of bodies' in the Hearts penalty area, and the referee awarded a spot kick to Celtic. Never one to look a gift horse in the mouth, Willie Orr scored the first penalty kick in a Scottish Cup Final while Hearts protests continued long and loud. This penalty kick remained until 1971 the only penalty kick that Celtic received in a Scottish Cup Final.

Hearts' protests were too long and loud for their own good, however. The game had another 35 minutes to run, and this was not necessarily a fatal moment for the Edinburgh men. But concentration sadly lapsed without Thomson to calm everyone down, and at the same time Celtic playing with the confidence that success brings, took over with wing halves Young and Hay surging forward and spraying passes.

Celtic's further two goals came within minutes of the disputed penalty and both were remarkably similar. In both cases there was a long ball from midfield out to the dazzling Alec Bennett on the right wing who beat a couple of men and sent over a cross for Peter Somers to tap in while Hearts defenders concentrated on the mighty Quinn.

The final whistle came with Celtic well on top, and Davy Adams in the Celtic goal distinctly underemployed. Celtic had now won the Scottish Cup five times, second only to Queen's Park's ten, and if there had been the slightest doubt before the game about Celtic being the team of the decade, there was none now. The glory days were nothing like at an end.

Hearts, although still sore about the penalty, conceded graciously. This result would be a watershed in their history, for it would be almost 50 years before they would once again be a power in the land. Mistakes were made at management level e.g. the selling of players like Davie Axford to Raith Rovers.

Hearts would always be a respectable team, hard to beat particularly in Edinburgh, but success in any national trophy would not come their way until 1954-5 when they won the League Cup, and the Scottish Cup would spend exactly 50 years away from Tynecastle from 1906 until 1956. They would have their moments and their fine players - Bobby Walker would continue to thwart McMenemy's International aspirations for some time yet, and in the 1930's they would enjoy another Walker - Tommy of that ilk. But Edinburgh would always struggle to rid itself of the reputation for being a footballing backwater.

Celtic fans sang lustily on the way home. 1907 was their first League and Cup double - in fact it was a treble if you count the Glasgow Cup won back in October, and Maley could count himself happy to have such a talented bunch of players. Crucially, as well, they all had team spirit, they all loved the team, and Maley whose mission in life often seemed to be to make the Irish respectable and accepted in Scotland could point with justified pride at the team that he had built, containing as it did quite a number of players who were neither Irish (first, second or even third generation) nor Catholic. Mr Maley had every cause to smile benignly at everyone at the post match banquet as he admired once again the handsome Scottish Cup.

— 6 —

ALL THE TALENTS
1908

Before 1967, there was never any great doubt about what was the greatest Celtic team of all time. This was the XI of 1908 whose names would trip off the tongues of children whose grandfathers were alive in 1908 - Adams, McNair and Weir; Young, Loney and Hay; Bennett, McMenemy, Quinn, Somers and Hamilton. 1967 did however introduce an element of doubt about the best team of all time. Clearly arguments about their respective merits are singularly pointless - suffice it to say that each team won every competition open to them.1908 and 1967 saw nobody in Glasgow, Scotland or Europe who could challenge Celtic.

1908's team seemed to have a problem with the East coast of Scotland. Their three defeats in the League were at the hands of East of Scotland teams - Aberdeen, Hearts and Dundee, all of them away from home. Each of the three of them were dispatched more than adequately when they came to Celtic Park, however, and Celtic were never in any great danger of losing their fourth successive League Championship, finishing up four points ahead of second placed Falkirk.

It was frequently said that the reason for success was the comparative stability at Celtic Park. Very few players came or went - an exception being Bobby Templeton who returned to his native Kilmarnock, but was immediately replaced by Davy Hamilton who was at least his equal on the left wing and definitely a lot more reliable and level headed. Captain James Hay took ill with appendicitis the week between Christmas and New Year and was immediately replaced by the talented John Mitchell. With other fine reserves around like McLean, Semple and Kivlichan, injuries were seldom much of a problem.

James 'Dun' Hay's illness was quite a serious one. Appendicitis was a known killer in the early 1900's. It is sometimes claimed that King Edward VII was the first person to undergo successfully an appendicectomy in 1902. This is not exactly true, but he was one of the first and this very high profile surgical success was an indication of the progress that was being made in health. Nevertheless, an appendicitis operation would cause as much concern in 1908 as a major operation for cancer would now. 'Dun' however pulled through and indeed by the end of February was back in training, regaining his place from the worthy John Mitchell in early March. 'Dun' was clearly not done yet.

It is difficult for us to imagine the effect that the name 'Celtic' had on everyone in those early days. Something that had not yet seen twenty years of existence, it seemed, nevertheless, to inspire, to light up and to animate everyone and everything. For example, when they were drawn to come to Kirkcaldy to meet Second Division Raith Rovers in the Scottish Cup in late February, the whole town seemed to be at the station to meet them. The ground had had to have large 'banks', of earth presumably, put in and the local Trades Band was engaged to play 'Songs of Ireland' to make the visitors feel at home. A crowd of 23,000 was expected, but foul weather cut the attendance appreciably and prevented the band from playing. A couple of local lads stole a clock and pawned it. Their excuse before the judiciary magistrate was that they needed the money to get in to Stark's Park to see the 'Bould Celts'.

It was a matter of some disquiet, however, to the Celtic Park faithful that a team of such undeniable talent which paralysed almost all the opposition teams in Scotland and could with some justification claim to be the greatest show on earth, seemed to be so ludicrously under-represented in the Scottish International side. Only McNair, Bennett, and Quinn appeared for Scotland that season. The treatment of Quinn in particular seems odd.

On 14th March 1908, Quinn played at centre forward for Scotland against Ireland in Dublin. Scotland won 5-0 and Quinn performed the rare, although not unprecedented, feat of scoring four goals. The Irish crowd, although disappointed at their own team's performance, found the pill a little easier to swallow at the thought that Quinn played for Celtic and that he was virtually one of theirs. It was confidently expected that the mighty Quinn would be given the chance at centre forward against England in Glasgow in three weeks time. Yet the selectors chose Andy Wilson of Sheffield Wednesday at centre forward and put Quinn on to the left wing. Granted Wilson did score in the 1-1 draw, but Quinn in the centre might well have produced more.

A greater mystery seemed to overshadow Peter Somers. He had already played three times for Scotland at inside left, but had now lost his International place. Those who saw Peter play were at a loss to understand why. He was without any great doubt the brains behind the Celtic forward line, possibly even in 1908 a better inside man than McMenemy. Maley described him as 'Celtic's powder monkey' a reference to the boys who loaded the cannons in naval warfare. He was never a great personality player like McInally and Tully would be in later years, and he was possibly too slight of frame to have been much use in the strong arm stuff in which Quinn, for example, excelled, but his contribution was immense. Tremendous positional sense allied to passing ability, ball control and a cannonball shot on occasion made him one of the Celtic all time greats and certainly the most under-rated player of that exceptional side.

Somers also seems to have been a tremendous character with loads of wit and cheerfulness, something that a successful football team always needs. He was described as 'Celtic's Mark Tapley', Mark Tapley being the permanently cheerful character in Charles Dickens' 'Martin Chuzzlewit'. He was an accomplished pianist and would entertain the rest of the party when the team were away from home, staying overnight in a hotel or at Seamill Hydro. Some of his quips to opponents and his own team-mates were famous. He once kicked out at an opponent. 'What was that for?' enquired the aggrieved man. 'It was for you. Don't tell anyone!'. Davy Hamilton and he once fell out on the field after Davy had chased in vain for one of Peter's rare misdirected passes. 'Don't talk to me!' said the angry Davy as Peter tried to apologise. 'Well, can I write to you, then?' blandly asked Peter. Davy had to smile.

Alec Bennett was a magnificent player but still nourished a love for Rangers. He had been left out of the 1904 Cup Final team in anticipation of a move to Ibrox which never came off. His love for Rangers (whom he eventually joined in the summer of 1908) never prevented him from giving his best for Celtic and although he would win League medals with Rangers and indeed add to his collection of Scotish caps, his best playing days were in the green and white hoops of Celtic. In 1908 he was simply immense with the ability of a Jimmy Johnstone to tear a defence to shreds but with the added advantage of being more direct and being more able to send across inch perfect crosses.

Celtic's passage to the Scottish Cup Final that year had its moments. Although the Rovers of Peebles and Raith presented few problems, Rangers did, and Celtic were indebted to the two goals of William Kivlichan, deputising for the injured Jimmy Quinn to see them through. Kivlichan, one of the very few players to have played for both Celtic and Rangers, was never a regular for Celtic, but he was a fine player nevertheless and this particular day was clearly his moment. He 'wormed about like an eel' according to one report which must have been quite a contrast to Quinn who is more readily compared to a bison.

The Semi Final took Celtic up to Pittodrie.(This was before the days of neutral venues for Semi Finals). The behaviour of the crowd turned out to be a shocker, for although Aberdeen, then as now, enjoyed the reputation of having douce, respectable supporters who were all good Elders of the Church of Scotland on Sundays, there was nevertheless a wild element of 'loons' from the bothies of Buchan and the Mearns who came into town on a Saturday to escape from their sweated drudgery and could not handle the cheap ale.

Celtic had brought with them that day a large travelling support, many of whom enjoying their first sight of the Granite City and with a similar inability to handle the cheap ale at one penny a jug. One or two fights broke out at the match, and the Aberdeen fans were incensed at what they saw as the spoiling tactics of Sunny Jim Young.

Sunny, of course, revelled in this role as the villain making great play of dodging the bottles of the irate home fans and generally inciting everyone. McMenemy scored the only goal of the game for Celtic; and the Aberdeen Press the following week was full of censure for the 'hotheads' who had thrown bottles and stones at the 'Irishmen' who were 'themselves on a short fuse, in some cases'.Apologetic letters flowed between both clubs for a spell, for Aberdeen, only five years old, were aware of their precarious position in Scottish football and of how much they needed the political support of Maley and Celtic.

St.Mirren were to be Celtic's opponents in the Scottish Cup final of April 18th 1908. The Paisley men were one of the founder members of the Scottish League, had seen the demise of the other Paisley side Abercorn and had earned themselves the reputation of playing good football, but without having achieved any great success in so doing.They had produced Internationalists notably Tom Jackson, the stylish right back who on a famous occasion before the 1904 International against England had to be informed of his last minute selection by telegram on the Saturday morning. Jackson however had an 'injury' which may have been a euphemism for one of his periodic feuds with the club, and did not play in the 1908 Scottish Cup Final.

In truth, St. Mirren were nothing more than a team of honest journeymen against the greatest team on earth, and a Celtic victory was confidently predicted. This did not however prevent a large crowd of Buddies appearing at Hampden to swell the crowd to 55,000 a good 5,000 more than last season's Cup Final between Celtic and Hearts. The teams were;

A superb season – winners of the Scottish, Glasgow, Glasgow Charity Cups and the Scottish League Championship.

Top row: Directors Tom White, J. Kelly, Tom Colgan, John McKillop, James Grant, M. Dunbar. Middle row: Maley (manager), J. Young, P. Somers, J. McMenemy, D. Adams, J. Mitchell, J. Weir, R. Davis (trainer). Front row: D. Hamilton, D. McLeod, W. Loney, J. Hay, J. Quinn, A. McNair.

Celtic: Adams, McNair, Weir; Young, Loney, Hay; Bennett, McMenemy, Quinn, Somers, Hamilton.

St.Mirren: Grant, Gordon, White; Key, Robertson, McAvoy; Clements, Cunningham, Wylie, Paton, Anderson.

The game itself was a very one sided affair with the men from Paisley clearly owerawed by the sheer size of a Celtic Cup Final crowd, and right from the start Celtic's wing halves Sunny Jim Young and James Hay took command. The connoisseurs of football saw the game played at pace, with skill, and total composure of a team that just knows that it is going to win. Alec Bennett scored in each half, Quinn scored from a position that might have been marginally offside, and Somers and Hamilton also netted. This left McMenemy in the unfortunate position of being the only forward not to score, but it mattered not, for he was the man who had masterminded the forward line. St. Mirren scored a consolation goal through Cunningham, but quite a few people thought that Celtic deliberately eased off and that 5-1 was enough. Indeed it was and Celtic had now won the Cup six times.

On May 30th 1908, Celtic won the Glasgow Charity Cup when they beat Queen's Park 3-0. They thus won every competition they entered for in season 1907-08, a feat which would never again be equalled until 1967. Obviously there was no European dimension in 1908, but few could doubt that they would have carried all before them there as well. Comparisons between 1908 and 1967 are pointless; nothing can be proved or gained by that. Certain it is however that no other team in either 1908 or 1967 was fit to lace the boots of the men in green and white.

In the early sixties when things were not good, one could often spot vendors of photographs of famous Celtic teams. A youngster could buy one and instantly recognise the team of 1954 and 1957. 1931 was more difficult, but Dad could help there. 1908 however, although Grandad might be required to point out who was who, presented little problems in the nomenclature. It was such a shame that the team of 1962 and 1963 resembled 1908 only in the colour of the jersey. It was always said that the way to order three whiskies in a pub was to say 'Young, Loney and Hay'. Why? Because they were 'three halfs of the best'.

— 7 —

McATEE AND McATEER
1911

All good things must come to an end, it is said, and by season 1910 - 11, it was becoming obvious that the sustained success of Celtic's great Edwardian side was faltering; appropriately enough, perhaps, for King George V had by now succeeded King Edward VII. The hegemony of Scottish football was also slipping, albeit temporarily, towards the west of Glasgow.

Superlatives tended to become a cliche when Celtic's Six League Titles in a Row were mentioned. After 1910, however, things began to fall apart, and in the League table at the end of the 1911 season, Celtic were not even in the top three. Rangers had taken advantage of Celtic's weaknesses, had built up a strong team and were now slowly emerging as the Glasgow team which would challenge the Mighty Celts in years to come, possessing as they did a fine stadium which could contain large crowds. Their immediate catchment area of Govan was of course the vibrant engine room of the British Empire's shipbuilding, and it was natural that people should flock to the local team, particularly in the years immediately before the First World War when the race was on to have more ships than our Teutonic competitors.

The Home Rule struggle in 1914, the War itself, the Easter Rebellion, the Partition and the Civil War would of course focus the Irish problem in Glaswegian minds, but in 1911, Govan was not yet a sectarian place. They were however proud of their football team.

Perhaps it is in this context that we should consider the case of William Fulton Kivlichan. This interesting character who was subsequently wounded in the First World War and became Celtic's doctor in the 1930's (among other things attending to John Thomson's fatal injury), was not one of Celtic's great players. The point about him was that he was a strong practising Roman Catholic, and a member of the Third Order of St.Francis. In November 1905 he had no objections to joining Rangers, nor did they see anything wrong in signing this lad from St.Joseph's Dumfries. On January 1st 1907 at Ibrox, as Rangers inflicted a rare defeat on Celtic, Kivlichan scored the winning goal, but his form for Rangers was not consistently good enough for him to retain his place and he joined Celtic that summer. No doubt he was glad to join Celtic, but playing for Rangers does not seem to have been any big deal for this man, whose scapulars (shoulder straps) of the Third Order of St. Francis were one day seen over his Celtic jersey bringing 'tears of joy to the eyes of the Celtic Park faithful'.

I am grateful to 'An Alphabet of the Celts' (MacBride, O'Connor and Sheridan) for telling me this tale, and no doubt the tears in the eyes of the fans that day in October 1910 may have been because he scored the only goal of the game from 40 yards (perhaps the 40 yards and the tears are both examples of a contemporary chronicler being profligate with the truth!), but the point here is that we have this very devout Roman Catholic playing quite happily for Rangers (scapulars and all, perhaps) for a short time before moving to his more likely home at Celtic Park.

The problem at Celtic Park in 1910-11 was scoring goals. The defence was quite strong with 'Icicle' McNair at right back now partnered by James Hay with Joe Dodds now at left half. Even when Willie Loney broke his wrist against Clyde in February, Celtic immediately drafted in the much travelled and experienced Tommy McAteer at centre half. Tommy came from Croy, and had been picked up in summer 1910 from a dispirited Clyde side who had just lost the Scottish Cup to Dundee. Already almost 30, Tommy's joining of the club raised a few eyebrows, but events would prove that his arrival was a timely one.

The forward line was still suffering from the loss of Bennett in 1908 and the departure of Peter Somers to Hamilton Academical in 1910. Kivlichan was not as good on the right wing as Alec Bennett, currently winning the Championship for Rangers, McMenemy was simply having a poor season (his only one), Quinn, injury prone and slower, was a lot less effective, inside left saw Peter Johnstone (a fine player, but out of position as later events would show) and John Hastie (an honest trier) struggle and on the left wing Davy Hamilton also slowing up as his thirtieth birthday approached.

A shocking start to the season and a few indifferent runs at critical points meant that by the turn of the year, the League Championship was not to come home for seven years in a row, but there was still the Scottish Cup in which Celtic were looking for their seventh victory. They might have won it in 1909 but for riotous behaviour of fans who felt that they had been conned out of extra time in the replay, and in

1910 the Cup had broken new ground by going to Dundee after Celtic had disappointingly fallen to Clyde in the Semi Final.

The strength of the Celtic defence in that season was proved by the fact that the Cup was won without a goal being lost. On January 28th, St.Mirren were beaten 2-0 at Celtic Park, then Galston had a day they would never forget at Celtic Park, performing wonders to restrict Celtic to a solitary Quinn goal. Celtic's luck in earning home draws continued when Clyde were the next visitors to Celtic Park on Cup business. This time it was 'Napoleon' McMenemy who scored the only goal in a game where Clyde looked the better team especially after Celtic lost the services of Willie Loney who fractured his wrist in a fall. 48,000 came to Celtic Park to see the fast developing Aberdeen side (which included, at right back, Scottish cap Donald Colman) in the Semi-Final. Once again, the score was 1-0, thanks to Quinn, and thanks also to a mightily impressive display by reserve centre half Tommy McAteer who saved the day with his timely interventions on more than one occasion.

Ibrox Park was the venue for the Scottish Cup Final on April 8th 1911, and the opponents were Hamilton Academical. The men from the Ducal toon had done well to win their way to the Final, defeating among others the holders Dundee who had been beating them 2-0 at one stage, yet their League form was poor. They finished up 16th in the table, and on the only occasion that they had played Celtic that season, had lost 0-1. Yet their team was not without its interest to the Celtic fans.In the first place Peter Somers was now at Douglas Park, and although he was no longer commanding a first team place thanks to injuries and the fact that he was now almost 33, yet his influence was such that very soon after he retired, he was made a Director.Half back Phil Watson had been a Celtic player from 1902 -3, and in addition, Hamilton had a forward called J.H.McLaughlin, son of the Celtic founding father of the same name. (McLaughlin senior had been one of the men who had pushed Celtic to pre-eminence and had served the club in various capacities. He had died in 1909.)

45,000 saw the following teams take the field:

Celtic: Adams, McNair, Dodds; Young, McAteer, Hay; Kivlichan, McMenemy, Quinn, Hastie, Hamilton.
Hamilton Accies: J.Watson, Davie, Millar; P.Watson, W.McLaughlin, Eglinton; J.H.McLaughlin, Waugh, Hunter, Hastie, McNeill

The pitch was hard, Celtic were poor and Hamilton, although clearly overawed by the occasion, played the better football, but neither team was able to find the net. Contemporary accounts are unanimous in saying that it was one of the poorest Cup Finals in recent years. A few jokes were made about Hamilton (i.e. Davy on Celtic's left wing) v. Hamilton (i.e. Accies), and there is the statistical oddity of both inside lefts being called Hastie, but apart from that, there is little for the historian to enthuse over in this game. Rangers, the hosts, even claimed their ball back at the end, instead of giving it to someone as a souvenir!

Such a miserly attitude did not prevent Rangers being allowed to host the Replay a week later. The dismal fare of the previous week had deterred people from returning and the attendance was a little more than half of those who attended the first game. For the replay, Maley, realising that the Accies had little to offer and that the Cup could be won by a little more adventurous play, made two changes. One was to push the attack minded Joe Dodds from his customary left back slot to left half, and bring Captain James Hay back to left back ('Dun' had increasingly become a defender of late in any case—what modern theorists, thinking themselves innovative, class a 'double centre half' or a 'sweeper').

It was the other change however that would have longer reaching consequences. John Hastie was dropped (he had been ineffectual in the first game) and Kivlichan of the brown scapulars was moved to inside left, leaving a vacancy on the right wing for a prodigious youngster called Andy McAtee.

Maley was prepared to back his judgement on this youngster who had already played several games on both wings and in the centre. He was stocky and burly, his legs famously described by more than one historian as resembling those of a billiard table; he had the impeccable Celtic credentials of coming from Croy Celtic and Mossend Hibs. He had a thunderball shot, was deceptively fast and even in his short time with the club, had revealed total commitment. His inclusion meant that the mining village of Croy, Celtic daft anyway, had at least three men in the green and white with intimate connections in the village - Andy McAtee, his near namesake Tommy McAteer and of course Jimmy Quinn.

The Hamilton team was unchanged, but Celtic now fielded Adams; McNair, Hay; Young, McAteer, Dodds; McAtee, McMenemy, Quinn, Kivlichan, Hamilton. The start of play was delayed by the appearance of a rabbit on the pitch. Jokes were cracked about him not being the only rabbit, but it took some time before he was eventually worn down - the honour of catching him going to Davy Hamilton.

When the game eventually did start, it was obvious from an early

39

stage that this was a hungrier Celtic team and the faithful were soon giving them every encouragement. In particular, they were encouraged to note that McMenemy was back on song with his mazy runs and splendid ball distribution. He also was wise and shrewd enough, remembering perhaps his own timid initiation into the big time, to bring, very gently at first and then with perhaps a little more demand, young McAtee into the game. Young McAtee began to power down that right wing in such a way that questions were being asked about why he had not played in the first game.

But Hamilton defended desperately and reached half time with the scores still level. Celtic, however, an experienced side and cajoled by Young and Dodds, kept at it and on the hour mark earned their due reward. McAtee picked up a loose ball on the half way line and slipped it inside to McMenemy. 'Napoleon' then started on one of his runs, not a mazy one this time, but directed straight at goal. He had evaded one or two challenges, got inside the penalty box and when every one expected him to shoot or pass, across ran Jimmy Quinn to take the ball off his foot and score in what was obviously a well rehearsed move.

There was now no way back for Hamilton, for Celtic's defence had given little away all season. Alec McNair was quiet and dignified, James Hay was constructive as he broke up any attack and Davy Adams in goal was having a lonely afternoon. Imagine, however, the feelings of Tommy McAteer as full time drew nigh. A year ago, as centre half of Clyde, he had been two goals up with very little time left before an own goal was lost and then Langlands hit home a corner to give Dundee a Replay. A further Replay followed before Dundee won it. Poor Tommy must have been suffering agonies, but this year brought the highlight of his varied but none too successful playing career.

Full time was almost there and Celtic were pressing. Unwisely perhaps, Tommy had followed play upfield leaving only Alec McNair to deal with any desperate Hamilton breakaway. Then a run by Andy McAtee, a cross, the ball only parried by a Hamilton defender, the ball bobbing about outside Hamilton's penalty area, then Tommy saw a chance. He pounced on the ball and unleashed a screamer into the top left hand corner of the net. The Cup was Celtic's and Tommy had at last won his medal. There would be dancing in the streets of Croy that night.

It was a peculiar triumph, made all the sweeter because 1911 was a poor Celtic side. Clearly in the throes of transition, they were nevertheless able to lift the Scottish Cup to keep faith with their fans.

Another truly great team was developing, as could be seen in the blooding of young Andy McAtee and the 1911 Scottish Cup was Celtic's way of apologising to their fans for losing the League. The Cup, however, would do for going on with.

— 8 —

ENTER PATSY
1912

In season 1911-1912, Celtic improved on their performance of the previous season in that they came second in the League (Rangers won it again) and once again carried off the Scottish Cup, for the eighth time. It could not truthfully have been said to be one of the greatest Celtic sides of all times, but this season did see the blooding of the famous Patsy Gallagher.

In the eyes of the few (the very few still alive who actually saw him) there is little doubt that he was the greatest of them all, beating Puskas, Pele and Maradonna by some distance. It is of course very difficult to argue that he was or he wasn't, yet there is a surprising unanimity of all those who played with him or against him that he was unbeatable for ball control, dribbling, passing and sheer footballing skills. Bob Kelly and James McGrory say he was the best, Davie McLean (who, although an ex Celt, played only against Patsy) also says so and many an old timer has now gone to his grave with the unshakeable conviction that he saw the greatest football player there has ever been. During the First World War, it was said that the talk in all the Scots regiments was of little other than Patsy Gallagher.

Unlike most Celts of his time, Patsy actually was an Irishman, born in Ramelton, Co.Donegal in 1893. His name ought to be spelt the Irish way - Gallagher, although his family after their move to Clydebank when Patsy was a young boy were willing to call themselves Gallacher (which was more Scottish, they felt) after their nameplate on the door had been erroneously spelt that way. Patsy was little more than 18 when he was signed from Clydebank Juniors in October 1911.

Frankly, he looked more like a candidate for a sanatorium than a football field with his slender build, lack of inches (little more than 5'6") and spindle shanks. When he was introduced to his team mates, Quinn and others were said to have made disparaging comments about being done for manslaughter if he was put on the park. 'The last time I saw a pair o legs like that, there wis a message tied tae wan o them' said the worldly wise Sunny Jim. It would not be long however before the magical wee man would make them eat their words.

The inside right position had been a problem that season for Celtic. McMenemy was out injured, and his deputy Paddy Travers was not a success. Accordingly on December 2nd 1911, Maley decided to back his judgement and risking the incredulity of the fans and disbelief of the players, put Gallagher out as inside right against St.Mirren at Celtic Park.

He need not have worried about the reaction of the fans. Fans always love a small person, he was an Irishman to boot and he looked like Charlie Chaplin, already the darling of the infant cinema industry. As well as all that, the team won that day and Gallagher played well, showing a certain amount of ball skills. He retained his place until Christmas, even on December 23rd when McMenemy returned, forcing 'Napoleon' to play at inside left. The move was not a success however on a boggy pitch, and Patsy was soon dropped. It was an idea that Maley would return to however.

James Hay had by now gone to Newcastle United and Sunny Jim Young now served as captain. Sunny Jim proved a determined leader, much loved of the Celtic Park faithful and his inspiration of the team was always a factor in the team's performances. Willie Loney was now back as centre half and in 'Dun' Hay's place, we now find Peter Johnstone, a fine strapping Fifer whose defensive capabilities would allow him to take over Loney's position at centre half in years to come but whose career and life would be cut short in the carnage of the First World War.

Behind the half back line, McNair and Dodds had now established themselves. McNair, deservedly called 'The Icicle' because of his unflappability, brought a dignity to the right back position that has seldom been equalled. A quiet spoken, retiring man, Alec McNair would deservedly be held in awe by the Celtic fans for over a decade yet, and then for all time as the legends grew up about him. Left back Joe Dodds was very much an attacking full back. He had started life as a forward, then was a fine wing half, but would earn immortality as a left back. In goal, Davy Adams was now suffering problems with rheumatism and his eyesight, and by December had given way to comedian John Mulrooney.

Mulrooney was not a handsome man with his large nose and protruding ears. His face however fitted him for the role of court jester and entertainer on away trips. When it was becoming apparent that Adams was beginning to struggle, Maley had signed Mulrooney in

November 1911, and given him his chance on December 9th on a snow covered Hampden Park against Queen's Park. John took the opportunity and the side lost more than one goal on only one occasion for the rest of the season.

The forward line was more problematical, with only Andy McAtee the hero of last year's Cup Final replay on the right wing being reliably able to produce the goods. On the left wing was John Brown for most of the season - an honest journeyman from Dysart in Fife but little more, and the inner three were much changed with the injuries to McMenemy and the recurrent breaking down of Quinn. Paddy Travers (later to become manager of Aberdeen and Clyde), Andy Donaldson and Willie Nicholl were only intermittently successful and Patsy Gallagher had not yet developed.

A Quinn hat-trick over Rangers on New Year's Day at Celtic Park seemed to rekindle Celtic's fading hopes of the Championship, but in truth they were probably too far behind following a dreadful autumn. The Scottish Cup however beckoned once again, and Celtic entertained Dunfermline Athletic for the first time in a competitive game at Celtic Park on January 27th. The Fifers, clearly relishing their big day out fought well, and a John Brown goal was all that separated the teams at full-time. East Stirling were then disposed of without a great deal of trouble, but Celtic faced real danger up at Pittodrie in the Quarter Final.

Only twenty minutes were left and Aberdeen were 2-0 up. Both goals had arrived unexpectedly and against the run of play, Celtic had missed a penalty and the Aberdeen fans in the huge 30,000 crowd were already celebrating a famous victory. Celtic had several players out of touch and in spite of their enormous pressure, just could not score. They would have been forgiven for thinking that this was not to be their day, but it was then that Sunny Jim adopted an inspirational role, thrusting forward, encouraging the half-fit McMenemy, cajoling the ageing Quinn and crucially feeding the young McAtee who was now clearly getting the better of the tiring left side of the home defence. It was McAtee who made space on the right and crossed for Quinn to pull one back, and then when a similar situation developed towards the end and the black and golds expected another cross, Andy ran in himself and scored from a tight angle to the rapture of the visiting support for whom the long journey and the expensive train fare had suddenly become worthwhile.

Celtic celebrated their escape by winning next week's Replay by two goals from Paddy Travers, and were thus through to the Semi Final at Ibrox Park against the strong going and much fancied Heart of

Midlothian. This was the first year that Semi Final venues were held on neutral territory, and 43,000 people were attracted to this tie.

The game was full of interest, for Hearts were going well, and Maley had returned the previous week to playing McMenemy at inside left, dropping Travers and introducing young Gallagher at inside right. This move had not been a great success when tried in the heavy conditions of mid-winter, but had seemed to work in a 1-1 draw at Pittodrie the previous week in the League.

Supporters were concerned about this, however, for a Semi Final did not seem the best place for an experiment, especially when Travers and Donaldson were available. Their concerns were unjustified, for Patsy won the hearts of all but the Hearts by a brilliant display of dribbling and ball control, distracting the Edinburgh defence and allowing the new left wing partnership of McMenemy and Brown to run riot. 'Napoleon' in particular who had not had a great season with injury and loss of form (involving the loss of his Scotland place to Bobby Walker of Hearts) now showed his versatility and revelled in his new role, scoring two goals of high quality and feeding John Brown on the left wing for the other. The supporters were as excited about next week's Scottish Cup Final as were those lucky people booked to sail to America in the maiden voyage of the ship called the *Titanic*.

Prospective travellers on the *Titanic* might have been upset at the vehemence of the wind which prevailed at Ibrox on April 6th 1912. The opponents were Clyde who had barely recovered from their Cup Final defeat two years ago against Dundee after they had seemed to have had things all sown up. En route to the Final, Clyde had experienced a torrid time against Rangers in a tie which the Ibrox men conceded following violence among their supporters. The Clyde back-room staff were not without significance in the history of Scottish football. The manager was Alec Maley, brother of Celtic's Willie Maley and thus brothers were rival managers in a Scottish Cup Final for the first time. (This would happen again with the Maleys in 1923 when Alec had moved on to be the manager of Hibs, and it would not be until 1991 that it would occur for the third time with Tommy and Jim McLean of Motherwell and Dundee United.) Clyde's trainer was one William Struth, who after the war would become manager of Rangers.

The teams at windswept Ibrox before 45,000 fans were:

Celtic: Mulrooney, McNair, Dodds; Young, Loney, Johnstone; McAtee, Gallagher, Quinn, McMenemy, Brown.

Back row: Directors M. Dunbar, J. Shaughnessy, J. McKillop, T. Colgan. Middle: W. Quinn (trainer), W. Loney, J. McMenemy, J. Dodds, J. Quinn, P. Johnstone, J. Young, W. Maley (manager). Front: J. Mulrooney, A. McAtee, J. Brown, J. Kelly (chairman), P. Gallagher, T. McGregor, A. McNair.

Clyde: Grant, Gilligan , Blair; Walker, McAndrew , Collins; Hamilton, Jackson, Morrison, Carmichael, Stevens.

In such hurricane conditions reminiscent of the 1900 Cup Final, good football was always going to be difficult, and Clyde who won the toss decided to play against the wind first. They were delighted to go in at half time only one goal down. That had occurred when a free kick taken by Alec McNair floated into the goalmouth, was missed by several Clyde heads who had misjudged the wind and came gently down to the feet of the unmarked McMenemy. This was on the 30th minute mark, and although Celtic then pressed furiously for the remainder of the half, no further goals were forthcoming.

The second half was a great test of the Celtic defence, but it was the Celtic midfield of Young and Johnstone who took control with Johnstone in particular appreciating the techniques of playing against the wind. Short passes along the ground were the order of the day and much use was made of the dribbling inside men McMenemy and Gallagher who were clearly under orders to retain as much possession as possible. Mulrooney in the Celtic goal was also in inspired form, being particularly adept at judging the swirl of the wind, and twice in the space of five minutes, his huge limbs sprang to either side of his goal to deny first Stevens and then Jackson.

Mulrooney's form was clearly inspiring those in front of him and

McNair's coolness was similarly reassuring to the lads in green in the stands and terracing, as wave after wave of Clyde attack surged against the steadfast Celtic rearguard. Yet the Clyde attacks grew less frequent as the half wore on, and Peter Johnstone in particular was outstanding in midfield. Time was wearing out for luckless Clyde when Andy McAtee broke down the right wing and sent over a cross, aiming for behind the goal but knowing that the wind would hold it up. The ball hung in the air almost on the Clyde goal-line, up jumped John Brown, who headed the ball down to the inrushing Patsy Gallagher who finished the job.

Clyde now had nothing left, and Celtic had won their 8th Scottish Cup. It was a tremendous triumph for the club with so many players (Mulrooney, Johnstone, McAtee, Gallagher and Brown) in either their first or at most their second season at Celtic Park. Rangers may have won the League, but with Celtic developing fast, it would clearly not be long before a challenge for the Championship would be made. In the meantime, the joy of victory was sweet, and young Patsy Gallagher had made the first step to becoming Charles Stuart Parnell's replacement as the 'uncrowned king of Ireland', at least in Glasgow!

— 9 —

NOT MUCH WRONG WITH THE WORLD 1914

Season 1913-14 was a magnificent season in the history of the club. Apart from losing in the Glasgow Cup to Third Lanark in October 1913, the team won every competition that it entered , comprehensively wrenching from Rangers the League Championship which they had held for the last three years and playing football that would live long in the memories of those for whom the next few years would bring a sort of hell that the civilized world had never yet experienced.

It was hard to find any kind of fault with the side. The facts speak for themselves. In all games between October 7th 1913 and February 28th 1914, they lost only one goal - to Raith Rovers at Stark's Park in December. Willie Loney was now away to Motherwell, but he was immediately replaced by Peter Johnstone who showed the same excellence at centre half as he had at left half. His place at left half was taken by Johnny McMaster. Sometimes erroneously called Jimmy, Johnny had the misfortune to have a most lugubrious countenance and was frequently referred to by the scribes as 'McMaster of the melancholy visage', yet his tackling was fierce, his clearances accurate and his distribution perfect.

Sunny Jim revelled in his role as captain and was a household name wherever Celtic went. The distinguishing white hair had now mysteriously darkened, but little else had changed about this Hercules of a man. Sunny, deified by the Celtic support, also had the capability of inciting the opposition support as the following story well illustrates.

In February, Scottish Cup duty took Celtic to Forfar for an occasion which, even now, outshines wars and everything else, in the local culture. Celtic won 5-0 to no-body's surprise, but Forfar had one fine talented forward in Alec Troup, who with better support might have caused real problems to Celtic. (After the war, Troup would go on to shine for Dundee, Everton and win 5 caps for Scotland, threatening even the great Alan Morton's Scotland berth on occasion).

In fact, something rare was happening here, for someone was getting the better of Sunny. The locals roared their appreciation, and on more than one occasion Sunny downed the talented Loon, earning a reprimand from the referee. All this was too much for Troup's mother whose maternal instinct was not to be deterred by anyone, however illustrious. As the game finished, and the players came off, to the amazement of the rest of the crowd who were enjoying their eyeful of the demigods, Mother Troup leaned forward and battered Sunny with her umbrella saying the immortal words 'Tak that, ye durty Glesca bugger'.Sunny was not called Sunny for nothing though; he smiled serenely and walked on, his dignity earning him even more approbation. The local constabulary chose to turn a blind eye to Mrs.Troup's antics, but no-one would in future trifle with her 'Eckie', Sunny Jim or no Sunny Jim.

It was during the long time when no-one could get near to Charlie Shaw that stories grew about him, as they had about Davy Adams. He used to go home for his tea, he would leave the field to court his lady friend, he would wander round the track and ask if the other goalkeeper wanted a hand, he would ask the crowd if they wanted a game of cards and so on. 'Ten Internationals and Charlie Shaw' was often said. This was not true, of course, but there was a serious side to it in that poor Charlie never got a chance to shine and impress the selectors, such was the quality of player in front of him.

Any forward line that started 'McAtee, Gallagher...' would outclass anyone else, for Patsy, although irritatingly prone to overdo it on occasion and vulnerable to a coarse challenge from the thugs who occasionally maqueraded as defenders (one thinks of Jimmy Galt of Rangers who rejoiced in the nickname of 'Dirty Galt'), was inspiring and a joy to watch, and McAtee was fast, speedy and deadly accurate with the ability to run in from the wing and score goals. Centre forward was more of a problem, for Quinn was now clearly struggling against injury and age, and an adequate replacement had not yet been found. McMenemy at inside left had been out with injury for a long section of the season but had returned with a new lease of life, and on the left wing there was a sensational new discovery called Johnny Browning.

Browning (not to be confused with John Brown whom he replaced on the left wing) is an interesting character. A streetwise, menacing looking character, Johnny would after the war do time for match fixing, but in 1914 he quickly became another darling of the Celtic Park Brake Clubs. He had the ability to impersonate Charlie Chaplin, Harry Lauder and even Willie Maley, but on the field his speciality was, like McAtee on the other wing, charging in and scoring goals, so much so that it was often said that the lack of a first class centre forward at Celtic Park wasn't necessarily all that great a disadvantage.

The League was won by six points from Rangers, a purple spell in the crowded April calendar merely crowning the event, but most eyes were fixed on the Scottish Cup Final to be played at Ibrox on April 11th. The build up to the game would have sent shivers down the spine of many a modern manager for McNair, Dodds and McMenemy all played in the 3-1 victory over Third Lanark on April 1st, then in Scotland's 3-1 win over England on April 4th, then the 1-0 win over Kilmarnock on April 8th before turning out in the Final on the 11th. Little seems to have been heard of 'mental preparation' and 'shielding from the media' in those days.

This Cup Final was not the first 'all green' or 'all Irish' Scottish Cup Final, for the two had met in 1902 when Hibs had been triumphant. But in 1914, Ireland was very definitely in the news, and newspapers were saying what a great year it was for the Irish, for as well as the two teams in the Cup Final, there would surely very soon be an Irish Home Rule Act passed through Parliament. The Ulstermen could surely not prevent it, and the British Government now seemed at last willing to solve the Irish problem. It would have to be something pretty cataclysmic to stop it now.

The Suffragettes were also very much in the news. Last year one of them had thrown herself in front of the King's horse at the Derby to draw attention to their cause, and although that was dismissed as the lunatic fringe, there was now a strong body of opinion that Votes for Women was not as ridiculous an idea as first thought. After all, some of them had by now been to University, become doctors even, and there was no reason to believe among the Establishment that they would do anything daft like vote for this dangerous Labour Party.

Abroad, Britain still was the richest power on earth. The United States was fast catching up, but remote and none too interested in Europe. Germany was a potential problem, particularly with her strong navy, but the Kaiser, although prone to the occasional piece of idiotic behaviour, was the cousin of King George V and basically a harmless fool. Russia was backward, corrupt and useless; France was decadent, effete and venal, and besides we had some sort of an understanding with them.

Such weighty affairs of state were, one suspects, of little concern to the 55,000 who made their way to Ibrox on that day. Celtic were the clear favourites, but Hibs were well known as tough competitors, and as was the way with Irishmen, had no great love for other Irishmen,

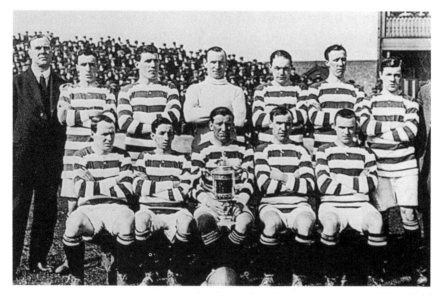

The side who beat Hibs in the 1914 Scottish Cup Final.

Back row: W. Maley (secretary/manager) McMaster, Dodds, Shaw, McNair, Johnstone, McColl. Front row: McAtee, Gallagher, Young (captain), McMenemy, Browning.

particularly these astonishingly successful ones who had usurped their position as the Irish team of Scotland.

Hibs suffered one piece of indignity in that their charabanc could not cut its way through the crowds. Appeals from the passengers that they were indeed the Edinburgh opposition made no difference to the thronging Glaswegians, nor the Glasgow Police who would not be persuaded that this was indeed the famous Hibernian F.C. It was rather like the story of the crowds rushing to watch a hanging and preventing the cart which carried the hero of the hour from getting there. 'What are you all hurrying for? There'll be no show until I get there' he is reputed to have said. Hibs manager must have said something similar to a perceptive policeman, for they eventually reached Ibrox.

The weather was fine, dry and windy and the teams were:

Celtic: Shaw, McNair, Dodds; Young, Johnstone, McMaster; McAtee, Gallagher, Owers, McMenemy, Browning.
Hibs: Allan, Girdwood, Templeton; Kerr, Paterson, Grossert; Wilson, Fleming, Hendren, Wood, Smith.

The famous referee Tom Dougray of Barrhead, later of Bellshill was in charge, and seldom can he have had an easier 90 minutes. It was clear from the start that Hibs' tactics were to contain and then to try to hit Celtic on the break. This led to mutterings from the packed terracings about wanting a replay for another big gate etc., but this was less than fair to a fine Hibs defence who gave the wingers McAtee and Browning their quietest afternoon for some time.

If the frustrated Celtic fans were looking for a scapegoat, they found one in centre forward Ebenezer Owers. Even in 1914, Ebenezer was a name that only appeared in Dickens' novels, and the poor Englishman was subject to an amount of ridicule. He also had a hard act to follow in that he was Quinn's replacement. In fact he did score 11 goals (including 4 against Ayr United in the week between Christmas and the New Year) that season, but sadly none of them in the Cup Final. Several sitters came his way, and he muffed them all, and his Celtic Park career rapidly came to an end.

In fact, Hibs grew in confidence as the game progressed, hitting the post late on and doing enough to worry the supporters. Full time came however with no score, and it was a disappointed crowd that returned home that night. The slightly snooty West End however was treated to the peculiar sight of two sets of supporters singing 'The Wearing o' the Green'.

It was on the Sunday that Maley made his fateful decision. The likeable Londoner would have to be dropped, at least for the game on Monday against Queen's Park at Celtic Park. In his place came 21 year old Jimmy McColl who had already been blooded that season. The Amateurs were cuffed 5-0, McColl scored twice and was kept for the Cup Final Replay at Ibrox on Thursday 16th April.

This was the only change in the Celtic side and Hibs were unchanged. Considering it was a Thursday evening with a 5.45 p.m. kick off, the attendance of 36,000 was quite remarkable. This time the outcome was in little doubt with young Jimmy McColl striking twice and early to kill the game almost before it started. In the eighth minute a Browning corner crossed the goalmouth and was headed back by McAtee to the excellently placed McColl who had clearly read the situation. Three minutes later, a shot from the youngster was saved by goalkeeper Allan, but McColl in spite of having stumbled, rushed in between two defenders to net the rebound.

A two goal start for a team of the calibre of the 1914 Celts usually meant no way back for the opposition, and this was what happened here. Celtic now started to turn it on, and the crowd were able to revel in the excellence of Gallagher and McMenemy, the visionary passing of Sunny Jim and the speed of wingers McAtee and Browning. It was

Browning who scored the third before half time when he ran in from the left, was fouled several times, but was able to keep going. Mr Dougray, a lover of good football, played advantage, and Browning scored a magnificent third.

The songs of triumph were heard all through the second half as the crowd obviously swelled with the presence of those late in getting away from work. In truth, the second half was a trifle tedious as Celtic saw no point in humiliating their rivals, and played out time. Browning scored another of his specials following a brilliant crossfield pass from Andy McAtee directly to his feet, and could have scored more. Some claimed to have seen manager Maley in the stand gesturing to his players to ease up and to Mr Dougray to blow for time, but Hibs did get a consolation goal and a cheer from the predominantly Glaswegian crowd when Smith put one past a somnolent Charlie Shaw who thus conceded his 14th goal of the season and his fourth since the New Year. Even that one was lucky for it hit a post first.

The final whistle was greeted with great cheers from a crowd who thus saw their team's ninth Scottish Cup. They were rapidly catching up on Queen's Park's ten, and surely by 1916 they would be ahead, for there was nothing in all Scotland who could live with that mighty team of 1914. There are some Celtic historiographers who think that 1914 was a better team than 1908 or even 1967. Sadly, they did not get a chance to prove it, for carnage and suffering beckoned. Nobody knew that though in the triumphant march home, with the accompaniment of bugles, to the East End on that fine spring twilight evening of April 16th 1914.

— 10 —

THE CASSIDY CAVALCADE
1923

They were of course to call it the war to end all wars, a classic misnomer if ever there were one. That it was manifestly untrue was proved by the continuing state of unrest that Europe found itself as millions tried to come to terms with the appalling loss and the changed world. The Irish community of Glasgow had suffered as much as anyone in the conflict with thousands on the Rolls of Honour as they were well meaningly but unhelpfully called; thousands more were now living under the handicap of permanent disability and disfigurement.

When one considers that there was also a trade recession (inevitable after such a grievous war), major labour problems in the mines and elsewhere and a very real fear (or was it not a hope?) of a Communist Revolution, the early twenties were an interesting, although terrifying time. But football once again provided a welcome relief to the masses of Industrial Scotland.

Even there, however, there was evidence that things would never quite be the same again. In the first year after the war, for example, Kilmarnock won the Scottish Cup beating equally unlikely finalists Albion Rovers. The following year it was Partick Thistle (Jimmy McMenemy and all) who won it on McMenemy's old stamping ground of Celtic Park, then Morton chipped in with their first success in 1922.

Celtic had had a fine side during the war, in spite of seeing many fine players go off to the front and, as in the case of Peter Johnstone that fine half back and some others, not returning. They had struggled in 1920 and 1921. They won the League in 1922, however, in a torrid game at Greenock which had been lucky not to be abandoned because of organized crowd trouble, and in season 1922-3, great were the hopes of a return to the pre-war glory days.

The season however started without the services of the 'boy wonder' Tommy McInally. Arguably, one of the greatest ball players ever to don the green, Tommy, an orphan boy from Barrhead and brought up by the mother of another Celt Arthur McInally, never knew any sort of stability. His early years seem to have been tough, his teenage years were scarred by that dreadful war, and Tommy could not cope with the rigid discipline, so necessary in a footballer, however talented. Maley had tried hard to be a father figure to the storm petrel, but there were too many times when Tommy turned up late for training or smelling of alcohol. In summer 1922 when Tommy did an Oliver Twist and asked for more wages, Maley had had enough, called Tommy's bluff and sent the Celtic daft youngster on his reluctant way to Third Lanark, where he would pine for home over the next three years.

Another who fell foul of Maley's discipline was the powerful Johnny Gilchrist, successor to Sunny Jim at right half. He was a fine player, and certainly in the previous year of 1922 (in which Gilchrist won his only International Cap), the powerful half back line of Gilchrist, Cringan and McMaster had won the Championship as much as any other department of the team. Johnny was yet a firebrand, full of himself and ready with his tongue. More tactfully handled, he might have been a great Celt for many years, but Maley was in no mood to thole any sort of rebellious behaviour, and in January 1923, ironically after a game against Tommy McInally's Third Lanark, Gilchrist was shown the door and moved to Preston North End.

Celtic Park was also stunned in September 1922 when the death of Sunny Jim was reported. Although he had retired from the game some five years ago, Sunny was still considered a God among Celts. Current Celtic historiography rates Sunny as the greatest Celt of them all, and his early death at the age of 40 stunned everyone. He was a pillion passenger on a motor bike which collided with a lorry between Hurlford and Kilmarnock. He died instantly in what was a surprisingly common type of accident in these pre-crash-helmet days. Maley, apparently, was inconsolable at the loss of his greatest ever player.

League form in the first half of the season was inconsistent, and the two defeats at both Celtic Park in the autumn and at Ibrox on New Year's Day to Rangers meant that there was no realistic chance of a challenge for the League against a consistent, if unspectacular, Rangers side. Yet the team did have some fine players, notably centre forward Joe Cassidy whose goal scoring exploits were legendary.

Originally an inside left, Cassidy had served in the Black Watch during the War winning the nickname 'Trooper' and earned his spurs and the undying gratitude of everyone by his two goals against Rangers at Ibrox on New Year's Day 1921. Contemporary accounts tell of brake clubs on their triumphant return from Ibrox with banners and placards mentioning Cassidy in the same breath as Sinn Fein and Rebels.Cassidy had been inside left that day, but the departure of McInally to Third Lanark moved him to centre, where the goals kept coming. With his good looks and pictures of him that twinkled everywhere, Joe was a hero in times which desperately needed one.

Another side effect of the move of McInally was the bringing in to inside left of Adam McLean and the introduction on the left wing of Paddy Connolly. McLean, grossly underated and falsely underestimated because of his quiet demeanour on the park would turn out to be a great Celtic hero until the late 1920's and Connolly who would eventually become as great a success on the right wing, was noted for his speed down the left and his inch perfect crosses. Once again, a quiet, soft-spoken, modest Celt whose contribution has often been neglected.

The Scottish Cup opened for Celtic at Lochgelly in Fife on January 13th with Celtic in the middle of a depressing spell of form which had effectively surrendered the League to Rangers. Gallagher was out injured, so Jimmy Cairney was given one of his rare outings for Celtic at inside right, and at inside left was Jean McFarlane. This mighty man would be quite at home in Lochgelly for he had played so much of his early football in Fife, including spells for Cowdenbeath and Raith Rovers. His name was John, but was changed to Jean, perhaps under the influence of the French which was so much in currency after the War, or perhaps because he wrote a column every week for the *Weekly News* whose main cartoon characters in the 1920's were 'Jock and Jean'. Wherever, he got his name from, he is one of the few footballers ever to be given a woman's name, and not apparently to be upset about it.

It so happens that this game at Lochgelly is on film. A local cinema owner decided to film the game with the obvious purpose of attracting people to his cinema the next week merely to see themselves at the match. Football historians however are disappointed when so little is seen of the play, understandably perhaps when one considers the sheer weight and unmanoeuvrability of these early cameras. You can see Jean McFarlane running past, and there is a shot of Charlie Shaw, but Joe Cassidy's hat-trick is sadly unrecorded. In fact, it was a totally unconvincing performance by Celtic, for Lochgelly fought hard, scored twice and with a bit of luck could have equalized at the end. Cassidy's hat-trick was the difference between the two sides.

The next round saw Hurlford at Celtic Park. Maley's disatisfaction with the Lochgelly performance had led him to introduce another youngster the following week against Third Lanark. The team had lost again to Thirds, but the youngster was worth another go at inside right for the visit of Hurlford, and his name was James Edward McGrory. Hurlford were swept aside to the tune of 4-0, and this time it was four goals that the mighty Cassidy scored. A fortnight later, East Fife were despatched 2-1 and the goals were scored yet again by Joe Cassidy. Thus Celtic were in the Quarter Finals of the Cup, had scored nine goals and Cassidy had scored them all.

Raith Rovers now came to Celtic Park for the Quarter Final in late February. The Kirkcaldy side were now going well and contained a talented inside man by the name of Alec James. The denizens of Celtic Park had a good laugh at the baggy pants that were already a hallmark of the youngster (the origin lay in his susceptibility to rheumatism) but had to be impressed by his trickery as he gave both McStays, Cringan and McFarlane a hard time of it. He did over elaborate however, clearly revelling in the reluctant applause from the Celtic Park crowd, and the more direct Celtic forwards won the day. Such had been the reputation and the crowd's expectation from their darling Joe that Rovers always had at least two men on him. Exploiting such a hole in their defence, Adam McLean squeezed through for the only goal of the game.

The Semi Final at Ibrox was against the strong going Motherwell who had their answer, they claimed, to the goal scoring machine of Joe Cassidy. This was Hughie Ferguson, a remarkably free scoring goal-scorer. In 1927, he would be known as the Scotsman who took the English Cup to Wales when he scored for Cardiff the only goal of the F.A.Cup Final against Arsenal. Yet when depression and homesickness brought him back to Scotland, to Dundee, a catalogue of misfortunes in his private life led to him tragically gassing himself in the stand at Dens Park in January 1930.

In 1923 however, the popular and apparently happy Ferguson was knocking them in for Motherwell (he would eventually net almost 300 for them), and the newspapers built up the confrontation between the two goalscorers. But Celtic's captain, centre half Willie Cringan, who had been under a great deal of pressure from the support and indeed the manager Willie Maley for poor performances, rose to the occasion. He stayed with Ferguson the whole game and totally nullified the threat, while meanwhile at the other end, goals by Andy McAtee and Joe Cassidy (of course!) saw Celtic home to an all green Cup Final against Hibs.

The last time that these two met was in that fine spring of 1914

Top row: Ed. McGarvey (captain trainer), A. McNair, W. McStay, C. Shaw, Hugh Hilley, W. Maley (manager), J. McStay, J. McFarlane, W. Quinn (trainer). Bottom: A. McAtee, J. Cassidy, A. McLean, W. Cringan, P. Gallagher, P. Connolly.

when the world had seemed such a totally different place with optimism and vibrancy and 'dreams and songs to sing'. Now 9 years later, the world was depressed in every sense of the word, and the future was uncertain and gloomy. The streets outside Hampden Park, for example, on that agreeably early day (March 31st in contrast to 1995 when it was May 27th!), were festooned with beggars, some with one leg and placards saying 'Woonded (sic) at Somme', others with poorly clad children, some playing mouth organs, others singing disharmonic ditties which extolled the values of Scotland, Ireland and my darling Clementine. Basically good humoured, yet on occasion, money was asked for with a little more than a piteous cry as a knife was produced to show that business was meant; women, most of them hideously past their prime of life or perhaps merely old before their time plied with a nod, a wink and a toss of the head their none too subtle trade. Others sold favours in green with 'Have a go, Joe' written on them, and there were the all too familiar lines of urchins, the lucky ones shod, begging to be lifted over the turnstile to see the Cassidy who would make them forget that they might not eat that night.

It was a sight that would leave its mark on many a visitor. Some 70 years later an old timer would recall the sight of the man with one eye, burn marks on his face and no teeth singing;

When this bloody war is over
No more soldiering for me
When I get my civvy clothes on
Oh, how happy I will be!

He couldn't finish the song because his throat filled up monstrously with phlegm, and he collapsed in a heap, coughing and spluttering and shouting to his puzzled listeners 'Gas'.

The game itself was a poor one. The crowd was 80,000 and the teams were:

Celtic: Shaw, McNair, W.McStay; J.McStay, Cringan, McFarlane; McAtee, Gallagher, Cassidy, McLean, Connolly

Hibs: Harper, McGinnigle, Dornan; Kerr, Miller, Shaw; Ritchie, Dunn, McColl, Halligan, Walker.

The line ups were interesting for several reasons. Hibs centre forward was Jimmy 'Sniper' McColl who had played for Celtic in 1914 and scored two goals in that outstanding replay, and for the first time ever, two brothers were playing in the Final - Willie and Jimmy McStay. Brothers were also the managers - Willie and Alec Maley - not for the first time however, for the same two had faced each other in 1912 when Alec managed Clyde. Both teams had one player who would play in the England v. Scotland International in a fortnight's time - goalkeeper Willie Harper of Hibs and centre half Willie Cringan of Celtic, and Celtic had one who would play for Ireland in the team that beat Wales 3-0 at Wrexham that same day. He was, of course, Patsy Gallagher.

Accounts of the game are unanimous in that it was a dull game with neither side really getting going and Gallagher in particular having a poor game. Praise is heaped upon defenders like Hibs' McGinnigle and Miller, and in particular on 'The Icicle', Alec McNair of Celtic. Alec was now nearly 40 and had played for Celtic half his life. As always he was faultless, retaining the love that the fans had for this quiet spoken and most gentle of men.

The game had gone about quarter of an hour into the second half when an aimless punt in the general direction of the Hibs' goal by Jean McFarlane was missed by goalkeeper Harper and Joe Cassidy was on hand to head into an empty net. It was a soft goal, but greeted with rapture by the crowd and with acclaim by those outside who knew by the cheer that Celtic had scored. 'It must have been Joe!' said our disfigured friend who had now recovered from his coughing fit.

Twenty minutes later,as the exit gates were opened to let the crowd out, they all rushed in to see the last quarter of an hour and revelled in the coolness of McNair, the composed play of the brothers McStay, the domineering Cringan and the authority of Charlie Shaw as the desperate Hibs' attacks fizzled out. Full time came, Celtic had won the Cup for the tenth time, equalling Queen's Park's record, and 'Erin's Green Valleys' was belted out from the packed terraces.

— 11 —

GIVE YOUNG McGRORY THE CUP!
1925

The mid twenties were shaping up to be unsatisfactory years at Celtic Park. More than once, talented Celts were shown the door, some for good reason, some for bad. Tommy McInally, for example, was still half-heartedly playing for Third Lanark, yet 'pining for home', as Maley himself would later put it. Johnny Gilchrist had perhaps been a real discipline problem, but the only thing that Willie Cringan seemed to have done wrong was to put in a dignified request for an improvement in conditions.

The brooding, introverted style of management as practised by Maley within the confines of Celtic Park was at odds with his external image where he was always genial, generous and kind, always willing to talk to the Press and on occasion on the infant method of communication called a radio for those lucky enough to possess such a machine and patient enough to listen to the dreadful crackling and hissing that it made.

That things were not well at Celtic Park was proved by the failure in 1923 and 1924 to make any sort of impression on the Scottish League. The fine Rangers side which contained Meiklejohn, Archibald, Cairns and Morton received little challenge and such challenge as there was came from the unlikely source of Broomfield, Airdrie where ex- Celt Willie Orr had welded together a talented side which included the likes of Bob Bennie, Hughie Gallagher and Bob McPhail to be a force of importance in Scottish football, and who won the Scottish Cup in 1924.

Season 1923-4 for Celtic however had been a singularly depressing one, yet there were some excellent players on view at Celtic Park. Patsy Gallagher was still the best inside man around, but now injury prone and moody. At inside left however, Celtic had introduced a Fife youngster by the name of Alec Thomson from Buckhaven. Like Gallagher, a little on the frail side, Alec was nevertheless determined and committed, and for him season 1923-4 was a learning process.

In summer 1924, while Britain tried to come to terms with a Labour Government, albeit a minority one, Celtic supporters remained cautiously optimistic that the coming season would see a fine blend of youth and experience, and that the Ibrox stranglehold on the Championship would be challenged. But then on the very eve of the season came the news that shattered everyone, namely that Joe Cassidy was transferred for a minimal fee to Bolton Wanderers. The Cassidy lovers were immediately plunged into grief; those of a more sanguine temperament hoped that pride could be swallowed and that the money could be used to bring back Tommy McInally; but this turned out to be one of Maley's more astute dealings.

In the first place, he was now able to introduce to the centre forward position the lad that he had farmed out to Clydebank, one James Edward McGrory. McGrory reputedly when he heard the news of his recall 'grabbed my cap and ran all the way'; in this youngster, there were definite resemblances to the mighty Jimmy Quinn. Secondly, Cassidy, great hero and character that he had been, was now in his late 20's and beginning to feel the pace and the pain of the many injuries that centre forwards got in these days. He would be less than a total success at Bolton, he moved to Preston for a spell before returning to Scotland to play for Dundee. In 1927, on the day of John Thomson's debut at Dens Park, the ageing Cassidy was making little progress against John Donoghue (not by any manner of means the greatest of centre halves) and his old fans sang more out of affection than anything else the old Negro slave song,

> 'I'm coming, I'm coming, though my head is bending low,
> I hear the gentle voices calling 'Poor Old Joe'.

'Poor Old Joe' did however have a few years of football left in him, but not at the highest level. He would never be considered as anything other than Joe Cassidy of Celtic.

In playing terms, the misery continued throughout 1924 -5. But the fans were justifiably proud of the young McGrory whose mid season lay off through injury was directly responsible for an abysmal run of games, and another youngster seemed to be coming through as well. This was Peter Wilson. Peter was a simple country boy from Beith in Ayrshire whose unfamiliarity with city life got him into difficulties more than once. He didn't know the way to Celtic Park, he couldn't handle trams and train timetables, he got lost in Woolworth's and the more street wise of his team mates mercilessly made a fool of this awkward looking youth whose clothes didn't fit and out of whose hair, reputedly, straw grew.

But slowly the kidding stopped as, throughout this season, Peter claimed the right half spot for himself. He may have been gauche off the field, but he was an expert on it with a fine positional sense, a tackle which was surprisingly strong in one so slight and an ability to pass an inch perfect ball across the field. He stroked and caressed the ball, and like a snooker player on a break, could think ahead and be in the right place for the return pass. His bucolic expression soon became a study in concentration and effort, and he was very soon a darling of the Celtic Park crowd. Celtic's history is rich in right halves; he can be paid no greater compliment than that he is freely mentioned by historians in the same breath as Sunny Jim and Bobby Murdoch. Such talent however does not always come to fruition overnight, and the 1924 - 5 season was very much a learning experience for the callow Peter.

The path to the Final in 1925 was not without its moments. Third Lanark were hammered 5-1 at Cathkin on a Saturday which may well be unique in Scottish footballing history. There was an eclipse of the sun, so serious that the gentlemen of the Press were give candles to help them write their reports. It cannot have been a total eclipse for Jimmy McGrory was able to see where the goal was well enough to score his first Scottish Cup hat-trick.

Then Alloa were defeated at Celtic Park before the quaintly named Solway Star paid one of their rare visits to Glasgow to play very well and hold Celtic to a 2-0 scoreline. There then followed a prolonged struggle against St. Mirren with a draw both home and away, then Celtic leading very narrowly by a single goal at neutral Ibrox when a St.Mirren forward was brought down just inside the penalty area as culprit McFarlane would later admit. Famous referee Peter Craigmyle of Aberdeen awarded a free kick just outside the box: St. Mirren wouldn't have it and refused to play on. It was an impasse, and Craigmyle, after ostentatiously looking at his watch, blew for time up, picked up the ball and walked off to the fury of the sulky Saints, but it was they who had refused to play.

Craigmyle was probably relieved to get rid of that one, for that was Monday 16th March and the Semi Final was scheduled for Hampden on the following Saturday against Rangers. Rangers at that time were undisputedly the best team in Scotland. They were the Champions of Scotland for the past two years and were unlikely to be caught this year either. In the rear they had the mighty Robb; Manderson and McCandless, in midfield the mighty Davie Meiklejohn, on the right wing Sandy Archibald and Andy Cunnigham, a whisker weaker than their left wing of Tommy Cairns and Alan Morton. Man for man, they were far superior to Celtic and had already beaten them three times that season, each time with more than a degree of comfort.

Celtic had only two things to comfort them as their fans in the 101,000 crowd made their way to Hampden for the Semi Final. One was that their players were younger - not necessarily a great advantage because younger meant less experience and striplings like Wilson, Thomson and McGrory might well freeze in the huge cauldron that Hampden would be. The other had to do with the supernatural, and it was that Rangers seemed to have a problem with the Scottish Cup which they had last won in 1903. A combination of the Hampden riot in 1909, the War and a fine goal for Greenock Morton in 1922 had prevented that, and jokes abounded about wounded soldiers recovering from shellshock and asking whether Rangers had won the Cup yet. Talk of hoodoos and jinxes prevailed, and this was the very point that Patsy Gallagher made to Celtic in the dressing room, indicating that the longer the game went on without Rangers scoring, the more it would play on their nerves. Accordingly, Celtic would start with a cautious, defensive formation.

The game did indeed start quietly, and with both Jimmy McStay at centre half and Peter Shevlin in goal in fine form, Rangers visibly began to fret as their outfield superiority brought no tangible reward. Then gradually and unobtrusively, Celtic's inside forwards Patsy Gallagher and Alec Thomson began to move forward, as Rangers players began to snarl at one another. The first goal however came from Peter Wilson who released Paddy Connolly. He then beat Irish International Billy McCandless, swept down the wing and crossed for young McGrory to score. It was a perfectly executed counter attack and remained long in the memory.

The second half saw Alec Thomson earn his spurs. In future years he would become known as 'McGrory's fetch and carry man', but on this occasion he sprayed passes all over to McGrory indeed, but more to wingers Connolly and McLean. These two roasted the panicky Ulstermen Manderson and McCandless and supplied countless balls into the penalty box.In the 60th minute, Connolly's corner kick was headed home by Adam McLean who was lingering unsuspected as two defenders followed the decoy McGrory. A fine one-two between McGrory and Connolly led to number three and McGrory's second; Alec Thomson then headed home a rebound from goalkeeper Robb, and Robb's miserable afternoon was completed when Adam McLean prodded home a misguided pass back from Manderson.

The 1925 side who beat Dundee in the final.

Top row: W. Maley (manager), W. McStay, P. Shevlin, H. Hilley, Tom White (chairman). Middle row: P. Wilson, J. McStay, J. McFarlane, A. McLean. Bottom row: P. Connolly, P. Gallagher, J. McGrory, A. Thomson.

The Celtic end erupted at all this of course, and the veteran's recollections were one of ecstacsy and dancing while at the other end, spaces opened up as disbelieving Rangers fans disappeared from the humiliation. It was quite clearly Celtic's greatest result since the War, possibly of all their 37 year history, and would stay that way for a long time, and the tradition began of Celtic being a weaker team than Rangers but capable of dishing out the odd spectacular hammering.

After all this, one would have expected the Final against Dundee on April 11th 1925 to have been an anti-climax. Not so, for it turned out to be one of the most famous in our long history, and one curses television for having been so slow to be invented, so that we cannot see the two most talked about and famous goals in green and white mythology.

75,137 saw referee Mr Dougray begin the game between the following two teams:

Celtic: Shevlin, W.McStay, Hilley; Wilson, J.McStay, McFarlane; Connolly, Gallagher, McGrory, Thomson, McLean.
Dundee: Britton, Brown, Thomson; Ross, W.Rankine, Irving; Duncan, McLean, Halliday, J.Rankine, Gilmour.

The run of play is easy to describe. Celtic were always on top but Dundee went in one up at half time after ex-Celt Davitt McLean was on hand to hammer home a rebound off the bar at the King's Park end of the ground. The second half was one of prolonged Celtic pressure until the 75th minute when Patsy Gallagher scored his famous goal. Various accounts are given, but very few people really had a clear view of what occurred. It appears that about 19 of the 22 players were in the Dundee penalty area at the King's Park end of the ground when Patsy Gallagher tried to dribble round them all. When tackled by a defender, he fell, but kept the ball tightly between his feet and somer-saulted into the net. He certainly had to be disentangled from the back of the net, but what exactly happened is not clear although McGrory was certainly in a good position to see and his account in 'A Lifetime in Paradise' is detailed and lucid.

For the winning goal with five minutes to go, we must move forward forty years and more to a Celtic household most Hogmanays and the occasional Saturday night. The father would tell everyone to clear the settee, the son and his friends would deferentially obey, the mother would look embarrassed but reconciled to what was to happen. 'You be Jean McFarlane and I'll do the rest', the father would say. The son would pull up his socks, as Jean had apparently done that day, and prepare to take the free kick. Sometimes a balloon was used; other times one's imagination, but after 'Jean' had lofted the 'Ball', James Edward McGrory dived horizontally over the settee crying 'A green and white figure catapulted forth...' The next prop to be used would be the silver teapot, and the action was now the Celtic charabanc. The son was now McGrory, the friends were the adoring masses, and the father was now Maley. 'Give young McGrory the Cup!' said the paternal Maley referring to the boy who had so recently been bereaved of his own father.

Celtic had now won the Cup for the 11th time, and Queen's Park's record had gone!

— 12 —

THE BARRHEAD BOY
1927

1927 saw Celtic's 12th victory in the Scottish Cup competition. The previous year in which Celtic had won the League, saw them unaccountably fall foul of St.Mirren in the Scottish Cup Final and lose in a way which baffled their supporters. Clearly, the supporters would settle for nothing less than the immediate restitution of the piece of silver which even in these days the supporters considered their own.

The man of the moment was Tommy McInally. His return home from Third Lanark in 1925 had been greeted with rapture by his many admirers, and the winning of the League the following year was due in no small measure to the Barrhead Boy. In his first three years at Celtic Park, the terms 'boy wonder' and such like had been applied to him, and his goals had been a permanent source of delight to the crowd, who had rejoiced in his clowning, his antics and his sense of fun.

Yet, as his critics were keen to point out, Tommy for all his talent achieved relatively little. His three years at Third Lanark were wasted ones, for his heart was not with him. For all his independent nature, he was Celtic to the core, and Maley who always claimed 'to have a soft spot for the boy' brought him back, but without totally being able to tame the wilder side of the boy.

Recent research has pointed out that Tommy was not who everyone thought he was, for there is no Thomas McInally born at Barrhead at the appropriate time. His brother Arthur can be found, but the evidence would seem that Tommy was an orphan or an illegitimate son of a relative whom Mrs.McInally (Arthur's mother) brought up as her own. Certainly, it does not seem possible for Tommy to have been the biological son of Mrs McInally. If Tommy was a 'changeling child', as adoptees were then known, there may here lie a clue to his bizarre, unpredictable and disturbed behaviour.

By 1926, Tommy's reluctance to train as hard as he should and his indulgence in the good life (although his friend Bob McPhail of Rangers tells us that he never swore or used bad language) meant that he had put on a lot of weight, and was now given unkind nicknames like 'the

Glaxo baby'. This was about an advertisement for baby food with a fat rosy cheeked infant extolling the virtues of the Glaxo variety, an advertisement which struck a chord with the undernourished of Glasgow.It was certainly now a far cry from the time in October 1920 when the slim Thomas beat the famous sprinter W.B.Applegarth over 100 yards.

Stories abounded about him leading Maley a merry dance at Hydro hotels, performing loads of practical jokes on his mates but like most such people, unable to take it when it was done to him. He was however essentially the punters' player, and it was difficult to enter a hostelry in West Central Scotland in the years between 1925 and 1928 without hearing a remark, complimentary or otherwise, about Tommy McInally.

Very few complimentary remarks were heard however about Celtic's Jekyll and Hyde performances in the Scottish League. A purple patch in November and December with McGrory hammering in 5 against Dundee United and 4 against Dunfermline led supporters to believe that the Championship could once again return to Celtic Park. But crucially the New Year's Day game at Ibrox was lost—narrowly and unluckily according to some reports, and in any case not in itself fatal. But on the following Monday, they also managed to lose to Queen's Park at home, and never really recovered from that.

Yet there was much about their play that was commendable. McGrory fed avidly off McInally's promptings and the spiritedly consistent play of Alec Thomson, now revelling in his role of 'McGrory's fetch and carry man'. Wingers Connolly and McLean were a constant thorn in the flesh of opposition defences and the midfield of Wilson and McFarlane (now a little past his best perhaps) was often a joy to behold, as indeed was the defensive work of the brothers McStay, Willie the full back the acknowledged Scotland International who could play in both berths and was twice on the winning side against England, and Jimmy unlucky not to be capped. He was at least the equal of the many good centre halves around, including Meiklejohn of Rangers, but the selectors tended to go for Jimmy Gibson of Partick Thistle.

Goalkeeper tended to present a problem, for Shevlin, although competent, did occasionally have a bad day and lacked in any case the charisma and presence of Adams and Shaw. Maley had been toying with the idea of replacing him after the disastrous New Year period, but decided to stick with him meantime.

The Scottish Cup opened with a rare visit to Palmerston Park,

Dumfries and an appalling performance in which the Doonhammers with better finishing might well have precipitated a major Cup upset which would have seen Rabbie Burns turning in his grave. The game finished scoreless, however, and Celtic managed to make things up to their supporters the following Wednesday with a 4-1 win at home in the Replay before an almost deserted Celtic Park. In these days, long before floodlights, Replays had to be played on a Wednesday afternoon, and very few people could dare to risk taking an afternoon off their work, particularly as this was in the aftermath of the catastrophic General Strike the previous May.

The next round put Celtic to a similarly far flung outpost of the Scottish football empire at Glebe Park, Brechin. It would be a game not without significance in the history of the club, and was quite clearly the biggest event in the history of the small Angus town. Enterprising local businessmen hired lorries and charged 6p so that people could have a better view, and the local railway station gave every impression of being unable to cope, including the sending after the game of a trainload of Glasgow fans in the direction of Montrose and Aberdeen before the mistake was spotted and rectified.

4,000 people were dangerously overcrowded into a ground which normally held 500 when the event occurred which all Angus still talked about a good fifty years later and which had the indirect effect of causing Scottish football's most melancholy tragedy. Wattie Gentles, himself reputedly Celtic daft like half the Brechin team, scored a soft goal in the first few minutes of the game. The soft ground could not excuse Shevlin's mishandling and Willie McStay was heard to bellow 'Get to that ball a little faster next time, Peter'. In the minuscule and primitive stand, Maley although beaming congratulations to the sycophantic Brechin officials, was fuming, and the decision was taken that Shevlin would have to go.

In the meantime gallant Brechin, playing their hearts out in the watery weary winter sun and the pitch which was visibly churning up with every tackle, were raising an eyebrow or two by their standard of play, until the inevitable happened and the roof fell in or as they said in Angus 'The wheels fell aff the certie'. McGrory ended up with four goals and won the hearts of all those who were seeing him for the first time. The game finished 6-3 and the two goals that Brechin scored were merely nails in the coffin of Peter Shevlin.

Celtic would now come to Dundee two Saturdays in a row, once for the League and once for the Cup. Maley decided to drop Shevlin and try the lithe young Fifer who had been attracting such rave reports at training (John Thomson). He was only 18 but seemed so good that only the pressure of a game against Dundee could tell if his reputation was justified. En route to Dens, the youngster sought out the companionship of his namesake and fellow Fifer, the kindly Alec, who did his best to reassure the youngster and avoided the banter of the wilder spirits like McInally who might undermine his confidence. He had to laugh, mind you at Tommy's continual clowning, and imitating of Maley and authority in general.

The youngster from Cardenden had a nightmare of a start as he fumbled a ball to allow Dundee to score. This reverse however steadied the nerves of the lad as Dundee, inspired by ex-Celt Joe Cassidy piled on the pressure. But the young John dived, jumped, caught, punched and positioned himself brilliantly to deny Dundee in such a way that two latecomers at the other end found themselves saying to each other 'This is the best we've ever seen Shevlin (sic)!'

Celtic went on to win that game, and also, more spectacularly, the Cup tie the following week before a 37,000 crowd packed into Dens Park. This was one of the finest games ever seen at that grand old stadium, and the 4-2 scoreline reflected the excitement as Celtic turned on the sort of display that they only seemed to reserve for Cup ties.

The third exotic venue for Celtic in that interesting campaign of 1927 was Bo'ness. This time 5-2 was the score, and Celtic were now in the Semi Final to play Falkirk. Falkirk had delighted their fans (and those of Celtic) by their removal of Rangers in the previous round, and they had with them now a star player by the name of Patsy Gallagher whom Celtic had released prematurely, it now seemed. A month previously he had been considered still good enought to earn another Irish cap (against Scotland in Belfast) and he would play for the 'Bairns' as late as 1932. Certainly the Celtic fans thought that he had had a few good Celtic years left in him when he was released, for it would be their habit in years to come whenever Falkirk where the opponents to sing

Better loved ye canna be,
Wull ye no come back again?

And what could be more fitting? As the Jacobites would sing of their king, so would Celtic supporters sing of the man commonly referred to as 'the uncrowned king of Ireland', now that Charles Stuart Parnell was long gone.

Even Patsy however could not stop Celtic that Semi Final day at

Here you see Celtic with the Glasgow Cup and the Scottish Cup.
Back row: P. Wilson, J. McGrory, W. McStay, J. Thomson, J. McMenemy,
J. McFarlane, E. McGarvie (trainer). Front row: T. McInally, P. Connolly,
A. Thomson, A. McLean, J. Donoghue, J. McStay, H. Hilley.

Ibrox, for Celtic were far superior to Falkirk and were further ahead
than the solitary Adam McLean goal would suggest. The team were
now in the Final against of all people - Second Division East Fife.

The Fifers who were not even challenging for promotion to the First
Division had owed their progress to the Final to a little luck and the
plucky determination to represent a deprived community. This was
1927, remember, and although the General Strike of May 1926 had
been a short-term and colossal fiasco, the miners' strike had gone on
for a long time after, in fact was still going on in some areas.

During all this time, East Fife's Cup run had provided a welcome
source of light relief to the beleagured community. Gates were low,as
they were everywhere, but the Fifers, with the help of two Hearts
reserves on loan, managed to get the better of Aberdeen in a Replay,
and then Partick Thistle in the Semi final to allow those of their
followers who could afford it the chance of a trip to Glasgow to see
their favourites against the mighty Celtic.

Celtic, although clear favourites, had one major problem, and that
was an injury involving broken ribs to free scoring McGrory in a game

at Falkirk ten days before the Final. With McInally and McLean both injured for that game, and their favourites going down 1-4 to the 'Bairns', the Jacobite anthem had added point,as the supporters sang for the return of Patsy. But by the Final, McInally and McLean had returned, and Maley put McInally at centre forward for the injured McGrory (that was where Tommy had played during his first three years with the club), and allowed in at inside left John McMenemy the son of the great James 'Napoleon' McMenemy.

John was a young lad of whom much was expected. His better days would come in the fine Motherwell side of the early 30's, but this was to be his big moment in the green and white. He had played only a handful of first team games for Celtic (without any great distinction) and was only told half an hour before kick-off on Saturday April 16th that he was playing. He was understandably shaking in the dressing room and unable to tie his laces when Maley came up to him and said 'What are you shaking for? It's those miners from Fife who should be shaking! It's an honour and a privilege to wear those green and white jerseys! Get out and bring me back that Cup! Your father did it often enough! It's your turn now!'

The crowd was a shade over 80,000 including a commendable support from Fife, and for the first time ever the Scottish Cup final was broadcast on radio. This did not, of course, mean in 1927 that everybody in Scotland had a chance to hear the game, for a radio was still very much a luxury item and even those who were lucky enough to possess one required a great deal of luck with geography and atmospherics. It would have been interesting to hear a tape of the game.

The teams were:
Celtic: Thomson; J.McStay, Hilley; Wilson W.McStay, McFarlane; Connolly, Thomson, McInally, McMenemy and McLean.
East Fife: Gilfillan; Robertson, Gillespie; Hope, Brown, Russell; Weir, Paterson, Wood, Barrett, Edgar.

The game was bizarre. Wood of East Fife scored in the sixth minute, then right back Robertson scored an own goal following a free kick which he himself had conceded, and from then on the game was no contest with McLean scoring in 35 minutes and Connolly in 46. The poor Fifers then struggled to get over the half way line, as fine play, particularly from Peter Wilson created loads of chances for McInally to waste. It took the 80,000 crowd and the radio commentator, presumably, some time to realise that the chances were missed deliberately, either not to humiliate the Fifers or simply because Tommy enjoyed acting the goat.

The match finished with McInally standing on the edge of the penalty area, asking for the ball and whenever he got it booted the ball into the terracing. He was 'delighting the now happy Celtic choristers with a few of the balloon variety' as a contemporary source put it. On one occasion, he booted the ball the other way to keep John Thomson from falling asleep, as he later put it himself, and the crowd revelled in the great day of their hero who at full time made a point of slapping the back of every East Fife player and encouraging the crowd to cheer each one of them. That Celtic had won their 12th Scottish Cup was almost incidental to the Tommy McInally show.

— 13 —

WELL, WELL, WELL, THE CLOCK'S TICKING WELL 1931

If any one year were to sum up the history of Celtic F.C. with all its magnificence, its romance, its tragedy and its dynamic unpredictability, that year would surely be 1931. The tragedy would come in September with the death of John Thomson, and 1931 would also be the year in which Celtic took the Scottish Cup in a shopping bag to the U.S.A. - a massive undertaking in 1931 with the five day Atlantic crossing and additional travel difficulties within the U.S.A.

The 1931 team itself, although not in all truth anything like the best in the team's history - they were some distance away from winning the Scottish League championship, for example, is one of the best known; there was one old timer, for instance, who when playing with the toes of his baby grandaughter did not say 'This little piggie went to market etc.' but rather quite simply 'R.Thomson, A.Thomson, McGrory, Scarff and Napier'.

The late twenties had not been good for Celtic. Ground improvements (in particular a new stand) had necessitated the sale of players like McInally and McLean, and there had even been a despicable attempt to sell the unwilling Jimmy McGrory to Arsenal which had not come about because the player was so much in love with Celtic. The general impression was that Celtic were more interested in money than in having a team, and gates fell accordingly. In addition, the Wall Street Crash of 1929 had triggered off a major global economic collapse, and the Irish community in the West of Scotland had suffered more than most.

Spring 1931 saw a resurgence of sorts on the football field, although there was a continuing worldwide economic decline. In Britain unemployment was disastrously high as the Labour Government of Ramsay MacDonald struggled unavailingly to solve the problem and elsewhere people like Adolf Hitler in Germany began to cash in. For Celtic, a realistic Championship challenge was mounted but fell because of Celtic's strange failures against Glasgow clubs with defeats at the hands of Rangers, Clyde and Partick Thistle at crucial points. Against that, McGrory, with Celtic apparently written on his heart, was still consistently banging in the goals, and one or two new players had emerged from the dark days of 1929 and 1930.

There was for instance Charlie Geatons from Lochgelly. Charlie was born Gattens, but his family changed the name during the 1st World War, presumably, because it had a German sound to it, and he arrived at Celtic Park in 1927 and was now breaking through at left half to take the place of Jean McFarlane. On the right wing, there was now Bertie Thomson, a difficult, rebellious character whom Maley was just about able to manage and a fine speedy player, and the left wing now had Peter Scarff, a gritty determined character and Charlie Napier.

Napier in particular was a great favourite with the fans. His springing stride made him look like a ballet dancer and he soon earned the nickname of 'Happy Feet'. The supporters would sing 'Clap, clap hands here comes Charlie' and his appearance on the jungle side of the ground would always earn a special cheer and a murmur of anticipation. Full backs Willie Cook and William 'Peter' McGonagle had also appeared in recent years, and thus the team had a fine balance with the new players complementing the experienced Jimmy McStay (the captain now since his brother had gone to Hearts in 1929), McGrory, Wilson and Alec Thomson. There were three Thomsons now in that team—goalkeeper John, right winger Bertie and inside right Alec.

The wonder goalkeeper John Thomson won his first International Cap in Paris in Summer 1930, and no-one would challenge him for his place the following season. The detractors will of course say, pointing to the likes of Rudolf Valentino and John F.Kennedy, that an early death works wonders for a reputation, but there can be little doubt that he was held in high regard by everyone even when he was still alive. His performance, for example, for the Scottish League against the English League at Villa Park in 1928 is well chronicled with English journalists full of admiration for the young Celt. Parallels with Rudolf Valentino are indeed apt, for he was young, handsome, courageous and chivalrous, and represented for the women of the time the possibilities of escapism that could not be found anywhere else.

The Scottish Cup campaign that year was a hard one. Narrow odd goal victories at Bayview and Tannadice Park were followed by fine performances against Morton at Cappielow and Aberdeen at Celtic

Park, and in the Semi Final against Kilmarnock (who had won the trophy two years previously) to set up an engrossing Final against Motherwell.

The 'Well', as they were known, had never reached a Scottish Cup Final before, but were a fine footballing side. Managed by John 'Sailor' Hunter, who had won a Cup winners medal for Dundee in 1910, Motherwell had shown the world what could be done on a limited financial budget even in an area where the trade recession had caused even more than the normal level of unemployment. Their star men were their legendary left wing pair of George Stevenson and Bobby Ferrier. George Stevenson was a brilliant dribbler, a fine accurate passer of the ball and had total understanding which bordered on telepathy with Bobby Ferrier. Stevenson played 12 times for Scotland, more often at inside right than inside left, never with less than distinction, and Bobby Ferrier was uncapped for Scotland only because he was an Englishman. The scribes of the time frequently bewailed this fact because he would have been the natural successor to Alan Morton.

That these were indeed great days for Scottish football was evidenced by what happened at Hampden Park two weeks before the Cup Final. Scotland beat England, the only International opponents that mattered in these days, for the third season out of four, by two goals to nil and the goals had been scored by the two most dangerous goalscorers of the respective Cup Final opponents, namely George Stevenson of Motherwell and Jimmy McGrory of Celtic.

Jimmy McGrory scores the first goal in the famous fightback against Motherwell.

On Saturday 11th April 1931, unemployment or no unemployment, almost 105,000 turned up to Hampden Park in brilliant spring sunshine to see the Cup final that everyone had been talking about. It was the first Hampden Cup Final in which it was noticed that Hampden Park had a serious car parking problem, for the amount of cars seemed to give the lie to talk about mass poverty and so on, and the motor car, which was providing so much employment to the Midlands of England, had steadily grown in popularity throughout the 1920's to such an extent that the Government was already contemplating legislation preventing people from driving a car unless thay had passed a test.

Those who took up their position on the North terracing slightly towards the King's Park end of the ground would get a good view. In the event, all four goals would be scored into that goal, there would be a fine display of the Motherwell supporters' orchestrated holding up of placards to spell out 'Motherwell' - an American idea which someone must have picked up from a Hollywood movie. More sinisterly, one or two blue favours were seen at that Mount Florida end, and the odd anti-Catholic song, so that one wondered whether Motherwell were taking on board some Rangers ideas for the day, or whether (more likely) some Rangers fans were there to rejoice in the downfall of their opponents or simply to cause a little trouble. But the great advantage that the North terracing brought was the view of the giant clock on the South Stand which would play such a vital part in the procedings.

Both teams were as expected:
Celtic: J.Thomson, Cook, McGonagle; Wilson, McStay, Geatons; R.Thomson, A. Thomson, McGrory, Scarff, Napier.
Motherwell: McClory, Johnman, Hunter; Wales, Craig, Telfer; Murdoch, McMenemy, McFadyen, Stevenson, Ferrier.

The referee was Peter Craigmyle of Aberdeen, and his part would also be decisive. Motherwell were attacking the King's Park goal, and they may have been unnerved by the huge Celtic support, but certainly did not show it. They had of course at inside right John McMenemy who had won a Cup Winner's medal for Celtic in 1927 and whose father Jimmy had won a record seven, six for Celtic and 1 for Partick Thistle. John's career had not developed to anyone's satisfaction at Celtic Park, but he was now flourishing at Motherwell.

McMenemy was instrumental in Motherwell's bright opening.

They took the lead in the sixth minute when Stevenson shot home from outside the penalty box. There was a touch of luck about it, for it took a slight deflection off the leg of McStay. Quarter of an hour later, they were two up, this time from a McMenemy shot and this time from a more obvious deflection off the outstretched leg of McStay.

This was making things look very rosy for Motherwell, for Celtic did not appear to have any answer. Motherwell then made the fatal mistake of easing off a little, happy to keep a two goal lead until half time at least, and allowing Celtic's influential men like Peter Wilson and Alec Thomson to play a part in the game. Motherwell who had the benefit of the wind, gusty and capricious though it was, would have been better advised to go for a third before half time which would certainly have killed Celtic.

Half time came to complete gloom on the North and East terracings. All they could do was curse luck, and hope for better things in the second half. Better things did not seem to be forthcoming, for although Celtic piled on hysterical pressure, the Motherwell defence, well drilled and organized, withstood all that they could hurl with centre half Alan Craig conspicuous in the taming of McGrory. Meanwhile, that wretched clock on the South Stand kept moving round to the witching hour. The second half had started with the large hand between five to and four o'clock, so the game would finish between twenty and quarter to five.

The large hand was perpendicularly pointing to half past when the first sight of the breaking of ranks took place, and one or two fans started to drift away, leaving the rest in sullen silence observing the rainbow of Motherwell colours, the frantic but fruitless action on the field, and the clock moving round. Motherwell were quite happy to concede free kicks outside the box; they handled the ball in ways that would earn a modern player a red card; they gave away corners if they had to, pulled back even Stevenson, McMenemy and Ferrier to defend, leaving John Thomson a lonely figure in the distant Mount Florida goal. Twice Mr Craigmyle refused Celtic clear penalties, and once he was chased round the posts by Scarff and Bertie Thomson, but Celtic still did not get the break.

The clock was at twenty five to five when Celtic won a free kick outside the box in more or less the same place that Jean McFarlane had taken his for McGrory to head home in 1925. But this was where the cunning brain of Charlie Napier came into play. Motherwell had formed a wall for Charlie had given every indica-

Top row: W. Maley (manager), C. Geatons, W. Cook, John Thomson, W. McGonagle, P. Wilson, W. Quinn (trainer). Bottom: C. Napier, P. Scarff, J. McGrory, J. McStay, R. Thomson, A. Thomson.

tion of shooting; all he did however was to hoist the ball gently over their heads for McGrory to lunge forward and toe poke the ball home.

Celtic now came to life; the departing supporters now stopped in their tracks; McGrory charged back up the field pointing to the clock; there were six minutes left. The six minutes however flashed past, it appeared, and with the hand pointing unmistakably to full time, Bertie Thomson had the ball at the corner flag. He may have dabbled with the idea of having the ball at full time so that he could keep it, but he glanced up at the clock saw from that angle that there was still time left, and sent the ball more in hope than expectation to the goalmouth.

McGrory went up for it, so did Motherwell defender Alan Craig and his goalkeeper Alan McClory. Craig got there first, perhaps he was slightly deceived by the breeze, but he did not head the ball cleanly. The ball hit his head and zipped into his own net. What happened next stayed clearly in the mind of a spectator for over 60 years. The Celtic support went crazy, McGrory did a dance but what stuck in the mind was the prostrate figure of Craig hitting the ground with his fist again and again until the referee, the kindly Mr Craigmyle, a team-mate and McGrory himself, ever chivalrous and magnanimous, helped the distraught man to his feet. Hampden had never before seen such drama, nor would it ever again.

Craig's agony will be sympathised with by anyone who has ever played football at any level. It was all the more tantalising for him after the game to realise that there were already some evening newspapers on the street proclaiming Motherwell as Scottish Cup winners. Yet his career recovered. He had already been capped twice for Scotland, and would play for the International side again, and in 1933 he would be transferred to Chelsea.

After all that, it was perhaps inevitable that Celtic should win the Cup Final Replay on the following Wednesday. They were after all on a high. Yet it was no easy victory, for Motherwell fought well, and but for a totally crazy game by goalkeeper Alan McClory, might well have won.

The teams were the same for the 5.00 p.m. kick off the following Wednesday evening. The crowd was down a little at 98,000 and the weather was a lot worse with consistently heavy rain. Celtic scored first when Bertie Thomson netted in a scramble after McGrory and McClory had gone up together for a high ball. McClory was convinced that he had been impeded or that McGrory had handled, and his chasing of the referee to the centre line showed that he was in danger of losing the place.

Although Motherwell equalized through Murdoch in the twenty fifth minute, there was a feeling about them that Celtic had already been allocated the 1931 Cup by some sort of divine providence. They were lethargic, slower to the ball and disjointed - a state of affairs that the immense Peter Wilson took advantage of. In the thirtieth minute an aimless lob across goal was totally missed by goalkeeper McClory, and McGrory had the easiest of tasks to put Celtic ahead. More praiseworthy was the third goal which Bertie Thomson squeezed home from an acute angle following a Geatons free kick. This was on the thirty fifth minute mark and the half ended with no further scoring.

In the second half, Celtic had to face the driving wind and rain and a somewhat more determined Motherwell team. Stevenson pulled one back in the 70th minute and it looked as if we could be once again in for a grandstand finish, but Celtic's half back line of Wilson, McStay and Geatons asserted themselves after a frenetic spell of Motherwell pressure. A break down the left led to Alec Thomson crossing for McGrory. Once again, goalkeeper McClory came out, missed totally and James Edward McGrory had a free header into an empty net. He didn't normally miss these! Only minutes remained, and Motherwell had nothing left.

Thus Celtic had lifted the trophy for the 13th time, and the famous old pot could travel with the club to the United States and Canada and be shown off to the very many Celtic fans in the New World. Motherwell emerged however with great credit. Their moment of triumph would come next year.

— 14 —

THE SAFTEST O' THE FAMILIE
1933

In 1933 the shadows of depression hung over Celtic Park in all sorts of ways. There was of course the depression of unemployment which the National Government of Ramsay MacDonald and Stanley Baldwin (a most unholy alliance) were not significantly easing. This certainly did affect Celtic attendances if not the enthusiasm of the supporters. Many well documented accounts exist of supporters walking all the way to Dundee and even Aberdeen, and if they had enough money to earn admission, well and good. Otherwise they would wait outside the ground until the exit gates were opened with about ten minutes to go, and they would then rush in and enjoy what they could.

There was also another kind of depression, and this was the sort which prevented Celtic from having a good team. John Thomson had died on September 5th 1931 - a dreadful blow.

There was another tragedy about to happen as well. Soon after the Thomson tragedy, gritty inside left Peter Scarff developed an alarming cough. Once after training he coughed up blood; once in a friendly game against Ayr, he was unable to resume for the second half, such was the problem with his breathing. Such symptoms were the all too obvious ones of the 1930's and shortly after New Year 1932, Peter was admitted to Bridge of Weir sanatorium, suffering from tuberculosis or as it was more graphically called 'consumption', as that is what it is - the eating away of a lung. The sheer horror was that it took Peter almost two years to die, and Maley, devout and conscientious, attended Peter regularly. He could not shake off his own depression, however, and the team, a potentially talented bunch, suffered.

No challenge was forthcoming for the League in either 1932 or 1933, but Celtic supporters were relieved that in 1932, Motherwell won the League stopping Rangers at five consecutive League Championships. Apart from that, the supporters had a genuine regard for Motherwell whom they acknowledged to have been just a little short of luck in the 1931 Cup Final.

Season 1932 -33's League campaign gave little sign that Celtic were shaking off the slough of depression that threatened to envelop them. Twice they earned respectable draws with Rangers, they similarly shared the points with Motherwell with a win each, but defeats at the hands of Partick Thistle (twice) St.Johnstone, Falkirk and Aberdeen indicated what every supporter knew - that this team, although possessing loads of talent, was not being lead in the right direction.

Yet the players were there, those lost since 1931 being adequately replaced. Goalkeeper was now Canadian Joe Kennaway whom Celtic had first met on the 1931 tour of North America. He was a Canadian Internationalist, and would play for Scotland eventually, but there is no evidence that he ever played for the U.S.A., as some books claimed. There was loads of evidence however that he was a fine goalkeeper, and this he would prove throughout the 1930's.

To cover for Peter Scarff, Napier moved to inside left and his left wing place was taken by Hugh O'Donnell, a man whose very name endeared him to the faithful as the doughty deeds of 'Dauntless Red Hugh' who used to give the Saxons hell were recalled in song.

Many a heart shall quail under its coat of mail
Deeply the merciless foeman shall rue
When on his ears shall ring, born on the breezes' wing
Tyrconnel's dread war cry, O'Donnell Abu!

This Hugh, although lacking his namesake's red hair, would cause similar panic down the left wing, possessing as he did a tremendous amount of pace and a cannonball shot. His brother Frank was also a fine forward, but tended only to play when McGrory or one of the Thomsons was injured.

In December 1932, much to the dismay of the fans, Maley sold Willie Cook to Everton. Cook, an Ulsterman, may have had problems at Celtic Park, but there was no indication of this to the fans, who always admired his tenacious tackling and solid no-nonsense approach to defending. It was a curious business, for it came as a total surprise, and the more perceptive fans were not at all convinced that he had gone to Everton to 'better his position' as was said. It did however give Celtic the chance to bring in the gritty Bobby Hogg, a tough no nonsense right back who would stay with Celtic until 1948 and more than pay his way. When Everton won the F.A.Cup in 1933, Cook, incidentally, became the first, and possibly only, Irishman to win both a Scottish and an English Cup winner's medal.

With League form so unpredictable, it seemed by the New Year that

Celtic would have to look to their favourite competition once again, if they were to give any silverware to their fans, who themselves found the loss of Thomson, the agony of Scarff and the scourge of unemployment hard to accept. The road to the Final was an odd one.

Dunfermline were crushed 7-1 at East End Park in January, then Falkirk were competently despatched by two McGrory goals in early February. Partick Thistle, even in 1933 unpredictable and certainly Celtic's bogey team, then came to Celtic Park. They took an early lead against a Celtic side who were without the ill Kennaway and the injured Geatons, and were holding it well late into the second half. A massive crowd given as 55,000 (a somewhat dubious figure, one feels, for that would be about 4 times what Celtic's average League gate was in 1933) in the early spring sunshine, however, roared Celtic on to victory with McGrory (who else?) and Bertie Thomson getting the goals.

March 4th saw Celtic paying a rare visit to Cliftonhill to meet Albion Rovers, and an even rarer chance to meet Sir Harry Lauder who was presented to both teams, and who responded to the cheers of the crowd by raising his famous crooked stick. The Rovers did themselves proud, and earned a draw and the respect of the Celtic support who were grateful for Charlie Napier's goal. The replay at Celtic Park was predictable, but the Semi Final against Hearts was tight, Celtic emerging 2-1 winners in a Replay after a shocker of a goalless draw in the first game, which Hearts felt that, with a little luck and a few breaks from the referee, they might have won.

The opponents in the Final were, for the second time in three years, Motherwell. These were heady days at Fir Park under the guidance of John 'Sailor' Hunter. Everybody knew that only seconds remained in 1931 when Craig scored his fatal own goal, and everyone was delighted for them when they won the League Championship in 1932. They amassed 66 points, 5 more than Rangers, and scored 119 goals of which centre forward McFadyen netted 52.

In season 1932 -33, although they would eventually just lose out to Rangers, Motherwell's fine form continued, and McFadyen set up a record by scoring 15 goals en route to the Final, including 5 against Montrose and four against Kilmarnock. But it was not only the forward line that was outstanding. Rarely, among provincial clubs, they possessed an International full back pairing. In January of that year, they had bought Jimmy Crapnell from Airdrie who played 9 times for Scotland, and at left back they had Ben Ellis, one of the very few players who have played in Scottish football and been capped for

Wales. To complicate matters, Motherwell's right half was called Hugh Wales and he played for Scotland! Craig, the tragic hero of 1931, had now gone to Chelsea, but replacement centre half Blair would also earn his International colours.

Centre forward for Scotland was a coveted honour, and both teams here felt that they had a grievance against the powers that were. Celtic felt that McGrory, for all his exploits, was ludicrously undercapped, including the sad fact that he never played at Wembley; and Motherwell's supporters pointed to McFadyen's form over the past two seasons and asked why he had never yet been capped (he would the following year) having to stand aside for McGrory or Neil Dewar of Third Lanark.

It was however McGrory who had got the nod for the game against England at Hampden Park on April 1st 1933, and the edge was taken off Motherwell and everybody else's objections when McGrory scored both goals in the 2-1 victory. One of them is claimed to have produced the first and the greatest Hampden roar, when McGrory finished off a move involving the two Rangers players Marshall and McPhail and sent a nation into delirium, spawning hundreds of verses, songs and almost a new folk culture about the day that Scotland beat the English:

But wait a bit, don't be so fast,
We've left the star turn till the last,
There in the midst o a his glory,
Our champion scorer, James McGrory!

Ten years later in North Africa, or Italy or even the distant Burma railway, whenever any Englishman was foolish enough to make a disparaging comment about 'Jocks', he would be reminded of that goal. McGrory himself in 'A Lifetime in Paradise' gives a good account of the goal, but being the man he was, he underplays his own role in it and emphasises that of McPhail.

The Scottish Cup Final of April 15th 1933 attracted another crowd of over 100,000 a testament to the attracting power of these two teams, not matter how bad the economic circumstances of the day. The weather was dull and overcast as the follwoing teams ran out:

Celtic: Kennaway, Hogg, McGonagle; Wilson, McStay, Geatons; R.Thomson, A. Thomson, McGrory, Napier, O'Donnell.

Top row: W. Maley (manager), A. Thomson, R. Hogg, J. Kennaway, C. Napier, J. McGrory, W. McGonagle. Front row: R. Thomson, C. Geatons, J. McStay, P. Wilson, H. O'Donnell, J. Quiskley (trainer)

Motherwell: McClory, Crapnell, Ellis; Wales, Blair, McKenzie; Murdoch, McMenemy, McFadyen, Stevenson, Ferrier.

Much was expected of the game, but the Motherwell crowd, well aware of their crushing disappointment two years previously, were noticeably more muted. This was perhaps due as much to the poor standard of the game as anything else, for the game seldom rose above the mediocre with both defences well on top.

If a Man of the Match had been awarded in those days, it would probably have been given to Celtic's Jimmy McStay. Captain since the departure of brother Willie, Jimmy had never been given the recognition that he deserved. Certainly, he was never capped for Scotland, although he had played for the Scottish League. Now at the age of 38, he could justifiably feel that he had done his bit for Celtic, having captained them in turbulent times, but to-day would be his finest hour. His task was simply to prevent McFadyen from scoring, in the same way as he had once prevented Dixie Dean from scoring for the English League against the Scottish. This he did, never disdaining the punt up the field if necessary, and as Hogg and Wilson were effectively able to neutralise the left wing menace of Stevenson and Ferrier, Motherwell's much vaunted attack never got going.

Neither, truthfully, did Celtic's. The only goal of the game came fortuitously. Bertie Thomson manfully worked his way into the penalty area some four minutes into the second half, tried a cross, the ball cannoned off two Motherwell defenders across goal into the onrushing path of McGrory who never missed them. It was a poor goal, fitting for a poor Final. Around that time, the great Harry Lauder, whom Celtic had met at Coatbridge before the Quarter Final had a song called 'I'm the saftest o' the familie'. A journalist on the following Monday would name that McGrory counter just that - the saftest o' the familie.

The desperate Motherwell now threw everything upfield, but with Peter Wilson and Chick Geatons controlling the midfield and McFadyen still shackled by McStay, scoring opportunities were few. Once however Stevenson got through, but Kennaway saved from point blank range. Full time came with Celtic still winning the midfield battle and winning one of their less distinguished Cup Finals. Not that the supporters minded about that as they trooped back to their trains that night. The Cup had been won for the 14th time and Glasgow belonged to Celtic.

Meanwhile at Bridge of Weir Sanatorium, the ailing Peter Scarff had been able to listen to the game on the primitive radio, and Maley brought the Scottish Cup along to show him a day or two later. The fellow patients and nurses had a treat that day, for Maley, whatever his private feelings of depression, was always able to turn a genial exterior for the benefit of others. 1933 was not great in the history of Celtic Football club, and worse was fast appearing on the horizon, but there was still some balm in Gilead, for the Scottish Cup was back on familiar territory.

— 15 —

THE SARDINE FINAL
1937

The world was a strange place in 1937. You did not know whether to be happy or to be sad. It was painfully obvious from current events in Austria, Spain and Czechoslovakia that war was coming, war, even more dreadful that that of twenty years ago with all its evidence of slaughter, carnage and the sight of piteous men, now in their forties, hobbling about with one leg or selling newspapers with one arm. This war would be worse with hideous fears of what aerial bombing could do to cities and civilians and Rumour, that creature of one hundred eyes and one hundred ears, delighted in the progress of chemical and bacterial warfare.

On the other hand, you were more likely to have a job. The preparations for war, however sporadic and fitful in some respects, had led to a demand for everything from aircraft and tanks to air raid masks and jute for sandbags. The economy was on the move, the crowds of street corner boys were beginning to diminish and the evils of unemployment and short time were going.

Celtic too, one felt, had turned the corner. 1934 and 1935 had been absolutely dreadful with low gates and almost the belief that it was God's will that Rangers would win everything, such was the appalling lack of challenge from Celtic. Motherwell were past their best; Aberdeen were yet to come. The world looked to Celtic for an answer, but answer came there none.

1936 however changed all that. A dreadful Scottish Cup exit at the hands of the incredulous St.Johnstone was followed by a run of 11 games without defeat in which McGrory scored at least once in each game apart from when he was injured in the last one, and the League was annexed. High were the hopes for 1936-7 but sadly inconsistency and the chronic inability to win the New Year's Day fixture at Ibrox meant that Rangers would once again triumph.

But the team was good. Some new players had arrived more or less simultaneously in the bad days of 1934 and 1935, and were rapidly approaching maturity. There was of course Jimmy Delaney on the right wing, arguably Celtic's best ever player had not the War coincided with his best years. He was tough, fast, powerful and a potent supplier of material to the ever alert McGrory. On the left wing was Frank Murphy of the centre parting. Often unfavourably compared to Delaney, Frank was in the opinion of many supporters, just as good, if a shade less flamboyant. Inside men Willie Buchan and Johnny Crum complemented the wingers and made it a fine forward line. Crum in particular was a darling of the Celtic Park crowd, simply because he was so obviously one of them - a gallus, Glasgow keelie from Maryhill and proud of it.

Behind these magnificent forwards stood a half back line to compare with the best. Chick Geatons had moved flank to fill Peter Wilson's place, his place at left half was taken by the reliable George Paterson and at centre half was captain Willie Lyon. Willie was not a Celt by birth - he was an Englishman who came to Celtic via the unusual route of Queen's Park. His gentlemanly air and somewhat aristocratic appearance with his calmness and unflappability under pressure did not however hide a steely determination. His appointment as captain soon after his appearance in the jersey was a strange one, it appeared, but he was exactly the man for the job, calming Crum, cajoling Delaney and exhorting the last ounce of effort from the willing but ageing McGrory.

There's surely no denyin,
Wi oor captain Wullie Lyon,
We will win the Scottish Cup once again.

The team worked hard for each other, and never more so than at Stenhousemuir in the first round of the Scottish Cup. Goalless until late in the game, Celtic scored, then Stenhousemuir equalized and in a frantic dash for the winner, seemed to have earned a penalty when left back John Morrison handled. Veteran referee Peter Craigmyle would have none of it, though, and Celtic lived to fight another day. The replay was won, albeit unspectacularly, and East Fife and Albion Rovers were then dealt with.

A penalty would be significant in the Quarter Final against Motherwell also. Late in the second half, and down 4-2 to a confident Motherwell side, who had more than a few Scottish Cup scores to settle with Celtic, things looked over and done with. But in a manner reminiscent of the 1931 Cup Final, Celtic fought back and eventually won a penalty when Delaney was brought down in the box. *Noblesse oblige*, and captain Willie Lyon took the kick himself, scored, then inspired his men to greater efforts to get the all important equalizer which came agonizingly late through Willie Buchan. It was the same player who again scored a late winner in the Replay.

Clyde were the opponents in the Ibrox Semi Final which attracted an astonishing 76,000 on April 3rd. They saw a dull game in which defences were on top until McGrory scored, then Clyde's defender Robb, still upset by allowing McGrory in for the first goal, made a dreadful hash of clearing a corner kick and put through his own goal.

Rangers had unexpectedly gone out of the Cup at an earlier stage of the tournament to Queen of the South at Palmerston Park, so the way was open for the other form team of the season to come through and claim a place in their first ever Scottish Cup Final. This was Aberdeen.

Football had been slower to develop in Aberdeen than in other parts of Scotland. Aberdeen Football Club had only been formed in 1903, after some tortuous amalgamations, and the indisputable fact that Aberdeen was a different kind of city from the others in Scotland hindered development. For one thing, Aberdeen lacked the heavy industrial base of Glasgow, Dundee and Edinburgh, being mainly a fishing port and a market city for the surrounding community. For another, Aberdeen lacked any significant Irish immigrant population, so that a 'Celtic' did not spring up, nor indeed a counterbalance. Accordingly, since 1903 Aberdeen F.C. have been the only team in the Granite City.

But the other main problem was that of geographical remoteness. The railways of the 1840's and subsequent decades seemed to have mitigated that problem to a certain extent, but Aberdeen is still some 60 miles away from its closest rivals in Dundee. For a long time, Celtic found travelling to Aberdeen a pleasant day out, but usually an unhappy result at the end (November 1925 was the last time that Celtic had won a League match at Pittodrie), and conversely, Aberdeen's jaunts to Glasgow with a very small travelling support were normally unfruitful. Perhaps because Aberdeen were seen as the outpost of the Empire, Celtic's support usually cheerfully accepted reverses 'up there' and looked upon their visits as social occasions, as distinct from the grim necessity of the likes of Motherwell or Kilmarnock.

Aberdeen, therefore, had not yet won anything of significance. They had had great players, it is true - Donald Coleman, Charlie O'Hagan, Frank Hill and Alec Cheyne who had scored that famous goal direct from a corner kick which had beaten England in 1929, and they had been second in the League as early as 1911 (they would equal that feat this year, as it turned out), but black and gold colours had not yet been wrapped round any major trophy.

Managed since the early 20's by Paddy Travers, who had played briefly for Celtic in 1911/12, Aberdeen had now built up an impressive side. The centre half and captain was Eddie Falloon, a fine player and totally reliable; they had a tricky winger in Jackie Benyon (sometimes spelt Beynon) who would almost certainly have played for his native Wales if the Welsh selectors had ever come up to watch him, and the centre forward was Matt Armstrong who with inside left Willie Mills formed a mighty goalscoring partnership which won them both Scottish caps. It was without much doubt the strongest team in the 34 year history of the northern club.

The interest in this game in Aberdeen and the surrounding area was intense. At the fish harbour, in refined Union Street, in the townships of Fraserburgh, Peterhead and Buckie, in the tiny villages of Maud, Tarves and Newtonhill, they talked about little other than the imminent visit to Hampden and the possibility of the first ever capture of the Scottish Cup. The International between Scotland and England on April 17th was followed by polite interest in the North East, and everyone was delighted to hear about Scotland's 3-1 win, but it was nothing to the passion that was already being engendered for next week's game.

Clearly too, Aberdeen was going to be a ghost city. The city of Aberdeen has always identified with its football club far more closely than any other city in Great Britain, and a feature of the Aberdeen support has always been the middle class women complete with their tartan rugs and flasks of half-time tea mingling happily with the working class punters and their bunnets and occasional couthy and earthy choice of language—'Get aff the park, ye durty green bastart' has a distinctive Aberdonian sound to it, as does the more genteel 'Stoap the game, ref , can ye nae see the loon's hurt?'

As early as Thursday troop movements south had been noted. Many travelled overnight on the Friday, special trains left Aberdeen station early on the Saturday morning, and the road out of the city resembled the Exodus of the Old Testament, as the douce citizens of Stonehaven, Brechin and Forfar watched shoals of buses drive past to support the black and golds with slogans like 'Rummle'im up,Matt Armstrong' or 'Mills'll score afore Lang' (Lang being the outside left) and odd references to the Lyon's den holding no fears for someone with a strong arm, or an arm strong.

Standing: C. Geatons, R. Hogg, J. Kennaway, J. Morrison, W. Buchan, G. Paterson.
Seated: W. Maley (manager), J. Delaney, J. McGrory, W. Lyon, J. Crum, F. Murphy,
J. McMenemy (trainer)

The authorities had clearly underestimated all this. The previous week had seen a record crowd of over 149,000 to see the International, and no-one could believe that this figure would ever be approached. Amazingly, 146,000 at least got into Hampden, and the probability was that thousands more climbed walls and rushed gates. Certainly, the streets around the ground were mobbed with disappointed humanity still trying in vain to gain entrance long after the turnstiles had been closed, and with battle inside joined.

The Celtic crowd had also been grossly underestimated by the authorities, as indeed had been the many neutrals whose annual day out to Glasgow was to see the Cup Final, no matter who played. A witness remembers seeing the crowds of beggars and unemployed people lining the route from Mount Florida station to the ground (nothing unusual about that) but this year, earnest young men and women in berets and dungarees pleading with supporters to join the International Brigades to fight the menace of Franco, aided by the Hitler beast and the Mussolini jackal in the Spanish Civil War, which was now almost a year old. Madrid had been saved by these glorious International Brigades at the Battles of Jarama and Guadalajara, but it was only a temporary reprieve. 'To-day Spain, to-morrow France, the next day - you' read the prophetic posters.

The teams were:

Celtic: Kennaway, Hogg, Morrison; Geatons, Lyon, Paterson; Delaney, Buchan, McGrory, Crum, Murphy.

Aberdeen: Johnstone, Cooper, Temple; Dunlop, Falloon, Thomson; Benyon, McKenzie, Armstrong, Mills, Lang.

Willie Buchan years later would recall that he honestly thought that he was going to pass out on the field immediately after they ran out, such was the wall of noise. Yet by the time that Mr Hutton of Glasgow blew to start the game, things had settled down. The weather was what the Aberdonians would call 'soor' - not much of a wind, dull, rain threatening and generally rather cold.

Celtic were attacking the King's Park end of the ground, and clearly their early ideas involved getting the ball to McGrory. The veteran, only a couple of days off his 33rd birthday, was playing in what would be his last Cup Final, and he had scored in 1925, 1931 and 1933, now possessed 'more records than Harry Lauder' in the goalscoring department, and he would clearly have liked to score to-day in front of what would be a European record for club football which would probably stand for all time. Alas, McGrory would not score that day, but he was instrumental in the first goal. He headed a Paterson free kick for goal, it was blocked, Buchan then shot strongly, but goalkeeper George Johnstone (who would play briefly for Celtic during the war) saved. This time however Johnny Crum nipped in to score an important, although hardly a classic Cup Final goal.

A minute later Aberdeen ran up and equalized through Armstrong following a deflection off the unfortunate Lyon. Thus the teams were level, thanks to two scrappy goals unworthy of the gigantic contest that was unfolding. Play raged from end to end in a way worthy of Homer's Iliad while the Gods watch before Zeus decides in what direction he is to place the weight on the scales and decide the issue.

It was decided in the 70th minute following a spell in which Aberdeen had been on top. Once again the influence of McGrory was there for all to see with a deft flick into the path of the oncoming Willie Buchan who made no mistake. From then on, Celtic with Geatons outstanding, took command, and although Aberdeen tried desperately, there was no equalizer. The game finished in a sporting fashion with the Northern supporters gracious in defeat, and Celtic supporters honest enough to admit that it might have gone the other way. For Aberdeen, their day would come, but the world would by then be totally altered.

Jackie Benyon would not long outlive this game. Aberdeen went on a close season tour of South Africa, minus the Cup, of course, but were feted by exiled Aberdonians and Scots everywhere. One night Jackie complained of abdominal pain, and sadly no-one was able to diagnose appendicitis early enough. Jackie died the following day, to the distress of football fans everywhere.

Celtic would continue to do very well the following year and celebrate their Golden Jubilee in some style. They would not, however, win the Scottish Cup in 1938 - they would go out to a Kilmarnock side which had a new manager, whose name was James McGrory. Thus McGrory found himself back at Hampden as manager in the next Scottish Cup Final, sadly to lose to East Fife.

— 16 —

'WE CAN NOW LOOK HISTORY IN THE FACE' 1951

There are times in history when Celtic just *have* to win a Scottish Cup in order to forestall serious unrest among their supporters. This was certainly the case in 1965, and in 1995, but seldom was it more incumbent on the team to win the Cup than in 1951. There was a serious lack of success, made all the worse by Rangers' good post-war team which had just completed a hat-trick of Scottish Cups.

The last trophies won by Celtic had been back in 1938, some thirteen long and eventful years previously, almost back into a totally different world, in fact. The war years had been totally barren for Celtic, whose Directors had not always given the impression of being totally committed to the idea of war-time football; and the immediate post war years, for which less excuse is possible, were grim with only the Victory in Europe Cup and the odd Glasgow Cup triumph to balance against consistent failure in the Scottish Cup, a total inability to make any sort of an impact on the new League Cup and a performance in the Scottish League which in 1948 left them on the brink of relegation.

But by season 1950 -51, a slight improvement was evidenced, not necessarily in the League position - they finished 7th (never having even made the first three since the War), but more by the standard of play and the emergence of one or two personality players, who could on occasion swing games for the team.

First in that category was the mercurial Charlie Tully. Tully had arrived from Belfast Celtic in 1948, and aided by an early spectacular performance against Rangers, the legend of Cheeky Charlie was born. The Celtic crowd had lacked a comedian since the days of Tommy McInally over twenty years previously, and certainly needed such a boost in those grim post war years. Yet it is very easy to be romantic about Tully. Certainly he had his great days, but there were also times when he looked lethargic and times when he gave the impression that he didn't care. He did not always enjoy the love of his team mates who resented his playing to the gallery - more than once stories emerged about fisticuffs in dressing rooms, and even the fans on occasion could become very frustrated at the showing off and the need to beat the same opponent twice. But with Tully on your side, anything could happen.

Then there was John McPhail. 'Hooky' or 'Mc-never-fail', he had joined Celtic in the dark days of the war, and although prone to an extraordinary amount of illness and injury, still retained the affection of the crowd, who saw in this bustling centre forward the qualities of a McGrory or a Quinn. Supporters of the time testify to the holding of breath as the forward line was being read over the tannoy, until McPhail's name was announced, then the loud cheer of relief would drown out the rest of the team. It is also an indirect comment about the amount of times McPhail was out of the team.

Bobby Collins had for the past year or two captivated the hearts of the Celtic faithful. Called 'The Wee Barra', he was a ubiquitous forward who could and did play in every position in the attack, although inside right was probably his best berth. He was a tricky dribbler, had a deceptive turn of pace and could shoot as well. His very size (about 5' 4") meant that the crowd could always identify with him in these days when the Welfare State was only in its infancy, and many punters were of the same height. There were very few however of the same footballing ability.

Arguably the greatest player at Celtic Park in those days, and perhaps even in Scotland over the next decade was Bobby Evans. This red head who had joined the club from St.Anthony's in 1944 had struggled in the forward line of the immediate post war years. Almost by accident, he stumbled into his true position of right half in the 'relegation' game of 1948 at Dens Park, and had inspired Celtic to a fateful victory. From then on he had never looked back. His finding of his real position was not unlike what happened to Bobby Murdoch in the mid-sixties, and he shared with Murdoch the tigerish qualities of perseverance, hard work and sheer class. It became a journalistic cliche to say 'Evans, as usual, was superb'. By Cup Final day in 1951, he has already played 10 times for Scotland, including the victory at Wembley just a week previously.

In addition to the class players, Celtic also had some honest to goodness triers like Joe Baillie, Alec Boden, Jock Weir and Sean Fallon, and there was enough of the Celtic spirit around for the fans to be confident. Goodness knows, they had needed a lot of spirit on the way to the Final, for there had been several close calls in an enthralling campaign in which there was seldom a dull moment.

Bayview, Methil was the first port of call against an East Fife team then in their heyday. They had already won the League Cup twice (unbelievably, they would win it three times before Celtic even reached a Final) and with players like Charlie Fleming, Henry Morris and Jimmy Bonthrone they were a force to be reckoned with. 14,000 fans crammed into the tight little ground to see a game in which Celtic just deserved their draw, being indebted to Bobby Collins for a late equalizer in which he belied his lack of inches by rising high to head home a Tully cross. The Replay at Celtic Park was a different matter, however, with Celtic winning comfortably 4-2. Duns were then accounted for in the next round, and Celtic were rewarded with a trip to Tynecastle.

49,000 is given as the attendance for that day; in fact there were thousands more allowed in when a fan at the Gorgie Road end opened the exit gates to allow his friends in. The crowd swayed dangerously on the packed terracing, crowd invasions happened more than once, and the referee and a senior policeman discussed at several points the possibility of abandoning the match. The referee was all for doing just that, but police opinion was that it was far safer to let the match proceed than risk the frustration of such a huge crowd erupting into violence.

Celtic won 2-1 and all the goals came in the first half, but the hero of the hour was 20-year-old George Hunter, Celtic's slim and youthful goalkeeper who was so reminiscent of John Thomson in build and even, from a distance at least, looks. Seldom has a goal been so much under seige from two directions—from Hearts forwards like Willie Bauld in front, and from fans allowed onto the track by anxious policemen behind it. But it would be George's day, and helped by a little luck, the outplayed Celtic defence yet triumphed.

The fans' appetite for football in 1951 was evinced by the 76,000 who turned up to watch Aberdeen at Celtic Park in the Quarter Final. Jimmy Delaney, that great ex-Celt had now found his itinerant way to Aberdeen, but Jimmy was well policed by Alec Rollo that day and the Aberdeen attack never got going in Celtic's classy 3-0 performance which really got the faithful believing that the Scottish Cup could be won that year.

84,237 attended the Semi Final against Raith Rovers. The Rovers were comparative newcomers to the First Division but had outstanding players like Andy Young (who had played for Celtic during the War), tricky right winger Johnny Maule and their great goalscorer Willie Penman. This was a fine match of football which could have gone either way. Celtic's first goal looked offside, but then the breaks evened themselves out when Boden scored an own goal. McPhail's goal late in the first half seemed to have won the game, until Penman rose McGrory-like to equalize. The last ten minutes saw Celtic, with Tully consistently brilliant, pressing hard. It was fitting that Tully should score the winner, although Harry Colville of Raith Rovers swears blind that McPhail held goalkeeper Johnstone and prevented him from jumping.

Thus after three very close calls, Celtic had reached their first post-war Scottish Cup Final. How poignant it was that the opponents would be Motherwell, the team with whom they had shared that epic Cup Final of 20 years ago! Yet what a different world it was, and how much had happened over these 20 years, arguably the most eventful 20 years of British and world history! Some things do not change however. Motherwell were still after their first ever Scottish Cup win, and had built up once again a fine side with many fine players who would soon be knocking on the International door.

131,943 people turned up to watch this game. The weather was bright and cheerful, and several people commented on the carnival atmosphere in and around Glasgow. Perhaps it was felt that the punters were simply due a break. The country had not yet recovered from the economic ruin of World War 2. The key word was 'austerity', and although 'austerity' meant far less to the working class with their grim memories of penury in the 1930's than it did to the middle classes now living through an economic crisis under a Government who did not consider their interests paramount, there were still a few tangible reminders of the problems of the day. Rationing, for example, was still in force on so called luxury goods like sweets.

In addition, Celtic's mammoth support had had few chances since the end of the War to have a day out, and Celtic's far flung allies rolled into Buchanan Street, Queen Street and Central Stations, not to mention the Broomielaw, all morning. Rarely had there been such an atmosphere in the city as there was that morning of April 21st 1951 with everyone, apparently, like the waitresses in restaurants, the barmen in pubs and the salesgirls in Lewis's Polytechnic asking the crucial question 'Are we gonna do it the day?'

There were the usual rumours of injuries, particularly as far as John McPhail was concerned. 'Big captain John', as a song of the time called him, had not played since the Raith Rovers Semi Final of March 31st, and Celtic had flopped badly in their three League games in April. Maybe Evans had picked up a strain against England last week - 'he

John McPhail, scorer of the winning goal, is chaired by his team-mates.
Left to right: Hunter, Weir, Rollo, Collins, Baillie, Boden, Fallon, Tully and Peacock.

was ootstaundin, by the way'; Jock Weir seemed to lack a little pace; Bobby Collins wasn't quite big enough - all these things preyed on the mind as we made our way by bus and train to Hampden Park.

The teams were read out, and big John was in! The teams were:

Celtic: Hunter; Fallon and Rollo; Evans, Boden, Baillie; Weir, Collins, McPhail, Peacock, Tully.

Motherwell: Johnstone; Kilmarnock, Shaw; McLeod, Paton, Redpath; Humphries, Forrest, Kelly, Watson, Aitkenhead.

The game was tense, but there was one surprise moment.Celtic supporters, who must have comprised at least 100,000 of the 131,000 were fiercely partisan, but the first time that Willie Redpath of Motherwell touched the ball, he got a rousing cheer. This was because Redpath, like Evans, had played last week in Scotland's win at Wembley. His second touch of the ball was less rapturously greeted however, for Celtic fans were aware of how good and creative a left half he could be.

Celtic were attacking the King's Park End of the packed ground, but making little headway against a determined Motherwell defence who had clearly been primed to expect an early Celtic onslaught. Then after about quarter of an hour had gone, Joe Baillie broke up a Motherwell attack in which Wilson Humphries was threatening damage, and sent

99

a high ball up the middle of the park to find McPhail who headed on past one opponent, evaded the tackle of another and then as goalkeeper Johnstone came charging out, lobbed the ball over his head from about the edge of the penalty area. Hampden erupted at such brilliance, and the rapture took a good five minutes to die down.

It was gradually replaced by icy realism however as Motherwell, determined and now having conquered their early nerves, came more and more into the game. Redpath was now showing just why he was a Scottish Internationalist, and the Celtic defence were at full stretch to ward off a fierce onslaught that came just before half-time.

The second half was long and painful for those who stood on the slopes, or more agonizingly, listened to Peter Thomson's radio commentary on those old radios which ten years ago were encouraging fighting on the beaches and talking about finest hours and so on. In this battle to-day, no blood was spilt, but the passions were no less fierce, as full backs Fallon and Rollo, their hair brushed back, took no prisoners or as one supporter put it 'tackled everything that crossed the half way line - linesmen, stray dogs, trainers, paper bags, the lot'. Evans, Boden and Baillie earned their place in immortality as attack after Motherwell attack was broken up before reaching the penalty area. Once, only once, was the defence almost breached, and that was in the 69th minute when the ball broke to Wilson Humphries who hammered it towards the top corner of the net, convincing the anxious behind that goal that it was a winner until George Hunter appeared from no place and saved the day with a marvellous save. An old timer behind the goal said 'Dan McArthur!' a comparison to Celtic's ace goalkeeper of the 1890's.

As the game crawled towards its conclusion, the feeling of optimism grew that Celtic would not now lose. But the irrational is always a part of football and it just needed one lapse of concentration to throw it all away. In the crucial last ten minutes, the Irish left wing pair of Peacock and Tully, quiet and anonymous so far, came into play by taking the ball for a walk to the corner flag, pausing with the ball, provoking the crunching tackle or trying to win a corner kick. Celtic were in fact enjoying their best spell of the game as the full time whistle came.

Total strangers hugged and kissed, shoes came off in the rapture of it all, the old timer who had talked about Dan McArthur was pummelled to such an extent that his son and grandson had to intervene to protect him, and allow him to see Lady McGowan present the Cup to John McPhail whose goal had made him the hero of the hour. The team would be going off to America on tour soon, and as 20 years earlier, they would take with them the Scottish Cup which they had won now for the 16th time.

That night, for the first time since VE Day of May 1945, there was once again dancing in the streets of the Gorbals.

— 17 —

DIMMING THE NORTHERN LIGHTS
1954

1954 was a curious year with prosperity and affluence gradually beginning to eat their way into the poverty and deprivation that had befouled British society for the past century and a bit. Nazism had been defeated for nine years, but the cost was still a grievous one for the inhabitants of the British Isles. Rationing had only recently stopped, but war and its attendant evils were still a very vivid memory in all but the youngest and the world was still not really a particularly safe place.

The atom bomb exploded over Japan in 1945 had two effects. One was a very potent reminder that the end could come very quickly (and evangelical and apocalyptic religious groupings were not slow to exploit that); the other was that it was now clear that the hegemony of the western world had passed to the other side of the Atlantic and that the United States (McCarthy, Korea and all) were now the world's policemen particularly as far as the prickly, sensitive tyranny of the U.S.S.R. was concerned.

And yet there was optimism too. The post-war babies had now started school, their parents grimly determined that this generation was not to be factory fodder, if possible. A young Queen with her young children seemed to symbolize hope. The saviour of the Western world (Winston Churchill) was still around, as bellicose and bulldogish as ever, but showing clear signs of mellowing by saying things like there is no finer investment for the future than putting milk into babies and proving that he could move with the times by not dismantling Labour's Welfare state and National Health Service.

For young men, there was the tiresome necessity of National Service. War was still considered so imminent against either the ambitious U.S.S.R. or a revived Germany having her third go at world dominion that the Government made every young man spend two years in the services. It was difficult to get out of—you needed a venal or a pacifist doctor who would swear blind to 'flat feet' or 'sore back' or 'heart murmur' , and it usually played havoc with careers and romances. Against that, it gave young men the opportunity to see the world— Cyprus, Aden or Singapore perhaps, even though brutality, bullying and bayoneting dummies were frequently the order of the day.

Where was football amid all this mayhem of a changing world? The answer of course was everywhere. It remained where it had been all century at the very forefront of working men and women, relegating work, business, religion, politics, marriage and even sex to very poor seconds in the conversation of everyday menfolk, and not a few womenfolk as well.

1954 saw the resurgence of Celtic at last, in the eyes of their loyal supporters. The green and whites had suffered terribly since the war with only the 1951 Scottish Cup to cheer them. The immediate preliminaries to the 1953 Coronation had seen a Coronation Cup played by eight invited British teams in Glasgow. Celtic were invited, hardly on the strength of recent form but rather on the strength of their massive support and had amazed the country by winning it.

Aberdeen had also participated in the 1953 Coronation Cup but their 0-4 thrashing at the hands of a very strong Newcastle United side caused less distress than their agonizingly narrow defeat by Rangers in the replayed 1953 Scottish Cup Final. The Northerners, now playing in red rather than their pre-war black and gold, had won the Cup in 1947 and were now quite clearly a strong feature on the Scottish scene, remaining, as always, notoriously difficult to beat at Pittodrie. Conversely travel sickness seemed to be a problem whenever they came to Glasgow.

Elsewhere on the football scene appeared something called the World Cup. Scotland had arrogantly refused to go to the 1950 World Cup on the grounds that they were not British champions, but now seemed willing to have a half hearted attempt in 1954 in Switzerland. Excitement had not exactly reached the hysteria that was to surface in the 1970's however, and the Press was very low-key about the whole business.

The main reason for this seems to have been the lack of television. TV had started in Scotland in 1952 but as yet, a television receiver was the possession of the rich, the pretentious, the eccentric and those who wished to show off. The watching of television was a haphazard affair. The 'set' needed five minutes to warm up, the screen was small, the reception was poor, the progress of your neighbour's motor bike up the avenue was monitored by a noisy burr and if you lived in the lee of a hill or near a noisy factory, you could forget it. The 1954 English Cup final was shown, as indeed would be the World Cup (the 0-7 thrashing from Uruguay remained a traumatic scar well into adult life) but no-body seemed at all interested in the Scottish Cup.

The lack of apparent interest shown by BBC TV (STV had not yet appeared) was in direct contrast to the passionate obsession as revealed in the streets of Aberdeen and Glasgow and indeed every other town and city in Scotland. Celtic had won the League for the first time since before the War and statisticians were not slow to point out that if they were to win the Scottish Cup as well, it would be for the first time since before the First World War, as the Great War or simply 'the War' was now called, that they had won the double. 1914 to be precise was when the double last came to Celtic Park when men like Sunny Jim and 'Napoleon' McMenemy were around.

Aberdeen had a mediocre League season, to be as polite about it as possible, but the belief in the North that something was stirring was given a tremendous boost in the Scottish Cup semi final when Aberdeen, in one of the tournament's greatest ever shocks beat Rangers 6-0. To say that this shocked them at Ibrox is like saying that the Hiroshima bomb caused a stir in Japan, and it was probably because of this that not a single Rangers man was picked for the 1954 World Cup trip. Yet for Aberdeen it was timely revenge for last year's Final reverse and confirmation that this team, under the management of Davie Halliday was on the brink of great things. It must have caused a few ripples of alarm down Celtic Park way as well, one can imagine.

The Cup Final arranged for April 24th aroused interest in a way that very few have before or since. In the first place, both sets of supporters had every reason to be confident—Celtic's because they had won the League and Aberdeen's on the back of that 6-0 thumping of Rangers. In addition, there was the inevitable comparison between the present day and the titanic struggle of 1937 when Celtic won 2-1. It was only 17 years ago, but it seemed a great deal longer when one considered what had happened to the world in those 17 years.

Any Sunday School trip from Aberdeen on 24th April 1954 would have had a major problem in finding a bus. The journey from Aberdeen to Glasgow in 1954 would have needed about five hours, and allowing for the traffic jams, if you hadn't left Aberdeen by about 7.00 a.m., your chances of reaching Hampden in time were slim. In fact, midnight seemed to be a popular time to depart the Granite City with the idea being that you could sleep on the bus and arrive in Glasgow in time for breakfast.

A comparatively new sound was heard on the southbound trains and buses. The Aberdeen supporters, so often douce, respectable, careful and fair with a large proportion of women and children, now had their own song. It is commonly assumed that 'The Northern Lights of Old Aberdeen' is a traditional song going back over the centuries, or at the very least a Victorian music hall ditty, rich in sentimentalism which used to reduce them all to tears in Canada last century or in the Flanders trenches in 1917. Not so! It was written in 1952, and thus was at the very peak of popularity in 1954, capturing the imagination in the same way as Andy Stewart's 'Scottish Soldier' would do a few years later or 'Amazing Grace' in 1972. 'Ah wish ald Wull wad shut up and lut we a get tae sleep' many a drowsy red bedecked Aberdonian must have said on these midnight buses, as the said 'ald Wull' did his Robert Wilson impersonation.

Much of the confidence in the Aberdeen ranks stemmed from their forwards. They had after all put six past Rangers, and that does not happen all that often in Ibrox history. Granted, hat trick hero Joe O'Neill was once again injured, but there was still Paddy Buckley in the middle, and much was expected of him. On the left wing was Jackie Hather, a talented and speedy harrier, and on the right was the

John Higgins jumps for joy as Neil Mochan's shot is deflected past Aberdeen's goalkeeper for the opening goal.

emerging talent of Graham Leggat, a baby faced youngster for whom beckoned a glittering career.In goal was Fred Martin, already on the brink of International stardom, an agile and confident fellow from the unlikely place of Carnoustie.

Celtic however, the deserved League Championship winners were adopting a curious ploy.Their defence was full of rugged defenders like Haughney, Meechan and Stein (definite leadership material in this bloke!) but the most rugged of them all, Irishman Sean Fallon found himself at centre forward.Injuries had compelled this ploy in the middle of March, but rather to the surprise of everyone it seemed to work with the stocky, thick set man from Sligo scoring at crucial times in the run-in to the Championship and being instrumental in the wrapping up of the first post war League flag.You cannot argue with success and the idea was persevered with, but not a few of the Celtic Park faithful were somewhat dubious about it.

The weather was not all that kind, but there was a definite carnival atmosphere in and around Hampden Park. Celtic supporters were boisterous and confident, singing songs about Charlie Tully 'How can you buy our Charlie' to the tune of 'How can you buy Killarney'.

How can you buy all the caps that he's won?
How can you buy old Ma Tully's son?
How can you purchase that son of a gun?
How can you buy our Charlie?

Aberdeen's hopefulls were equally noisy. If they were overwhelmed by the size of the crowd and the magnitude of the occasion, they certainly did not show it. Happily, both sets of supporters mingled freely and talked to each other, exchanging reminiscences about the great Jimmy Delaney who had played for both clubs or the recent 6-0 thumping of Rangers which had gone down equally well with both sets of fans.

The sheer vastness of Hampden Park was intimidating in itself. In 1954, it did not have that run down decrepit look that it was to have in the 1970's, and it had only recently celebrated its 50th anniversary. There was no segregation either in these days and thus green and red scarves mingled happily with the greens not outnumbering the reds by all that much, although there was the usual concentration of Celtic supporters at the King's Park end.

Pre-match entertainment saw majorettes, pipe bands and soldiers as the vast crowd built up.In fact, the attendance was just a little under 130,000, not all of whom saw the kick off such was the build up particularly at the Mount Florida end of the ground. The teams were:

Celtic: Bonnar, Haughney, Meechan; Evans, Stein, Peacock; Higgins, Fernie, Fallon, Tully, Mochan.
Aberdeen: Martin, Mitchell, Caldwell; Allister, Young, Glen; Leggat, Hamilton, Buckley, Clunie, Hather.

The referee went under the name of Charles Faultless, and although no fan would ever admit that he lived up to his name, he was generally admitted to be one of the best around at this time.

The game kicked off at 3.00 with a crescendo of noise and Aberdeen kicking towards the Mount Florida end of the ground.At several points the crowd swayed dangerously on the terracing as everyone stood on tip toe and moved with every ball.From early on, it was seen that Aberdeen's tactics were to use their wingers rather than their inside forwards to feed Buckley; it was equally obvious that Jock Stein had been detailed to mark the dangerous Buckley and that Evans, ubiquitous in defence, would sweep everything that Stein missed. Twelve years and more later, when Stein successfully deployed Clark in a similar role to cover for McNeill, it often seemed that he had this tactic in mind.

At the other end, the Celtic forwards, although brilliantly prompted by Willie Fernie, made very little of Aberdeen's excellently organised defence with Fallon looking ponderous against Young who won everything in the air, and Tully looking moody and lethargic. Not that this was anything for the green and white hordes to concern themselves about. One flash of Tully could win anything.

The first half came to a close with no scoring. Both goalkeepers had been in action but neither team felt robbed that they were not going in a goal ahead. The standard of play had been high.Often two good teams produce a stalemate, but not here. Goals would come in the second half, it was felt, although the Dons' supporters were reconciling themselves to the thought that there was to be no 6-0 thrashing as there had been of Rangers. If only Joe O'Neill hadn't injured himself...

And what was the said Joe thinking? Joe would have loved to be out there, but he had a problem. You see, he came from a Celtic family and unless you are actually playing against them, it is difficult to want them defeated. Once a Celt, always a Celt. He would have loved a Cup winner's medal, though. If only that game against Rangers had been the *Final!*

The teams re-appeared and battle raged again.Five minutes had elapsed when Celtic, now gradually asserting their superiority, scored. Neil Mochan, the cannonball kid, had the ball on the edge of the box. He was about to be closed down by two defenders when he tried one of his favourite ploys, which was to hammer the ball into the goal-mouth and hope for a deflection. His luck was in, for the ball ricocheted off the unfortunate centre-half, Young, and Celtic were a goal up—A lucky, but not entirely undeserved goal!

The rainbow of green and white favours which appeared at the far end of the ground had not yet reached its apex when the Dons equalized.A long ball found Hamilton who headed on to Buckley. Buckley was a good yard faster than Stein and this time Evans was not there to help. Buckley gave Bonnar no chance as the BBC Radio commentary caused a whole city 150 miles away to rise in acclaim. Mothers, wives and aged fathers from the Mearns to Buchan cheered as their team was now back in it.

But there were shamrocks bursting forth on the banks of the

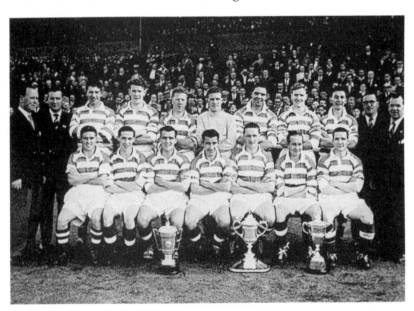

On display are the Coronation, League and Scottish Cups, 1954

Back row: A. Dowdells (trainer), Paterson, Haughney, Meechan, Evans, Bonnar, J. McPhail, Walsh, Peacock, Dr. Fitzimons, J. McGrory (manager). Front row: Collins, Higgins, Fernie, Fallon, Stein, Tully, Mochan.

Shannon when Celtic scored again ten minutes later with a goal fit to win anything. Willie Fernie, arguably Celtic's greatest post war dribbler, went on a mazy run beating several men and crucially drawing defenders away from Sean Fallon. Centre forward or no centre forward, the Irishman was waiting for the ball and could hardly fail to score when the ball came across.

The remaining twenty-five minutes saw the battle, if anything, intensify, as a nation listened to George Davidson on the Scottish Home Service and envied the 130,000 who could watch. Gradually, Celtic's two full backs Haughney and Meechan gained the upper hand over Leggat and Hather, thus forcing Aberdeen to try the long ball tactic towards Buckley. Once Buckley got past Stein Bonnar dived at his feet, reminding some of his brilliance in last season's Coronation Cup final.

Tully at last came into the game. 'Cheeky Charlie's capers' were exactly what Celtic needed at this point to take pressure off an exhausted defence. Those in the green however would have preferred an extra goal rather than the elaborate ball play that Tully purveyed, but he and Fernie were able to take the ball for a walk to the corner flag and spend precious time there.

Frantically Aberdeen, spurred on by fanatical cheers, tried one last attempt to save the game, but Evans again mopped up and the ball was cleared. Mr Faultless, handled the game faultlessly, one may say, and his pointing to the tunnel unleashed an orgy of acclaim as total strangers embraced and wept. Words of consolation and genuine admiration were offered to the red bedecked, and this was mirrored on the field as Buckley embraced Stein, Fernie shook hands with Glen and both goalkeepers warmly congratulated each other. Manager McGrory permitted himself a smile as the toothless Jock Stein collected the Scottish Cup for Celtic's 17th time.

After match scenes in Glasgow revealed a genuine emotion and mutual admiration between both sets of fans, as fans exchanged scarves and tried to learn each other's songs. 'The Northern Lights of Old Aberdeen' sound funny when sung by a Glasgow Keelie, but many tried. There had been a tradition of good relationships between Celtic and Aberdeen supporters, and it was never more in evidence than here.

Buchanan Street Station saw many disappointed northerners as they waited for the 7.30 train that night. But they could console themselves by the thought that success with that team was not too far away (they were to win the League the next year) and by their

109

making of many friends among the green and white brigade. And yes, there was that 6-0 thrashing of Rangers in the Semi Final to think about and savour.

— 18 —

THE DAWN OF THE FREE
1965

Without a shadow of a doubt, 1965 was the most important year in the history of the club. It was the turn of the tide, the year that launched Celtic into being a world class team. We might have seen the slow lingering death of a once great club with a vast support, tremendous pedigree, equally tremendous potential but no present and little future. Instead, because of an honest admission of error and willingness to do something about it on the part of Chairman Robert Kelly, Celtic took off.

The early sixties had been grim. Promise had not been fulfilled, the 'Kelly Kids' who always threatened to 'arrive' were perpetually late, two Scottish Cup Finals were lost in Replays, one agonizingly close, the other humiliatingly one sided, the one world class player we had, Pat Crerand, walked out on us to Manchester United, and there was a perpetual complex about Rangers in whose presence we always froze.

Season 1964 -5 had however started with a bang. Crucially, we beat Rangers on a rainy day in September at Celtic Park in the League and reached the Final of the League Cup in October. The October 24th Final might have been Celtic's breakthrough. Instead we had the usual first half story of missed chances and refused penalties, then 2 professional goals by Rangers, followed by a Celtic fightback that was too late. Everyone agreed that Celtic deserved a draw at least, but it was Rangers who lifted the trophy. Yet, there is the Greek goddess called Nemesis which stalks and catches up with and punishes the wicked; she was waiting for Rangers.

It did not look like that however as autumn turned to winter and defeats from Kilmarnock, St.Johnstone, Dundee and Dunfermline piled up our misery. Bobby Murdoch, an indifferent forward, missed a penalty at Ibrox on New Year's Day after Johnstone had been sent off to give Rangers another lucky win. We then fell at Dundee United a week later, and on January 16th at a rainy Celtic Park, although Bertie Auld had now returned from Birmingham City, Celtic went

111

down to Hearts before a crowd of 20,000 which contained more Hearts fans than Celtic supporters.

This could not go on, for Celtic were almost finished as a force in Scottish Football. Then on that fateful Sunday at the end of January came the announcement that Jock Stein would take over as manager of Celtic just as soon as he could finish his notice with Hibs. Jock of course had been the Captain in 1954 when the team won the Double, had brought on fine youngsters like McNeill and Crer-and after that for Celtic in his capacity as youth coach, then moved to Dunfermline. There, in a space of less than 4 years, he had saved them from relegation, won the Cup (that painful Cup Final of 1961) and made them a force in Europe, and now was the successful manger of Hibs.

In spite of Bob Kelly's high regard for Stein, it must have been a stumbling block that he was a Protestant, albeit not a practising one. Certainly, this presented no problem whatsoever with the support who were keenly enthusiastic for Jock's arrival, but the suspicion remains that it must have hurt Mr Kelly, not only that he had to approach a man of different ethnic origins, but also to admit that his management policies were not working.

The Scottish Cup campaign thus started in early February on a bizarre note in that the players knew that they would have a change of boss in a month's time. It was all very well to speculate on Stein being a miracle worker, but the players would have to make sure that they were still in the Cup at the beginning of March to allow the miracle worker to have the chance.

This was however a changed Celtic team, changed as far as attitude was concerned, and outgoing manager Jimmy McGrory (who in the best of Celtic traditions was not to be sacked but made Public Relations Officer - a job for which the gentle Garngad man was so eminently suited) had now put on the left wing Lennox and Auld. Auld, of course, abrasive, lovable, streetwise, Glaswegian Bertie, so reminiscent of Tommy McInally of old in character, play, and his return to his first love, was an instant hit with the fans who loved his cheekiness, and Bobby Lennox, who had played sporadically on the left wing, now revelled in an inside position. The pair had a great understanding, and jokes began about rival team managers excusing their sexual inadequacies to their wives on the grounds that 'Ah'm gettin' auld' and she would say 'Get Lennox as weel, then'.

The First Round saw Celtic on very dangerous ground at Love Street, Paisley. St.Mirren, fine Cup fighters who had put Celtic out of the Cup in 1959 and 1962, were always good for an upset, but on this occasion they were swept aside to the tune of 3-0 and the Sunday papers claimed it was 'Auld Black Magic', in imitation of a current TV advert. Celtic were a lot less convincing against Queen's Park at Hampden in the next round, but once again the combination of Auld and Lennox was crucial, and Lennox scored the only goal of an otherwise poor game.

The Quarter Finals were played on March 6th 1965, the very eve of the arrival of Stein. Celtic had the strong going Kilmarnock (who would eventually win the League that season) at Celtic Park before a crowd of 47,000 in the pleasant spring sunshine. This was a fine game of football with Celtic just edging it 3-2 with goals by Lennox, Auld and that perpetually frustrating character big John Hughes, who when he was good, was very very good, but when he was bad... He had now however benefited from the general uplift of the team.

But there were significant developments in Edinburgh that day, and some people say that Stein actually won the Cup for Celtic that year before he became manager. He was in charge of Hibs for his last game in front of a crowd which had ambivalent feelings for him, resenting as they did his movement to Celtic in mid-season. Hibs were playing Rangers in the Quarter Finals of the Cup in front of a packed Easter Road. The game was fast and furious, but Rangers, clearly reeling under the news that Celtic had appointed Stein and that their days of getting away with mediocrity in Scotland were numbered, were struggling and had the deathwish on themselves long before Hibs' late, scrambled, lucky winner.

This was a bonus to Celtic and their supporters were happier that night than they had been for many years. The Semi Final Draw paired Celtic and Motherwell at Hampden Park, while Stein's two previous teams Dunfermline and Hibs fought it out at Tynecastle. The games were to be played on March 27th, but meanwhile all attention was focussed on how Celtic would play under Stein in the now meaningless League fixtures. There was a bright start at Broomfield when luckless Airdrie were thrashed 6-0, but then a shocker at Celtic Park when St.Johnstone won 1-0 and completed a rare double of beating Celtic home and away. Stein was quoted as saying 'I see what I am here for' and then made his first great managerial decision.

He pulled Bobby Murdoch back from the forward line to wing half. Murdoch, a talented player had lost his way somewhat since his beginning with a bang at the start of the 1962-3 season, and this move, which a fanzine called 'The Shamrock' suggested some time before

Happy Celtic players salute their fans after winning the 1965 Scottish Cup Final.

Stein's arrival, would resurrect a moribund career and eventually turn Murdoch into one of the greatest players in the world.

Thus Murdoch was at right half for the Semi against Motherwell. This time it was Billy McNeill who had a poor game, and Joe McBride of Motherwell (who would not have claimed otherwise than that his heart was at Celtic Park) did his cause of joining them no harm by scoring two good goals. Celtic, twice a goal down, did very well to fight back. Bertie Auld organized the rescue, feeding Lennox for one goal and scoring a penalty for the other. Celtic in fact should have won on pressure and indeed Auld scored in the last minute only to have it mysteriously disallowed. It only delayed matters however, for Motherwell had no answer to Murdoch and Auld in the Replay which

Celtic won 3-0 with goals from Chalmers, Hughes and Lennox.

Thus it would be Celtic v. Dunfermline Athletic in the Hampden Park Final on April 24th. This was a particularly ironic pairing for it inevitably brought back memories of 1961, and that particular result which seemed to symbolise all the suffering of the lean years. The sheer power of Pat Crerand had made Celtic seem worldbeaters in every respect bar one, and it was the vital one of goalscoring. Feckless finishing and lucky goalkeeping had made that night one of the most frustrating of anybody's life, and the Pars had run up and scored two goals, both well taken but at least one gifted by sloppy goalkeeping, to make it Dunfermline's greatest ever night, but Celtic's worst.

But now we had Stein. This would make the vital difference, we were told, but it did not seem that way as League form continued to be deplorable. Falkirk hammered Celtic 6-2, admittedly a weakened Celtic without McNeill and Clark, and then on the Saturday before the Final, when no excuses were possible on the grounds of injury or anything else, Partick Thistle beat Celtic 2-1 at an ominously silent Celtic Park. Yet on that same day, Dunfermline also lost in a game which mattered and which probably cost them the League Championship, a point raised by the more perspicacious of Celtic optimists before the Final.

The day of the Final also contained a dramatic finish to the Scottish League Championship. It all boiled down to Hearts and Kilmarnock. Dunfermline had lost it the previous week; Hibs and Rangers had fallen by the wayside, and unless Hearts lost by 2-0 at Tynecastle to Kilmarnock, they would be League Champions. Hearts would in the event live up to their tradition of blowing it on the last day by doing just that - losing 2-0 to Kilmarnock.

All this however was of precious little concern to all those 108,000 people who gathered at Hampden Park to watch the following two teams take the field:

Celtic: Fallon, Young, Gemmell; Murdoch, McNeill, Clark; Chalmers, Gallagher, Hughes, Lennox, Auld.

Dunfermline Athletic: Herriot, W. Callaghan, Lunn; Thomson, McLean, T. Callaghan; Edwards, Smith, McLaughlin, Melrose, Sinclair.

'We'll forgive everythin, Cel-lic, everythin, if ye's jist win the dae' screamed a desperate Glasgow voice in my ear as referee Hugh Phillips of Wishaw started the game. Celtic were playing towards their own supporters, although in truth, there were enough of them at the other end as well, and green and white favours seemed to outnumber black and white ones by about 20 to 1. The weather was fine - a bright spring day with more than a hint of a breeze.

The Pars drew first blood as Melrose hooked a ball from the edge of the penalty area after the Celtic defence had failed to mop up a throw in and goalkeeper Fallon had been caught off his line. Time 15 minutes and then Celtic began to surge forward, playing the sort of football that would become their hallmark in years to come. On the half hour mark, inside forward Charlie Gallagher picked up a loose ball and shot from about 25 yards. The ball hit the bar, and the cries of frustration from the packed Celtic end were strangled when it was seen that the ball, caught in a capricious gust of wind, did not fly over the bar, nor bounce back into play, but shot straight up in the air. The bar was still shaking with the vehemence of the shot as the ball came down, and the ever alert Bertie Auld kept his eye on the ball and headed in from about six inches out. It was one of the strangest goals ever seen at Hampden Park, but totally deserved, you felt, before about thirty strangers of all ages and sexes jumped on your back in ecstasy.

1-1, but then just at half time a cemetery silence descended once again on the Celtic End amid the odd call for the sacking of Queen's Park's public address system man. It was bizarre the way Dunfermline went ahead again. A soft free kick had been conceded outside the box. Melrose shaped to take it, but instead tapped the ball to McLaughlin. At that very instant the P.A. system announced a message that no-body heard but might well have gone down in infamy. The Celtic defence's concentration fatally wilted, and everybody hesitated as McLaughlin hammered a great goal past Fallon.

The half time whistle went soon afterwards, and everybody felt that this was rough justice. Celtic had played better football, had had more possession of the ball, and yet these two Dunfermline goals had given them a 2-1 lead. Half time was spent in a curious state of introverted pessimism and everybody was wishing they hadn't come and that they'd never heard of football or Celtic, for there was that sickening promise of another disappointment, one that would be hard to handle psychologically.

But this was a different Celtic team. This one had passion as well as skill. The days of the cavings-in had gone, and within five minutes of the restart, they were level again. It was that left wing pair of Lennox and Auld again! Auld had released Lennox, then had charged into the penalty area to receive the return pass, to hammer home a low shot at the very instant of being tackled.

It was now that we began to have our alternate dream and nightmare scenario, as both teams served up what would be described by all the papers as a great game of football. If anything, Dunfermline upped a gear once they got over the shock of the equalizer, and on at least two occasions Celtic were indebted to John Fallon for saving them. He may have been partly to blame for the first goal, but he made up for it now as first Edwards, then McLaughlin shot for him to save brilliantly. Then Celtic began to take command for a spell, as the feeling began to grow once we were in the last quarter of an hour that the next goal would be the winner.

Nine minutes remained as Lennox's speed won Celtic a corner on the left at the Mount Florida end. Charlie Gallagher took it, sent over a perfect ball and Billy McNeill appeared from nowhere to head home, taking radio and TV commentators as much by surprise as he did the Dunfermline defence.

This was indeed story book, B(h)oys Own stuff, full of romance and joy with plucky winners and gallant losers. But journalists and historians have tended to ignore the truth when they talk about Celtic's meeting with destiny and so on. The truth was that we had nine undignified minutes to live through. Nine minutes of sweating, praying, pleading, bowel churning, bladder bursting, promising to attend Church every Sunday for the rest of our life, agony to live through. Fortunately the players on the park were calmer than we were at the top of Gangway 25 as Bertie Auld pretended to trip over and stand on the pile of policemen's coats as he shaped to take a corner kick.

Hugh Phillips eventually gave way to the pressure of 100,000 hysterical voices and pointed to the dressing room. *Now* we could talk of Captain Courageous, of the old Celtic Cup Magic, heroes of the hour, and the glorious uplands of our august destiny. Why, somebody even said we could maybe win the European Cup - 'maybe no' next year, but the year efter that',and we all slapped him on the back as we shared his unfettered joy. We cried as they ran towards the Celtic End with the trophy, some whose childhoods had been flawed and underpriviliged but whose young manhood would now be rich with the joys of triumph. Introverted, sad children suddenly became alert, cheerful, confident young people, and life would never be the same again.

There was an appointment with history in one sense. Rangers

victory over Dundee in 1964's Scottish Cup had meant that for the first time since 1922, Celtic had slipped behind in the table of Cup Winners. Now we were back level again, for we had won the Scottish Cup for the eighteenth time. The pendulum had swung back.

— 19 —

A STEPPING STONE TO LISBON
1967

Although 1967 is, and always will be, remembered in the chronicles of Scottish football for the mighty deeds in Lisbon (as well as an honourable mention for Scotland's 3-2 victory over England at Wembley and indeed Rangers' reaching of the Final of the Cup Winners' Cup) it would be wrong to omit mention of Celtic's achievement on the domestic front. In fact, they won every competition for which they entered, thus putting them on a par with the giants of 1908. Now at last could somebody be mentioned in the same breath as Young, Loney and Hay!

It would be wrong to assume that Celtic had things easy in Scotland in 1967. On the contrary, one could put up a case for saying that the 1967 Rangers team was one of their best, and certainly better than quite a few, before or since, who have had more tangible rewards. Granted, they did fall on their faces spectacularly twice, but they pushed Celtic hard in the League with Celtic glad of a draw at Ibrox on that rainy day in May, and the League Cup Final at the end of October was a very tense affair which Celtic won by one solitary goal.

The only real problem that Rangers had in 1967 was that Celtic were better. The management of Stein had brought on some players, who moved from the ordinary to the superb, and had consolidated others who were already good by giving them that elusive quality of confidence and belief in ultimate success. In addition he had bought well twice. Joe McBride from Motherwell banged goals in at the rate of about one a game, and as if Stein was to know that Joe would be injured at Pittodrie on Christmas Eve, he had bought Willie Wallace from Hearts a fortnight earlier! Willie was a total professional rather than a dyed in the wool Celt, and to his credit, he made no attempt to hide that. But the fans made him welcome in his first Celtic Park appearance in a game against Motherwell by displaying a banner with 'Oor Wullie' written on it. In that same game incidentally, Motherwell's centre forward Dixie Deans was sent off.

The most romantic and unbelievable story was that of veteran goalkeeper Ronnie Simpson. It is all the more remarkable when one considers that it was Stein, as manager of Hibs, who sold him to Celtic. Argumentative people in pubs will always tell you that Stein bought Simpson twice, once for Hibs and once for Celtic. Not so! Simpson joined Hibs on October 4th 1960 when Stein had just started making something of Dunfermline, and he joined Celtic on 3rd September 1964 when Stein thought he was finished at Easter Road. Simpson gives the impression in his book 'Sure It's A Grand Old Team To Play For' that he and Stein did not altogether 'hit it off' at one point in the Easter Road days. So much more then to the credit of both men that they made such a success at Celtic Park!

Tommy Gemmell was a player whose career was in the doldrums until Stein arrived. He had never given the impression of lacking confidence, but Stein's arrival gave him that extra bit to justify his self-confidence, and with Stein's attention to discipline and detail, Tommy soon developed into Britain's number one attacking full back with the cannonball shot.

The midfield of Murdoch and Auld (by 1967 Celtic were playing a very fluid 4-2-4 formation, however much we diehards on the terracing still talked about wing halves and inside forwards) was without peer. Murdoch had been transformed into a world class player who sadly did not always impress when he got the chance for Scotland, and Auld was simply a genius—a Tommy McInally, a Patsy Gallagher and an Alec Thomson all rolled into one. A born show off with a tremendous sense of humour, he was much loved by the crowd and much admired and envied by supporters of other teams.

Up front, Chalmers had improved beyond measure, and Lennox had, thanks to intensive training, become the fastest thing on feet, frequently pulled up for offside simply because the linesman could not believe that he had such a turn of pace. Jimmy Johnstone was simply Jimmy Johnstone - brilliant one day, even more brilliant the next, and on his day, the best in the world. Capable of inspiring a team, not the least of his many qualities was courage in that he frequently would risk a broken leg by not shirking a tackle from some coarse defender.He did however have a problem with his temper and his sometimes cavalier attitude to discipline. This would more than once get him into real hot water.

Celtic's Scottish Cup campaign that year lacked any great tie or really any major difficulty before the Final. All their games were played at either Celtic Park or Hampden, and never were they in any real bother. The first game saw Arbroath at Celtic Park. The 'Red Lichties' from Angus were never really in it once Celtic scored three times in the first half hour, but that game was not the main topic of conversation, for that day 28th January 1967 brought about the astonishing scoreline of Berwick Rangers 1 Glasgow Rangers 0. Even the BBC queried that one and Celtic Park, so often fertile ground for baseless rumours about Rangers (there is no limit, after all, to what you will believe if you want to believe it!) was at first a little incredulous with loads of us refusing to accept it until we saw the evening paper. Even then, some of us considered it a very sophisticated wind-up!

But true it was, and East Fife supporters were less than happy at being knocked off the headlines, for they too had had a great win against Motherwell which would surely have merited the back page on any other day! In the next round, Celtic met more fishermen at Celtic Park when Elgin City came to town. They held out until just before half time, but lost three goals between the 43rd and the 45th minute! They eventually went down 7-0 but earned a huge cheque and a few cheers from the Celtic Park faithful. Some of them had admitted quite cheerfully before the game that they were Celtic supporters and they were singled out for applause whenever they took a throw in, for example.

More difficult opposition was forthcoming in the Quarter Finals in the shape of Queen's Park who managed to persuade Tommy Gemmell to score an own goal in the first minute, and from then on fought every inch of the way. Celtic won 5-3, but once again we had the strange spectacle of the Jungle applauding the opposition for their gutsy performance. There was however one unsavoury incident when Jimmy Johnstone appeared to head butt a Queen's Park player on the blind side of the referee and linesman. Most of the crowd were genuinely appalled at this behaviour, even though he did not necessarily make contact with the player, and Celtic Park lapsed into an embarrassed silence for a while. Jock Stein however acted swiftly and decisively and imposed a club suspension of one week on Jinky.

This was the admirable side of Jock Stein, yet one wonders what would have happened if the Vojvodina game which had been played the previous Wednesday had been scheduled for the next mid-week? Would Jock have been quite so iron fisted, or would cynical pragmatism have won the day? As it was, it was excellent public relations for the club and a warning (sadly not always subsequently heeded) for Wee Jimmy.

Clyde were the opponents in the Semi Final. Clyde, managed by Davie White who later moved disastrously to Rangers, were having an excellent season. They would finish third in the League that year and possessed some fine players including Dick Staite, a classy defender, and Harry Hood whom the newspapers had been trying to sign for Celtic for some time, and would eventually succeed in 1969. Conventional wisdom dictates that 'you never get a good game wi' these two' East End rivals, and 56,000 saw a dreadful Semi Final with no goals, no football, although a blatant penalty was turned down in the last minute when Soutar elbowed a fast travelling Johnstone shot over the bar.

Conventional wisdom also dictated that Celtic seldom lose Semi Final Replays, and Wednesday night brought another crowd of over 50,000, some of whom must have missed Lennox's second minute opener. Clyde knew the game was up then, and their suspicions were confirmed in 25 minutes when Bertie Auld showed what a great player he was. He got the ball on the edge of the penalty area, swivelled, controlled and then shot in almost one movement to the high corner of the net. We could have gone home then, for we knew that Celtic were in the Final to face a tough Aberdeen side who had defeated Dundee United by a freak own goal in the other Semi Final.

The much talked about Cup Final between Celtic and Aberdeen would take place on April 29th. There was a great deal of interest anyway in the game, but in its immediate context, it was so much greater for on the previous Tuesday Celtic had qualified to be the first British team to play in a European Cup Final. This they had done by a totally professional performance against Dukla Prague. They had won the 1st leg 3-1 at Celtic Park and by uncharacteristic defence had kept everything low key and 0-0 in Prague. They had arranged to fly back that very Tuesday night immediately after the game, and everyone landed happy except right back Jim Craig who had picked up a fluish chill and was sent home immediately to bed, isolated from the others in case the infection spread.

Celtic thus thoroughly deserved the plaudits, but Aberdeen meanwhile, under the leadership of Eddie Turnbull, were quietly confident. On the eve of the season they had committed a major blunder in transferring talented half back Dave Smith to Rangers, but had slowly built up a good side. They were hardly the attacking cavaliers of Scottish football, but had earned two draws against Celtic that season in games which they had killed stone dead, and with experienced players like Harry Melrose and Frank Munro around were nobody's pushovers. They had bought from Leeds Jim Storrie who had been a great success at a packed Pittodrie in their Quarter Final Replay against

Hibs, and their star man was Jimmy Smith who like Jimmy Johnstone had the nickname 'Jinky'. There had been a certain amount of speculation linking this Smith as well with Rangers, but I was reliably informed on the seething East terracing that day that this could not ever happen because 'Jimmie Smith cannae play for the Gers. Jimmie Smith's a Tim! His uncle used tae play wi me'. So that was that, and I was grateful to the man with a huge scar and no teeth for informing me.

The teams that day were in front of 127,117 fans were:

Celtic: Simpson, Craig, Gemmell; Murdoch, McNeill, Clark; Johnstone, Wallace, Chalmers, Auld, Lennox.
Aberdeen: Clark, Whyte, Shewan; Munro, McMillan, Petersen; Wilson, Smith, Storrie, Melrose, Johnston.

We had noticed that when the Aberdeen bus appeared, there was no Eddie Turnbull in charge, and he could not be seen on the trackside, nor in the Directors' Box either. It transpired that he had taken ill with a viral complaint at Gleneagles Hotel and could not make it to the game. Possibly influenced by this, Stein decided to flummox the Dons and indeed the crowd by moving about Jimmy Johnstone who did not line up in his usual inside right position. 'Big Jock's gaen Wee Jimmy a rovin' commission the day' said my new friend with the scar and no teeth.

This ploy certainly worked for the Aberdeen defence were running around like headless chickens for a while, as Celtic settled into their normal game. Jim Craig had clearly shaken off his 'Dukla flu' and played an outstanding part in this game. Both sides had chances, however, in a somewhat mundane first half, characterised by the booking of Jimmy Smith by referee Willie Syme for a foolish tackle. This particular indiscretion possibly cost him his chance of a transfer to his beloved Celtic, although he would be on their books on loan at the end of his career in 1976.

Celtic opened the scoring in the 42nd minute following some fine play by that left wing pair of Lennox and Auld. Lennox reached the dead ball line, and when the Aberdeen defence was expecting a long cross, Bobby cut back to the awaiting Willie Wallace who stabbed home a simple goal, as Chalmers raised his arms in triumph. Loud and long was the cheering at half time, and a few minutes into the second half, Celtic made it two. In some ways it was a remarkably similar goal to the first, but this time it was Jimmy Johnstone on his own right wing

Billy McNeill and Ronnie Simpson in a dance of delight.

who cut the ball back to the unmarked Willie Wallace, and those of us low down on the King's Park terracing had a great view of the ball heading towards us before we were engulfed in the tide of ecstasy.

There were still a good forty minutes of the Final to go, and although they took a long time to pass as Aberdeen did indeed make a good fight of things, there was yet something comforting about this Celtic team, something so slick, so professional, so assured. Even in the last minute when Aberdeen seemed to have pulled one back, Simpson who had been caught off his line, sprinted back to clear his line to a tremendous cheer from the distant Celtic end. This was Ronnie Simpson, son of a once-hated Ranger who was sitting in the stand cheering on Celtic, capped for Scotland two weeks previously for the first time at the age of 37 and 15 years after he won his first F.A.Cup Medal for Newcastle United, soon to win a European Cup medal in Lisbon. It was unbelievable, but the wonderful thing about Celtic is that you get romance as well as reality.

At full time we shook hands with the disconsolate pocket of Dons fans who had arrived on the East Terracing by mistake presumably and were now heading home. They were honest and likeable and we who had known the bitterness of defeat not all that long ago could empathise. Billy McNeill dropped the lid off the Cup as he lifted it up that afternoon, but at least he himself was O.K. unlike a month later when he looked distinctly ill at Lisbon following a well meaning pummelling from delirious fans as he lifted a larger and far uglier but more significant trophy.

— 20 —

THE RANGERS NIGHTMARE
1969

1969 was another remarkable year in the history of the club. Following the dizzy heights of 1967, it was perhaps inevitable that the team would slide a little in 1968 (some slide! They still managed to win the League Championship and the League Cup!), but by 1969, they had bounced back to sweep everything before them in Scotland and be a challenge once again in Europe.

Early on in season 1968-9, we were given a sight of the team's calibre. In the First Round of the European Cup, Celtic were drawn against St.Etienne the French Champions. 2-0 down from the First Leg, things were looking bad for Celtic especially as early League form had been none too impressive (Rangers had won at Celtic Park, for example, and a point had been dropped at Dunfermline) but the return at Celtic Park had seen Celtic fire on all cylinders and defeat the Frenchmen 4-0, with Joe McBride making one of his rare appearances and scoring a late goal.

The European challenge would sadly come to grief at the Quarter Final stage at the hands of the eventual winners A.C.Milan, but there would be another thrilling night at Celtic Park in November when Johnstone, bribed by the offer of not having to fly for the second leg in Yugoslavia, demolished Red Star Belgrade almost on his own.

The League campaign was not without its interest. Rangers beat Celtic home and away (luckily both times, it must be admitted) and maintained a credible challenge to Celtic until late in the campaign, but Celtic in spite of that double defeat from Rangers and being behind on occasion in the League race, were always favourites.

The team was more or less the same as the Lisbon winners, although hard tackling Jim Brogan had edged out John Clark. The strength however of the forward line was that Stein always had the ability to permutate. There were the five of two years ago and John Hughes who was having a superb season. Youngsters like George Connelly were introduced as well, and to further strengthen the line, Stein in mid

March bought Harry Hood from Clyde.He had also signed Tommy Callaghan from Dunfermline in November to bolster the midfield.

The League Cup was odd that season.Celtic had always looked the likely winners after they defeated Rangers twice in the Sectional Ties 2-0 and 1-0, and in both games won more comfortably than the scoreline would suggest. Partick Thistle, Morton and Hamilton Academical were all swept aside, but a few days after a narrow win over a determined Clyde in the Semi Final, a fire in Hampden's main stand forced a postponement of the League Cup Final against Hibernian until the spring. Thus the scene was set for Celtic's glorious April of 1969.

The opening of the Scottish Cup campaign in January did not find Celtic in the best of moods. Rangers had beaten them narrowly and luckily on New Year's Day after a string of unsatisfactory draws on the hard pitches of December had raised a few questions about the team's staying power. The 1st Round saw Celtic at Firhill and a good game which Celtic having been 3-1 up, threw away thanks to careless defending. The following Wednesday night at Celtic Park, however, showed the world what they could do with a spectacular 8-1 demolition of poor Thistle, and the 8 goals were shared among 7 players! Only Tom Callaghan spoiled the party by scoring two.

More Glasgow opposition was forthcoming at Shawfield against Clyde. The first game was dull, a 0-0 scoreline yet again underlining the point that Celtic and Clyde seldom play well against each other, but is significant for two reasons. One was that it was the beginning of the end for Ronnie Simpson who dislocated a shoulder early on and had to go off, being replaced by the ebullient and apparently super confident Tommy Gemmell; and the other was that it was probably this game which finally decided Stein to bid for the sharp Harry Hood who, with better support, might well have won the game for the Bully Wee against a makeshift goalkeeper who according to one fan, was put in goal so that he could save Celtic with his nose, if necessary. The Replay at Celtic Park was 3-0 for Celtic with Fallon in goal and Celtic's erstwhile goalkeeper, the loveable Big Tam, missing a penalty kick!

The next round against St.Johnstone was a thrilling affair. Under ex-Hib Willie Ormond, St.Johnstone had surprised and delighted everyone by emerging as one of the powers in the land with fine players like John Connolly and Henry Hall. Celtic were always ahead and with ten minutes left made it 3-1. Henry Hall pulled one back soon after, though, and the last five minutes were spent with the 40,000 crowd on tenterhooks for the Saints would have deserved a draw and a Replay at Muirton. They thoroughly merited their round of applause from a relieved Celtic Park crowd at the final whistle.

The Semi Finals now paired Celtic against Morton and Rangers against Aberdeen. One would have expected the Rangers game to be at Hampden and the Celtic one at Ibrox, but the S.F.A. annoyed Rangers by making them play at Celtic Park while Celtic went to Hampden. As it turned out the Rangers game attracted a slightly larger audience, so perhaps Rangers' gripe was justified, but it did show that in 1969 Celtic were now considered to be the bigger team by those in authority.

Both games were played on Saturday March 22nd, and the results were in little doubt. Yet Celtic surprised their supporters by wearing an all-white strip, so that when they appeared, some fans at the top of the East Terracing (a considerable distance away) refrained from clapping, thinking that it was Morton who had appeared. (Morton occasionally did wear all white). Such disorientation was not helped when Morton scored first, and a Greenock man beside me reminded me of 1948 when Morton did indeed beat Celtic in a Scottish Cup Semi. But Celtic equalized ten minutes later, went ahead before half time, added another two before full time and the game finished a somewhat one sided bore. Some supporters were upset that it was only 4-1, for Rangers had won 6-1 at Celtic Park.

But now some bizarre events only loosely connected with football began to take place. Rangers now had a Stein themselves, one Colin Stein whom they had bought from Hibs the previous autumn for £100,000. Fair haired, good looking Colin soon became the darling of Ibrox for his goal scoring exploits, most of them admittedly against weaker opposition. But he had a disciplinary problem which came to a head when he was sent off against Clyde at Ibrox after an incident with a Clyde player. Rangers were 6-0 up at the time and only seconds remained, so it seemed rather foolish to turn violent at that time.

He had earned quite a few disciplinary points over the season for both Hibs and Rangers and the upshot was that he would miss the Scottish Cup Final on April 26th.

It also became apparent that Jimmy Johnstone would be suspended for the Cup Final. This was in addition to the loss of John Hughes through injury, so perhaps Rangers had a slight advantage in terms of player availability. But Celtic had other things on their mind in that month of April, like the winning of two other trophies. The League Cup was won on April 5th by beating Hibs 6-2 and by playing glorious football even by the standards of that golden era. Less spectacular was the winning of the League Championship by means of two weak

THE RANGERS NIGHTMARE 1969

draws, one aginst Airdrie at home and one at Rugby Park on the Monday before the Cup Final.

The run up to the Final was hysterical in some sections of the Press. Much stress was laid on Rangers' naive announcement that there would be a victory parade at Ibrox on Saturday night for their fans. It reminds one of the Astoria Hotel in Leningrad where Hitler said he would have his celebratory banquet in 1941. No such prognostications were made at Celtic Park where Stein had decided to bring in young George Connelly who had only recently celebrated his 20th birthday. There would be two other changes from the Lisbon men - Jim Brogan, hard tackling and determined had now replaced the slightly more elegant John Clark at left half, and Simpson's injury in the game against Clyde had allowed back the ever loveable John Fallon.

The red headed, friendly Fallon was Celtic through and through. He had saved many games for Celtic particularly in the pre-Stein era, and already possessed a 1965 Scottish Cup medal; but he had also had some shockers, and in particular in the New Year's game at Celtic Park in 1968 he had given Rangers a draw by two crass blunders. This Cup Final would be a vital one for him, one felt.

The all ticket crowd of 132,870 saw the following teams run out on April 26th 1969, a pleasantly warm day;

Celtic: Fallon, Craig, Gemmell; Murdoch, McNeill, Brogan; Connelly, Chalmers, Wallace, Lennox, Auld.
Rangers: Martin, Johansen, Mathieson; Greig, McKinnon, Smith; Henderson, Penman, Ferguson, Johnston, Persson.

Celtic won the toss and found themselves playing down towards their own supporters. It was the usual Celtic whirlwind start, and off the second corner that they forced in as many minutes, they scored. It was so predictable. A high floating corner kick, the unmarked McNeill, the ball going in off the post, the momentary stunned silence then the rainbow of green at one end and the continuing stunned silence at the other. The aftermath of the goal saw John Greig asking Kai Johansen the question of why he was not at his post, for which no satisfactory answer would be forthcoming and Alex Ferguson collapsing head in hands for it had been he who had been told to mark McNeill at corner kicks.

Battle now resumed with Mr Callaghan the referee a busy man as tackles on both sides were fierce and the crowd, heavily committed on one side or another, intense in their urgings on of their heroes. If

Celtic celebrate their second goal in the Scottish Cup Final against Rangers.

anything Rangers had slightly more territorial advantage and John Fallon became the darling of the Celtic End on more than one occasion with saves from Persson, Ferguson, then Ferguson again when he dived courageously at his feet. Against that, Celtic had the ball in the net, but Mr Callaghan had already blown for a foul on the goalkeeper.

Towards half time, the pace noticeably slowed with both teams conserving their energy for the second half onslaught. Celtic appeared quite happy with their one goal lead, and Rangers reconciled to it, when there occurred the most amazing end to a first half in Scottish Cup Final history. On the halfway line on the main stand side of the field, Persson's pass to Mathieson was somewhat astray and young Connelly stepped in to prod the ball to Lennox. Rangers never could catch Lennox who ran the length of the Rangers half of the field before scoring effortlessly.

The Celtic End were still jumping on each other's backs when it happened again! This time it was goalkeeper Martin who tried to pass to Greig who was unprepared and George Connelly stepped in to round the keeper and score like a veteran. It was just as well for Rangers that half time came almost immediately after that, for they left the field a ragged bunch, lacking even the spirit to shout at each other. The Mount Florida end spent half time in a state of shock with several fans slumped over crush barriers unable even to communicate with friends, whereas the King's Park end had never seen anything like it since the 7-1 of almost 12 years previously.

To their credit, Rangers fought in the second half. Tackles continued to be fierce, and one player in particular, whose subsequent managerial record in both Scotland and England commands admiration, was very lucky not to be sent packing after what looked like a head-but on Bobby Murdoch. Celtic, however, were in command in midfield, with Auld, Connelly and Murdoch all superb. Half way through the second half Auld released Chalmers, who ran all of 35 yards, outstripping the exhausted Rangers defence, to make it number 4.

At this point, the Mount Florida End invaded the field. It was not, I think, any attempt to stop the game; rather it was an attempt to get home early to avoid seeing any more. However, the Glasgow Police forced them back onto the terracing and made them watch the rest of the game.

The ecstatic Celtic fans just could not be happier as the Cup was passed down the line of players (laps of honours were banned at that time) with each player receiving his own hurrah. Goalkeeper John Fallon got his own special cheer - he had already done a bow to his now adoring followers - and little seemed wrong with the world that spring day of 1969 on which Celtic won the Scottish Cup for the 20th time.

— 21 —

STEIN FIGHTS BACK
1971

Season 1970-71 was probably as successful a season as any in the Stein era, given the problems that faced him. The main problem was of course that the great side of 1967 was breaking up, and Stein's dilemma was always how to introduce youngsters gently into the side without upsetting any rhythm. There were indeed talented youngsters around, loads of them but everyone at Celtic Park was totally aware of the disastrous events of ten years previously when too many youngsters had been thrown in without the counterbalance of experienced men. On the other hand the Milan fiasco had shown that change was necessary.

Summer 1970 had seen Celtic lose the Scottish Cup Final very unluckily, but no excuses were possible about the European Cup Final against Feyenoord. Woods and Campbell in 'The Glory and the Dream' use the brilliant Old Testament analogy of the Genesis story:

The serpent of complacency had crept into Paradise.

Complacency and the naked desire for money and financial advancement on the part of some players who did not fully appreciate that money really has to be earned in football. A subsequent, pointless tour of America had seen poor results. Then Stein had suddenly departed for home without an adequate explanation. He would soon be followed by Gemmell and Auld, sent home, for similarly mysterious reasons, by Sean Fallon.

The season therefore began with Celtic apparently at sixes and sevens, and in October the League Cup Final was lost to Rangers who had hitherto been giving every indication of having a complex about Celtic. But Stein buckled to the task, was ruthless when he had to be, dropping Johnstone and McNeill on occasion and New Year was reached with the damage minimised. The team was only one point behind the strong going Aberdeen who had beaten them 1-0 at Celtic Park in December, and Celtic had once again reached the Quarter

132

Finals of the European Cup. Rangers in spite of their League Cup win were having a poor season and would clearly be looking to the New Year's game at Ibrox on January 2nd to resurrect their championship challenge.

That particular game however would become Scottish football's saddest day. It was a close fought encounter with honours even until the 89th minute when Jimmy Johnstone scored. Rangers fans, as is the way with supporters, turned their back on their team and headed down Stairway 13 for the exit. The vanguard were half way down, when a roar announced that Colin Stein had equalized immediately from the restart. Some turned to get back; others kept going because they could not stop themselves, many lost their footing and in the end 66 people were crushed to death. Scottish football would never be the same again, and the well attended Memorial Services in both Church of Scotland and Roman Catholic Churches showed perhaps that there was more to life than football.

Life however must go on and the following week Celtic played Hibs at Celtic Park. One might have feared that the minute's silence for the victims might have been profaned by the cries of the ignorant. Not a bit of it. Celtic Park was mute and respectful, a fitting tribute to 66 fellow football fans who were not really the enemy after all. It was a moving experience.

The Scottish Cup opened with a 5-1 demolition at Celtic Park of Queen of the South, but more difficult opposition was forthcoming when Dunfermline came to town in the next round, containing as they did ex-Celts in Joe McBride and John Cushley. True to form, Joe scored early in the second half to level the scores (he had already scored twice for Hibs against Celtic earlier in the season at Easter Road) and a Replay was necessary. Wallace had scored for Celtic before Joe's equalizer, and the only goal in the Replay was scored by Harry Hood. Thus all 3 goals were scored by Stein signings.

It is perhaps interesting at this point to notice that Stein seldom got a disappointment with his goalscorers. These three already mentioned paid their way (although McBride was unlucky with a bad injury) as indeed would Dixie Deans. It was almost like a conveyer belt of strikers which Stein seemed able to buy at bargain prices. He was less happy with his goalkeepers, and some of his talented youngsters let him down through emotional problems, but he had a good eye for a striker. Of course, the cynics will argue that it is easy to be a striker in a successful team, and this the Celtic team of the early 70's still were.

Raith Rovers, a poor outfit in 1971 were hammered at Celtic Park in the Quarter Final where Lennox scored a hat-trick and the headlines were made by John Hughes having an argument with Stein about not being selected and being asked to vacate the premises. This would be the beginning of the end for the mercurial Yogi Bear and within a few months he would be on his way to Crystal Palace.

The Semi Final placed Celtic against Airdrie and Rangers against Hibs. The Old Firm would eventually triumph but it was a struggle in both cases. Celtic's first game against Airdrie was a great spectacle but an unhappy experience for Celtic who were twice two goals ahead, yet the game ended in a 3-3 draw with both goals in the last ten minutes having lucky escapes. Young Dalglish, who was being brought in gradually, was given an outing for the Replay which Celtic won 2-0, but in which they again failed to convince their fans.

By the time that the Final came along on May 8th 1971, many changes had been made from the previous year. The most significant development over the past two years had been that of David Hay. He had the ability to play on either side of the defence, and was equally happy as a midfielder. His tackling was superb; his passing reminiscent of Pat Crerand a decade ago, and his speed was impressive. Already an established Scottish Internationalist, Davie Hay was widely recognized as being something special. George Connelly who had first come to prominence in January 1966 with a display of ball control at half-time in the European Cup Winners' Cup game against Dinamo Kiev, and had hit the headlines by his goal in the 1969 Scottish Cup Final, was now being given the accolade of one of the all time Celtic Park greats. He had replaced the magical Bertie Auld, and the personality problems that would ruin him a few years later were as yet under control.

Tom Callaghan had proved to be a shrewd buy for the midfield. Tall, lean with a slight resemblance to Hen Broon of 10 Glebe Street, Tom was used sparingly by Stein (as was everyone that year as Stein relentlessly experimented for his ideal formation) but to good effect. It is true that he did not necessarily become an instant hit with the Celtic Park faithful, but respect for him was growing.

The League was won officially on April 29th at Hampden (Celtic Park's stand was being repaired) against Ayr United, but effectively it was Aberdeen's failure to beat Celtic at Pittodrie on April 17th which won the League. Aberdeen had put up a brave fight that year, but fell a little short in the run in. Rangers would end up 15 points short of Celtic, so that a great deal hung on the Scottish Cup, as far as Rangers were concerned.

It would have to be admitted that Rangers must have found it tough playing at Ibrox, with considerable parts of it sealed off, after the tragedy of January 2nd. Celtic's fine team of 1931, it will be recalled, fell apart after the death of John Thomson. What was less easy to accept was the continuing self righteousness of all those in authority in Scottish football who refused to allow the Scottish Cup Final to be televised so that 120,000 tickets could be sold for the game. We even got excuses like 'It's safer in a large crowd than in a smaller one' and so on. Another objectionable part of the build up was the campaign by sections of the Press to bring in the Ibrox disaster with headlines like '66 reasons why Rangers want to win the Scottish Cup'. Both Celtic and Rangers fans found this distasteful, and wrote to papers to say so.

The first game was very competitive with Celtic seeming to be on top after Lennox's goal before half time. The anxiety at the Celtic end, however, was replaced by despair when Derek Johnstone, already an Ibrox hero after the League Cup Final, scored a painful late equalizer. The two teams could not be separated, so it was a Replay the following Wednesday night, May 12th, with TV once again being refused permission to show the game live, and another six-figure crowd of over 102,000 turning up.

There were of course murmurings about 'fix' from disconsolate supporters and allegations in pubs about pocket lining and so on with fingers pointed at the 1963 and 1966 Cup Finals which had both gone to Replays. More disturbing was the fact that Rangers had won both these games, and having had a let off on Saturday, would now have their tails up for this one, it was felt.

Stein had not been happy with the forward line on Saturday. He re-jigged it, dropped the ineffective Willie Wallace and brought in young Lou Macari whose appearances this season had been sporadic. Like Dalglish and Davidson, he was being introduced gradually, but there were times, Stein felt, when youngsters had to prove themselves on the big stage. One could not say that Lou would go down as one of the most popular Celts of all time, but no-body knew what his future would bring on that bright spring night.

Rangers made a major error in team selection. Right back Alex Miller was injured, and rather than make any further changes by re-drafting their defence, they brought in a young debutant at right back called Jim Denny. Their fans had never heard of him, unless they went to the reserve games, and it was a bold move which had the radio commentators wondering whether this was sensible or not.

The teams which referee Mr Tom Wharton brought to order were;

Celtic: Williams, Craig, Brogan; Connelly, McNeill, Hay; Johnstone, Macari, Hood, Callaghan, Lennox.
Rangers: McCloy, Denny, Mathieson; Greig, McKinnon, Jackson; Henderson, Penman, Stein, McDonald, Johnston.

From the start it was obvious that Celtic had been instructed to attack down the left wing where the Rangers youngster was. It was not unlike a boxer mercilessly going for his opponent's cut eye, hoping to expedite victory. The opening exchanges were as always hectic with Mr Wharton a busy man and both goalkeepers in early action. Penman could have scored for Rangers, but it was Celtic who opened the scoring. Callaghan had been superb in his orchestration of the left wing attacks and from a corner kick, Billy McNeill, the constant worry for Rangers at corners, dummied the ball which came to young Lou Macari who obliged.

This was in the 24th minute, and a minute later Celtic went two up when Jimmy Johnstone was manhandled off the ball by Ron McKinnon and a penalty kick awarded. Although both men embraced after this, and Johnstone would often describe big Ron as 'a smashin big man' in later years, this tackle would undoubtedly have earned McKinnon a red card in years to come. Not that it mattered when Harry Hood scored with the penalty to send 50,000 people behind that goal into a frenzy of ecstasy. It was the first penalty kick awarded to Celtic in a Scottish Cup Final since 1907.

The rest of the first half saw Celtic in almost total control, and without unduly exerting themselves giving the impression that more goals would be forthcoming. Yet the supporters remembered Saturday, and other defensive lapses that season, and worried that we might once again let Rangers back in. Connelly and Callaghan, however, were superb for Celtic in midfield as Tiny Wharton blew for half time to loud cheers from the Celtic end and a cemetery silence from the other end of the ground.

Rangers are not the sort of team who lie down however and came out battling in the second half. Although clearly outplayed in most departments, they covered every blade of grass winning a certain amount of appreciation from the Celtic end whose anxiety was in no way diminishing as the minutes began to tick away. Half an hour remained and Rangers pulled one back, but it was an error in the defence rather than any inspired play by Rangers. Not for the first time in his life, luckless Jim Craig scored an own goal for Rangers, and Rangers were back in it.

The hitherto taciturn lads in blue began to let it rip from down at the other end, and for a spell after that, Rangers did very well, winning balls and attacking down both flanks, but without gaining that midfield superiority which is so vital for any prolonged spell of pressure. After a frantic five minutes, it was obvious that Celtic were back in charge and those listening on radio began to breathe more easily as we heard ' and once again it is Connelly for Celtic who mops up and sends it down the left'. Poor Jim Denny. In truth, considering all he had to do, he coped admirably that night, but it was simply the wrong time to make a debut, and his career at Ibrox never really took off after that.

In the last five minutes, Rangers, throwing caution to the winds, brought on Derek Johnstone for the tiring Penman in the hope that he might save them (Celtic now had Wallace on for Hood) but to little avail until the very dying seconds when Evan Williams in the goal was hit in the chest by a Colin Stein shot from close range, but the ball bounced fortuitously clear and was booted upfield by Jim Brogan.

The full time whistle came soon after that, and Celtic had won the Scottish Cup for the 21st time, deservedly so. The game, although hard fought and tough on occasion, finished with both sides congratulating each other, but Jock Stein in the TV interview could not stop himself making a snide comment when he said that a scoreline of 2-1 for Celtic was a 'good result for Rangers'.

In fact it was probably Stein's best ever Scottish Cup from the point of view of it being a total recovery from the dreadful events of the previous summer when it seemed that the glory days of Celtic Park would be coming to an end. It also vindicated his own decision to stay on as manager at Celtic Park, when the Press were absolutely convinced (and succeeding in convincing the gullible of the Celtic support and the hopeful of the Rangers support) that he would move on to Manchester United.

— 22 —

THE DIXIE MELODY
1972

1972 was another great year in the history of Celtic Football Club. The League was won by ten points from Aberdeen and was probably the easiest Championship of all the nine-in-a-row, to such an extent had they paralysed the opposition, including Rangers. There was one spectacularly awful display in the League Cup Final, one crushingly unlucky night to put us out of Europe, but the rest of the time, it was almost entirely glory, glory all the way. And the Scottish Cup success for a variety of reasons was one of the most memorable in the history of the club. It has certainly become one of the most talked about on supporters' buses, pubs or even in the old Jungle on a dull day.

It was, funnily enough, the defeat in the League Cup Final against Partick Thistle which was the catalyst to glory that year. It was indeed a shocker, and although no-body could really grudge Thistle their moment of glory, it was still a stunner for Celtic. In a matter of days, Stein plunged into the transfer market, but his choice was surprising.

John Deans of Motherwell was allegedly nicknamed 'Dixie' after the 'Dixie' Dean of Everton fame in the 1930's. He was a fair enough goalscorer for Motherwell, but there seemed to be at least three reasons why the signing of Deans for Celtic was not a well thought out move but more of a knee jerk reaction to the Hampden humiliation of a few days previously.

In the first place, he was an unathletic looking specimen. His physique could be most charitably described as stocky, he was only 5' 7" when what seemed necessary for the Celtic forward line was a tall, high jumping, gangling, loose limbed character. But appearances could be deceptive, and in any case the moment he set foot over the Celtic Park door, he was put on a special diet and training regime which was as much like an assault course for the Army as anything else and a counterblast to those who thought that the life of a professional footballer was a glamorous bed of roses.

He would certainly have some time on his hands to get down to that schedule for he would not be playing football for some time. This was because he was in the middle of a suspension, the second of the apparent objections to Dixie. He did have a bit of a temper when fouled. His temper had got him into a great deal of trouble. Celtic supporters could remember him being sent off at Celtic Park in December 1966, the day of Willie Wallace's debut, and he was currently serving a six week suspension. This sort of ban made some think that a *sine die* suspension might happen some time, and he himself was becoming so depressed about things that he was actually thinking of giving up the game and taking up a job outside football altogether. As it turned out, Deans although signed in late October 1971, could not make his debut until November 27th.

The third objection might have lain in Dixie's past. He was a Rangers supporter. Now, this usually was not a great handicap at Celtic Park. After all, Stein himself was reputed to have had a few sympathies in that direction in his early life, Willie Wallace would admit to something similar, and the current prodigy Kenny Dalglish had had to remove pictures of John Greig and Willie Henderson from his room before his mother could allow Sean Fallon into his house. The trouble was that Dixie, being the ebullient person that he was, had made no attempt to hide his allegiance. The story even went that when he signed for Motherwell in October 1966, he was wearing a Rangers tammy. The Glasgow grapevine ensured that everyone knew about Dixie's sympathies long before his debut on November 27th.

But the wonderful story of Dixie Deans illustrates two things. One is that a professional football player will do his best for whoever employs him, especially if the structure is a good one. The other aspect of this is that it provided a perfect example of what Stein always said, albeit not publicly and not until years later, and that was that he would always make an effort to go for a Protestant player before Rangers could on the ground a Catholic would sign for Celtic anyway.

Dixie was given a great welcome on his debut at Firhill and scored a late goal in Celtic's emphatic triumph. He then managed to score at least once in each of his next 5 games. Such conduct is excessively endearing to the Jungle, and very soon his name was being chanted. He was quoted as saying how happy he was; he did not say 'All my life I wanted to play for Celtic' or any such cant, but expressed his admiration for Stein and the other players and realised he was part of a big team at Celtic Park.

The team was quite clearly firing on all cylinders, as if determined to apologise to the fans for the Partick Thistle fiasco. It could be argued that this was now a new team since the Lisbon triumph for in the course of the season Auld, Gemmell, Wallace, Chalmers, Clark and Fallon departed and had been replaced by the likes of Connelly, Hay, Dalglish and Macari - at least half a new team, and no-body in Scotland could live with them! These youngsters had been called the 'Quality Street Kids'. They had learned their trade at Celtic Park in the immediate aftermath of Lisbon, and now Celtic were reaping the harvest.

The route to the Final was one of the easier that Celtic have faced with only Hearts giving them the slightest bother. Albion Rovers and Dundee had already comprehensively bitten the dust when Hearts came to Celtic Park. Frankly, they were outplayed but Celtic made the fatal mistake of sitting on a one goal lead and Hearts managed a late equalizer.

Tynecastle was then packed for the Replay with 40,000 all ticket fans recalling happier days for the Edinburgh men. It was a tight encounter with Hearts putting up a great deal of opposition to Celtic, even after Macari had given Celtic a 35th minute lead. It turned out to be the only goal of the game, but Hearts might well have earned an equalizer once again but for an inspired performance by Evan Williams in the Celtic goal. It was good to see Evan doing well, for he had borne a disproportionate amount of the blame for the Partick Thistle League Cup Final disaster.

In the Semi Finals, Celtic competently disposed of brave Kilmarnock but Hibs refused to play according to script and dumped Rangers after a Replay. Rangers domestic woe was thus complete, but Celtic would not underestimate the Edinburgh greens, now managed by that gritty character Eddie Turnbull. But the Scottish Cup Final of 1972 can only be recorded in the context of dramatic and shattering European events of some 18 days earlier.

It was the night of the second leg of the European Cup Semi Final against Inter Milan at Celtic Park, 4 days after Celtic had clinched what was then a record breaking 7 Championships in a row at East Fife. Such was the strength of Scottish football in these days that there was actually another European Semi Final going on in Glasgow the same night, for Rangers were playing Bayern Munich in the Cup Winners' Cup. It is hard to imagine it happening again, but then again 1972 will be looked upon as a great time for Scottish football.

All was quiet at Celtic Park for the 90 minutes had come and gone with no goals, and, frankly, no great likelihood of a goal. The First Leg in Milan had also been goalless, so it was on to extra time with defences well on top. News had also filtered through that Rangers had made it

Hibs players looking dejected as Celtic celebrate.

to the Final of the Cup Winners' Cup, so there was a distinct absence of animation from the Celtic crowd when TV, having shown the Ibrox game live, crossed the city to Celtic Park to show the finale. For some reason never adequately explained, Deans started on the bench that night but had by now replaced the tiring young Dalglish, Stein hoping presumably that he would be the surprise weapon.

The game remained cold, however, and no goal came. Celtic were thus for the first time involved in a penalty shoot out in a major competition. Subsequent history would show that Celtic were not good at penalty shoot-outs (e.g. the Scottish Cup Final against Aberdeen in 1990, the Coca Cola Cup Final against Raith Rovers in 1994) and this would be the start of a melancholy tradition.

Mazzola, who had taken the penalty in the 1967 European Cup Final, scored first. Then came Dixie's darkest hour as he fired high over the bar. He was the only one who missed, and his thoughts could only be imagined. The cheers in the Rangers supporters buses as they listened to the radio were perhaps understandable; the heartless minority who expressed their frustration at Celtic Park by booing the desolate Dixie were harder to forgive. It was a shame because the European Cup that year might not have been totally impossible, even against the mighty Ajax who would beat the Italians 2-0.

Dixie however scored twice in the following Saturday against Motherwell, then once against Dundee United in midweek. But on the Saturday before the Final Celtic went down 4-1 to Hearts. Deans did not score nor did he in the game against Dundee which finished off the League season. This was enough to give him palpitations in case he would be dropped from the Scottish Cup final team and thus be denied the opportunity to pay back the Celtic fans for the way he broke their hearts in the European Cup game. Fortunately, Stein, however much he may have joked about it and hinted that he might not play Dixie, was not daft.

It is important to realise that this was actually a good Hibernian side, certainly fit to rank comparison with the Famous Five team of twenty years previously. Their names were complicated, though. There was a Brownlie, a Blackley and a Black in the defence, good players all. Their best player was Pat Stanton whose brief glorious Indian summer at Celtic Park was a few years away yet, and they had fine forwards in Alec Edwards and Arthur Duncan, and of course they now had Bertie Auld who was not slow in telling the Press what he would do to his old mates on Saturday.

Saturday 6th May was a wonderful day for football as the following teams took the field in front of a crowd of 106,102 people who would see arguably the greatest Scottish Cup Final of them all:

Celtic: Williams, Craig, Brogan; Murdoch, McNeill, Connelly; Johnstone, Deans, Macari, Dalglish, Callaghan.
Hibs: Herriot, Brownlie, Schaedler; Stanton, Black, Blackley; Edwards, Hazel, Gordon, O'Rourke, Duncan.

The referee was Alistair McKenzie of Larbert and the weather was fine with Celtic attacking the Mount Florida end for the first half. The game had only gone two minutes when a Callaghan free kick sailed across the Hibs penalty area and with the danger apparently gone, McNeill appeared out of nowhere to toe the ball home. Hibs equalized through Alan Gordon on the tenth minute mark, and as both teams were playing bright attacking football, the stage was set for the brilliance to come.

In the 23rd minute after Johnstone had been fouled, Murdoch took a free kick on the right. Murdoch had been suffering from his recurrent

Billy McNeill jumps with joy as he scores against Hibs.

problem of overweight, but after a battle which had included stays at health farms, he was back, not quite the Bobby Murdoch of 1967 and 1969, but still a tremendous player. His free kick found the head of Dixie Deans whose squat figure had outjumped the Hibs defence and he bulleted home a powerful header.

Thus Celtic went in 2-1 up at half time, but Hibs had fought hard. There were signs however that in key areas of the battle, Celtic were winning. Callaghan and Murdoch were powereful in midfield, McNeill had only once lost his joust with Gordon, and up front Deans was relishing every minute of the game. Whether this was because he still felt that he had his point to prove because of the European exit, nobody knew, but it was certain that he was after his first winner's medal.

The second half had gone about ten pulsating minutes when came the Dixie Deans goal which has become almost as famous as that of Patsy Gallagher of 47 years previously into that same King's Park goal. He picked up a ball at the edge of the penalty area on the left, beat Brownlie, then almost allowing it to run out of play, he beat goalkeeper Herriot, then Brownlie again before scoring and doing his famous somersault in front of the adoring multitudes. Glory be to the video invention which allows us to watch it again and again!

3-1 down and still Hibs did not give in, stunned though they must have been by that third goal. 15 minutes were left when Celtic put the issue beyond any doubt when Dixie scored his third, picking up a through ball from Tommy Callaghan and finishing clinically. Very few in the crowd knew at the time that his hat-trick had only been equalled once before and that was Jimmy Quinn in 1904 (other, earlier claimants are difficult to prove as the newspaper evidence is contradictory). Gordon Durie of Rangers would equal this rare feat in 1996.

As the minutes ran out, Hibs at last crumbled with not even the appearance of Bertie Auld to a loud cheer of acclamation from both sets of fans able to turn the tide. Celtic scored two more goals, both by Lou Macari, but each of them a combination of fine team work. The game thus finished 6-1 equalling the record of James Kelly's Renton a few weeks before Celtic's first game in 1888. The supporters were ecstatic, and Dixie Deans was now clearly re-instated in the eyes of everyone as the hero. He had gone from villain to hero in 18 days, and like so many other romantic episodes in the history of the club, this story would have been rejected by a publisher of fiction for being too far fetched.

Celtic had now won the Scottish Cup for the 22nd time, moving some distance ahead of Rangers who had reached 19 in 1966, but had stayed there. Stein was delighted, of course, and poor luckless Hibs were to suffer a lot more from Dixie Deans. When asked years later why he always did so well against Hibs, Dixie, in a clear tongue in cheek remark to his previous affections said 'I didn't like the green jersey!'

— 23 —

TELL ME THE OLD, OLD STORY
1974

It is often said that it is a good idea to keep politics and religion out of everything, especially football. Celtic and Rangers fans, of course, have always kept religion out of the game (Ho! Ho!), but politics only makes the occasional rare appearance (at the 1988 Cup Final everybody showed Mrs Thatcher a red card, and in 1927 in a game against Queen's Park, Celtic fans booed a Spider who had tried to break the General Strike of the previous year). In 1974, however, there was no choice. Everyone was up to his neck in politics, for it affected everyone and everything, including football.

Very briefly, the miners called an overtime ban and then a strike. The government responded with a three day week for everyone to preserve fuel stock, a Middle East war pushed up the price of oil and threatened its supply altogether, inflation was at a record high and threatening to go the way of the banana republics of the West Indies or Latin America, a general election resulted in a hung Parliament, and, generally speaking, it was a situation that could not be ignored.

For football, floodlighting was discouraged to save electricity, so that the League Cup Final of December 1973 kicked off at 1.30 p.m., and in early 1974, football matches were given the go ahead to be played on Sundays, as the three day week involved half the nation working on a Saturday. (On January 27th, Dixie Deans became the first player to score on a Sunday.) In an atmosphere like this, football was a strange business, rather akin to football during the Second World War - with everyone having very real doubts about the future, and football, though very competitive and providing light relief for spectators, not always the main topic of conversation.

But the game in Scotland had received a major boost. In September, Scotland for the first time for 16 years, qualified for the World Cup to be held in Germany in 1974. The joy was probably increased when England failed to do likewise in October, and there was real hope that Scotland, under the amiable and unpretentious Willie Ormond, could do well, for there were players of real quality, including Celts like David Hay, Kenny Dalglish, George Connelly and Danny McGrain, who seemed capable of turning it on for Scotland.

Celtic in the midst of all this were advancing towards their ninth League Championship in a row without ever seeming to be in any great danger. They didn't always impress either, mind you, and the feeling grew that they were sated with their own success, had grown complacent and careless, and that whenever Rangers, Aberdeen or Hibernian were to mount a strong challenge, they might be in real trouble.

They continued their melancholy tradition of losing League Cup Finals, this time to Dundee in circumstances already described on an unplayable pitch on a miserable December day and a sparse crowd watching one of the more depressing occasions of Scottish football history. In the spring, they would be kicked out of Europe by a bunch of desperadoes from Athletico Madrid.

There was also at Celtic Park a certain amount of unrest behind the scenes. Jimmy Johnstone, as usual exercised to the limit the disciplinary powers of Jock Stein, but the signs were that Jock was slowly winning this one, until, that is, the rowing boat incident of the spring when Jimmy was on Scotland duty. A more complex character was George Connelly. A player of undisputed talent and probably capable of becoming one of Scottish football's all time greats, George sadly was unable to cope with the emotional demands of the game. The emotional demands were considerable, and George for all his tremendous talent, lacked the stamina and stability. Instead of confiding in Stein or McNeill, his knee jerk reaction was all too often to walk out of training sessions for no apparent reason to the bewilderment of the management. This led to transfer requests being granted but no-one was willing to take on this tormented genius. Peace was made before the end of the season, but it was only temporary.

His friend David Hay had also been causing waves. Hay was undeniably one of the best players in the world on his day, and had been since his emergence in 1970. A regular cap for Scotland, Davie had been giving the impression that all was not well with himself and Stein for some time before he eventually picked a quarrel about some money owed to him and ending up suspended by the club. He was far too good a player however for the club to allow this to happen, and he was also far too sensible a man, so peace was restored. These events in the autumn of 1973 however did pave the way for his departure to Chelsea the following summer, where everything went wrong for the luckless Davie, and like many another, he would have been better staying with his beloved Celtic.

This season had seen the start of his Celtic career for Steve Murray. Murray had never pretended to be anything other than Celtic daft, and had already done sterling work for Dundee and Aberdeen, earning himself a Scottish cap in the process. Stein's signing of him in May 1973 had been nothing short of visionary, for his experience, enthusiasm and new lease of life as an attacking midfielder stood Celtic in good stead during that season of 1973-4.

His arrival did however have one side effect, and that was the departure to Middlesborough of Bobby Murdoch. Murdoch had been struggling to keep fit for some time and clearly unsettled by the changes all around him, was delighted to move on to Teeside where he very soon became a folk hero to the impoverished fanatics of the Boro for whom he played for another three years and subsequently became their manager.

A player who had quietly slipped into the team was Pat McCluskey. Pat had been at Celtic Park since the late 1960's. He tended to be a double centre half or sweeper of the John Clark type, and although his presence was seldom obvious or obtrusive, his influence was considerable, covering for the occasional lapse of Billy McNeill.

All this meant that there were now only three of the Lisbon Lions left at Celtic Park - McNeill, still going strong, Johnstone, tricky as ever and Lennox, now the highest post war goal scorer and although still a great deal short of McGrory, worthy of being mentioned in the same breath. The changes since 1967 had been subtle and gradual, and the team had kept winning the Championship to such an extent that a generation of boys were growing up unable to remember anyone else being Champions. A favourite quiz question was 'Who won the League Championship prior to Celtic's run?' and very few people got 'Kilmarnock!'

The Scottish Cup campaign for 1974 got under way on Sunday 27th January at Celtic Park, and not only did Dixie Deans score the first Sunday goal, he celebrated with a hat-trick in Celtic's 6-1 demolition of Clydebank. Clydebank, incidentally, included in their line up one Samuel Henderson who, we had all been told ten years ago, would lead Celtic to glory as the new Pat Crerand but whose career had failed to develop under Stein. 6-1 was also the score when Stirling Albion came to Celtic Park three weeks later. Stiffer opposition came our way however when Motherwell came to town in the Quarter Final, and the game finished 2-2 with both sides unlucky

Davie wins this tussle with Jimmy Johnstone in the 1974 Scottish Cup Final.

not to snatch it in the last 10 minutes and thoroughly deserving of the ovation at the end from the 46,000 fans who managed to reach Celtic Park in spite of Sunday's chronically awful transport problems. The Replay the following Tuesday was just as tight with only the one Dixie Deans goal separating the teams.

The city of Dundee was all agog at the prospect of an all Dundee Cup Final, for the Semi Final line up was Dundee v. Celtic and Dundee United v.Hearts. Dundee, in particular, were fancied for their first Scottish Cup success since 1910. Not only were they the holders of the League Cup, but they had also put out Rangers by the impressive score of 3-0 at Ibrox, a result that must have made manager Davie White happy, as he had been sacked from there some years previously. Clearly, the Dens Parkers had been influenced by the ebullience, *joie de vivre* and general confidence of Tommy Gemmell, but Big Tam did not always endear himself to his erstwhile admirers at Celtic Park by putting his name to euphoric stories in newspapers about what he would do to Celtic. Celtic's 1-0 victory was more emphatic than the scoreline suggested.

Eyebrows were raised on Tayside and elsewhere however by the performance of Dundee United. Always considered the poor man's team of the city, United had delighted their fans and surprised everyone by staying in the First Division throughout the sixties, and even having the odd spectacular performance in Europe such as the dumping of Barcelona in 1966. Since the appointment of ex-Clyde and Dundee favourite Jim McLean as manager in November 1971, the team had played consistently well and had built up a strong defence round two men called Smith - Doug, who had been with them since the early 60's and a fellow called Walter who might become a good manager one day, some people thought.

They now also had an exciting forward called Andy Gray whose 16 League goals that season had been impressive for an 18 year old in his first professional season. United defeated Hearts impressively 4-2 in the Replayed Semi Final. This game was played ludicrously at Hampden in midweek before a crowd of 12,000. Thus United managed to reach their first ever Scottish Cup Final, and there would be little doubt that the sympathies of the neutrals would lie with this brave little club taking on Celtic who were now playing their 6th consecutive Scottish Cup final of which they had won three. Some of the massive Celtic support as well would not have been too unhappy at a little success going to a very deserved quarter; the majority however were nothing like so magnanimous.

The crowd on May 4th 1974 at Hampden was 75,959, a considerable drop on previous years. Two years ago, for example, against Hibs, the crowd had been 106,000, and it was the first Saturday Cup Final that Celtic had played in since 1927 that the crowd had not reached the six figure mark. There were, of course reasons for this. Dundee United had a very small, although admirably vocal support, inflation and economic uncertainties played their part, but the real reason was a feeling of *ennui* among the Celtic support, who were becoming sated with success. The home attendances in 1973-4 had dropped considerably, and even Celtic supporters themselves were saying that there had to be a strong challenge to Celtic soon, or Scottish football would suffer irreparable damage.

The smallish crowd saw the following teams take the field:

Celtic: Connaghan, McGrain, Brogan; Murray, McNeill, McCluskey; Johnstone, Hood, Deans, Hay, Dalglish.

Dundee United: Davie, Gardner, Kopel; Copland, D.Smith, W.Smith; Payne, Knox, Gray, Fleming, Houston.

149

The referee was Mr J Paterson of Bothwell, and he could hardly have chosen an easier Scottish Cup Final in all its long history of 101 years to referee.

United started well, playing towards the King's Park end with its massed ranks of Celtic fans and seemed to have settled well in the great atmosphere. It may have been one of the lower Cup Final crowds but it was probably the biggest crowd that United had ever played in front of. As was now the tradition in Scottish Cup Finals, Jimmy Johnstone was given a roving commission and the United defence's normal organization was given a jolt by this necessity to detail one man to follow Jimmy wherever he went. At the other end it was seen that McNeill did not let the dangerous young Gray out of his sight.

In 20 minutes Celtic went ahead and it was a goal out of nothing. A long through ball from Deans seemed to be heading for the goal-keeper when in jumped handy man Harry Hood to head home. 5 minutes later, the game virtually ended when Johnstone and Hood combined well in the penalty area, and the ball came to the unmarked Murray who stroked the ball home.

The double whammy knocked the stuffing out of the gallant Tay-siders and the half time interval came with Celtic well on top. Jim McLean however must have said a few things to his men in the delightful uncomplicated approach which was his hall mark even as early as 1974, for they came out and for about ten minutes looked as if they could make a game out of this Final. During this time Denis Connaghan, who had enjoyed a strange mercurial sort of career at Celtic Park under Jock Stein, saved from Andy Gray, and one or two other half chances were not seized upon. Eventually however the Celtic midfield of Murray and Hay took command and did not relinquish it until the end of the game. The impression grew that even if United pulled one back, Celtic would up a gear and score again.

The game thus petered out, and the radio commentators were having quite a job keeping people interested, talking, even during the second half about forthcoming Internationals and Scotland's chances in the World Cup! TV was not allowed to show the game live, and although their contract specified that they could show the cup being presented at the end, STV jumped the gun and showed the last few minutes. Thus the nation saw Dalglish pass to Deans and Dixie hammering home the third goal in the last minute.

The sight of Celtic receiving the Scottish Cup for the 23rd time was a source of great joy to the fans, but it was very noticeable that this year's presentation brought claps of approval and benign smiles

150

rather than the ecstatic, hysterical howls of some previous years.The happiness reflected the realisation that although the Cup had been lost in 1973, it was now back where it belonged. Dundee United too received hearty and genuine applause as they collected their losers' medals. After all what harm could a nice man like Walter Smith ever do us?

— 24 —

PAUL'S DAY
1975

The phrase 'end of an era' is much over-used. 1975, however, could well be argued to have been just that as far as Celtic were concerned. Just how comprehensive an end to an era it was, did not become apparent until months after the season ended, but it was clear from an early point that season (soon after the New Year) that it was not to be ten in a row as far as League Championships were concerned, and Celtic's period of being a major European power came to a shuddering end on October 2nd 1974 when a third rate Greek team called Olympiakos, whom the great teams of 1967, 1969, 1970 and 1972 would not have seen in their way, defeated Celtic 2-0 in Athens following a miserable 1-1 draw at Celtic Park.

It would not be true to say that the team grew old together. In fact, only three of the Lisbon men - McNeill, Lennox and Johnstone - were left. But so many men lost form and fitness that season - Callaghan, Hood, Deans and even young Dalglish (not quite so young now) failed to deliver. Those whose memory is selective will claim that Kenny's performances in a green and white jersey were all outstanding. Not so! Memories remain of boos and catcalls directed at Dalglish in particular, probably because everyone, himself included, knew that he had the talent to do a lot better.

In addition, Rangers, disappointing in the Cup competitions, managed to concentrate enough resources for the League campaign which they eventually won by 7 points from Hibs with Celtic third. Celtic's acid test was on January 4th at Ibrox, when they lost 3-0. A defeat by a Willie Pettigrew-inspired Motherwell team at Celtic Park followed; then came draws with Arbroath and Dumbarton, a defeat by Hibs and a cave-in so comprehensive that Rangers won the League as early as March 29th.

On the up side however, Celtic at last won the League Cup, having lost in the Final of this trophy for the last four years. This year they beat Hibs 6-3 in a marvellous Final with a Dixie Deans hat-trick and some superb football. Poor Joe Harper of Hibs created some sort of a record by scoring a hat-trick and finishing up on the losing side! Never exactly the darling of the Celtic Park support, Joe did get a certain amount of credit and indeed sympathy from the Celtic fans. This game was also the last great game that Jimmy Johnstone played for Celtic. He was absolutely brilliant, so he was, scoring the first goal himself, laying on a few more and delighting his many fans. He did play for Celtic after this and indeed for Scotland, but his form and fitness declined to such an extent and so rapidly that he was given a free transfer at the end of the season.

George Connelly persisted in his soap opera antics which puzzled, mystified, bewildered and eventually angered the support. A player of tremendous natural talent, George simply could not cope with the emotional side of the game. On September 14th for example, he announced spectacularly that he was quitting the game. Nevertheless he was back on November 27th to somewhat less than a hero's welcome. His colleagues were distinctly unimpressed, and as Davie Hay, his best friend, was now away to Chelsea, he was still unhappy. His appearances were sporadic.

There were two good transfers this season. One was Ronnie Glavin, a ball player of some repute from Partick Thistle, who had never hidden his love for Celtic and who would ginger up the midfield, and the other was an unknown (in Scotland) goalkeeper called Peter Latchford, whose brother Bob's goalscoring exploits for Birmingham City and Everton were more famous. Peter turned out to be one of Stein's more successful goalkeepers, and in fact stayed with the club until 1987.

One young player developed that season and that was Paul Wilson. Paul was a utility forward and could play anywhere. He was powerful, a good header, a strong runner and had a tremendous shot. He scored 22 goals in total that season and earned his one and only cap against Spain in Valencia in February when he came on as a substitute. He had been at Celtic Park for a long time, was slow in developing, and sadly disappeared rather quickly from the scene.

Paul was Scottish, but his mother was Indian, and his complexion reflected this. This meant that he was the butt of racist taunts from the less well educated of the opposition support and even (incredibly) from some of his own on a bad day. On the day of January 11th when Celtic went down to Motherwell the week after a defeat at Ibrox, Paul was, like all the Celtic players, having a shocker. This did not in any way excuse the racist abuse which some of his own fans, a minority it must be stressed, in the Jungle hurled at him in one of my saddest days as a Celtic supporter.It was sad for two reasons - one was that it was hurled at one of our own, but even if it hadn't been, it was rather sad to hear the scions of an ethnic minority unable to accept another. Nothing could ever excuse such ignorance.

The Scottish Cup camapaign opened on January 25th with Celtic at Easter Road, Edinburgh. Celtic were very much in disarray at this stage of the season, and with Hibs having improved of late, it was confidently expected that Hibs might put the kybosh on Celtic's season and revenge that 6-3 defeat in the League Cup Final. In addition, there was more than a little spice added by the ongoing and public arguments between the two Boards about television coverage, entrance prices and this, that and the other. This feud would surface sometimes subtlely, more often less so throughout the 1970's and there was the unmistakable impression that Hibs were jealous of Celtic. Their jealousy was fuelled by the result for Celtic won 2-0, delighting their fans in the 36,000 crowd. Dixie Deans once again scored against Hibs, as he so frequently did. He 'didn't like the green jersey' - he would say.

This result was a welcome shot in the arm for the struggling Celts, but the League position had weakened considerably by the time that the next round came along and Celtic easily defeated Clydebank 4-1. They had terrified their fans by going one down in the 25th minute, but then an electrifying burst in the 8 minutes before half time saw Celtic score 3 goals and have their perplexed fans wondering why they could not do this oftener. A late goal finished the scoring after a dreadful second half. Billy McNeill had suffered the rare (although not unprecedented) humiliation of being dropped for this game.

In the Quarter Final on March 8th, Celtic had a very tricky tie at Boghead, Dumbarton. The Sons of the Rock were in the First Division (this was the season in which the top ten would qualify for the new Premier League) and had already earned a draw with Celtic a month previously. They had two 'old bhoys' in John Cushley, surely a fine centre half and unlucky to be at Celtic Park at the same time as Billy McNeill, and Willie Wallace, still fit and banging them in after a brief and none too successful spell with Crystal Palace. In addition there a couple of brothers called McAdam whose major mark on Scottish football had yet to come - Tom with Celtic and Colin with Rangers.

This game was an absolute thriller. 16,000 crammed into what was once known as 'fatal Boghead', and the pitch lived up to its reputation by being heavy. The entertainment was excellent and Dumbarton, most of whose supporters support Celtic as well, could have scored twice in the first five minutes before Ronnie Glavin scored first. Tom McAdam then equalized almost immediately, and the remainder of the first half was played at furious pace. Remarkably, the half time score was 1-1 when 5-5 might have been a fairer reflection. Inevitably, the pace dropped in the second half and full time training told in the end, but only after Paul Wilson had put Celtic ahead on the hour mark, and Dumbarton launched a major offensive, feeling aggrieved not to have been awarded at least one penalty.

And then to the somewhat familiar Dundee in the Semi Final. We had played them four out of the last six years at Hampden in the Semi Final. Equally familiar and a wheen more irksome was Tommy Gemmell's newspaper boasts about what he and the Dundonians would do to Celtic. This game was on the Wednesday immediately following the final surrender of the League, and it was a determined Celtic who took the field. It was also to the glee of some, but to the despair of others, Tommy Gemmell himself who made a major blunder in allowing Ronnie Glavin in to score the only goal of what was a singularly unimpressive occasion. Some sang 'Tommy, Tommy shut your mooth', others wished Tommy would retire and live on his extensive and well deserved memories of his valiant years with Celtic.

The opponents in the Cup Final would be Airdrie, making their first appearance there since the glory days of 1924 when, managed by ex-Celt Willie Orr, Hughie Gallagher and Bob McPhail helped to beat Hibs. Sadly Airdrie had failed to make the cut to play in next season's Premier League, but it was only by a matter of 2 points. They had played some good football, and Celtic needed only to look back to March 22nd when they dumped Celtic 1-0 at Broomfield, a result that more or less killed Celtic's slender Championship hopes.

There could be little doubt either that they would enjoy the support of most neutrals, for they had not yet acquired the infamous reputation that would follow them around in later years, and everyone in Scotland (including a few Celtic supporters) had tremendous respect and affection for Ian McMillan, the ex-Rangers inside forward, who had built up such a hard working side. There was also something quaint about their little ground, deep in a hollow it always appeared and possessing that romantic old pavilion at the corner flag - a pavilion that looked as if it should belong to some rural cricket team rather than a football team of industrial west central Scotland.

Hampden on May 3rd provided a splendid setting with lovely warm sunshine for the crowd which at 75,457 was probably Airdrie's largest ever crowd and by coincidence within a few hundreds of the previous year's attendance for the Celtic v.Dundee United final. Airdrie were out to enjoy themselves, Celtic had a point to prove. Once again, the authorities refused to bow to realism and allow TV coverage but they would have been as well to do so, for both channels showed the goals being scored seconds after they happened, interrupting their other sports coverage to do so. Thus the secret was to listen to the radio and watch TV with the sound turned down. You missed nothing that way!

The referee was Mr.Ian Foote of Glasgow and the teams were:

Celtic: Latchford, McGrain, Lynch; Murray, McNeill, McCluskey; Hood, Glavin, Dalglish, Lennox, Wilson

Airdrie: McWilliams, Jonquin, Cowan; Menzies, Black, Whiteford; McCann, Walker, McCulloch, Lapsley, Wilson.

It was a minor surprise that Celtic included Paul Wilson, for Paul's mother had died a few days previously. But Jock considered that the best way to honour her was for her son to win a medal, and having consulted with Paul, put him in, nominally at no.11 but with a roving commission to play all over the field if necessary. It would turn out to be one of Jock's better decisions. Celtic were playing towards the Mount Florida end in the first half, and after a bright start seemed to have faded a bit until in the 15th minute Dalglish fed McGrain on the right, got the ball back from him and crossed from the corner flag to find Paul Wilson's head. It was a good, quintessentially Celtic goal.

Airdrie however fought back and their nippy forwards were giving the ageing Celtic defence a great deal of bother. Half time was approaching when the Diamonds equalized. They had hit the post earlier and this time the Celtic defence should really have cleared the ball which bobbed about at the edge of the box before breaking to Kevin McCann. Kevin, unashamedly Celtic daft, would claim twenty years later that he thought it all out, taking into consideration the height of the defenders, the angle of the shot, the height of the bar and so on. In fact, he simply shot and the ball screamed into the roof of the Celtic net to a stunned silence from those behind the goal, in whose number Kevin might in other circumstances have been.

Those who in disgust turned for solace to the primitive pie stalls with their enormous queues, missed a tremendous Celtic riposte. The tiny outnumbered knots of Airdrie supporters at the Mount Florida end and in both stands were still celebrating when Celtic won a corner on the left. The evergreen Bobby Lennox took it, swung the ball over and up jumped Paul Wilson, unmarked by a strangely complacent Airdrie defence, to head home his second of the game. Half-time came soon afterwards, and Celtic went in 2-1 up with their supporters once again in raptures.

It was the buzzbomb Bobby Lennox who was instrumental in gaining Celtic's third goal within ten minutes of the re-start. He had charged down the left but didn't seem to be in a particularly dangerous position almost at the bye line at the edge of the box when he was unnecessarily pushed by an Airdrie defender. It was a silly penalty to give away and Airdrie paid the full price for it as Pat McCluskey slotted it away.

From now on the Celtic midfield of Steve Murray and Pat McCluskey exercised a stranglehold on the game. Airdrie battled, tried two substitutions in Reynolds and March, but if anyone was going to score it would be Celtic with Paul Wilson almost entering the hat-trick Hall of Fame beside Dixie Deans and Jimmy Quinn (the only players to have hit a Cup Final hat-trick). The noise began to increase as the minutes ticked away and phrases like 'It looks like Celtic' began to be heard more and more from the radio commentators. The game had long finished as a contest when Mr Foote pointed to the tunnel and Celtic had won the Scottish Cup for the 24th time.

The Cup was duly presented and the supporters went home happy. It was only on the TV Programme that night broadcast from Celtic's victory party that Billy McNeill announced his retiral from football. The past ten years had seen him lift a total of 23 winners' medals in all competitions, and he had been captain in them all. There is no need to expand on McNeill's playing career, for the penultimate sentence says it all.

—25—

STEIN'S SWAN SONG
1977

One of the hallmarks of Jock Stein's remarkable 13 years management of Celtic was his ability to bounce back. 1970-71 showed this characteristic perfectly. After a catastrophically disastrous loss of the European Cup, the team fought back to win the Double. 1976-7 was a similar sort of season; the difference lay in the base line. In 1970 Celtic were undisputed kings of Britain and second best in Europe, in 1976 the club were precisely nowhere.

1976 was the worst season that Celtic had experienced since 1964. A car crash had put Stein out of action for more or less all the season. Sean Fallon had tried manfully but too many of his players were old or uninterested. And the Dalglish problem was becoming acute. Kenny had turned awkward in summer 1975 and had had to be bought off with the captaincy. This move might well have worked if Stein had been in harness, but without Stein, things were allowed to drift and questions were asked whether Dalglish had the ability to lead at this comparatively early stage of his life. Too often his commitment to the club seemed to be in reverse proportion to his undoubted ability.

Thus when Stein took over again, changes needed to be made. In summer 1976, he appointed Partick Thistle man Davie McParland to be his Assistant with Sean Fallon still being retained but clearly in a back seat. It was indeed unusual for a man with no Celtic connection to be appointed to such a position, but the following months would be full of surprises.

Scotland was amazed in early September 1976 when Pat Stanton was signed from Hibs. Pat and Hibs were considered almost to be an immutable connection, and besides Pat was now almost 32. Stein however had always admired Stanton and thought that he would be a great boost to the other central defenders Roddy McDonald and Johannes Edvaldsson who were finding McNeill's act a hard one to follow.

Another apparently bargain basement signing came Celtic's way a couple of weeks later in the shape of Partick Thistle's Joe Craig. Joe was not exactly a household name outside of Maryhill, but Stein, on the advice of Davie McParland presumably, saw him as a successor to Dixie Deans who had now gone to Luton. This would continue Stein's impressive ability to find a striker whose career was apparently going nowhere and turn him into an Internationalist.

But the greatest signing coup of them all came in March 1977 when Celtic signed Alfie Conn. Conn, of course, had played for Rangers before going to Tottenham Hotspur where his career was stuttering. Rangers too were stuttering this year, losing out quite clearly to Celtic in the League.

Stein had seen the chance to put one over Rangers in the propaganda war. Calling a meeting with Kenny Dalglish and Danny McGrain (both, incidentally, like Stein, non Catholics) to ask their opinion and getting their support, he decided to go for Conn while Rangers still dithered. The papers were only told about it almost as the deal went through, and very soon the Jungle was singing to the tune of the Campdown Races 'He used to be a Hun but he's all right now - Alfie, Alfie!'. It would turn out to be a crucial, although short term success. He would play his part in Celtic's double, but his chronic injury problems continued. Rangers meanwhile were flummoxed and never recovered that season.

But it was not all sweetness and light for Celtic even though by the New Year they were up at the top fighting off Aberdeen and Dundee United. September saw a First Round exit from the UEFA Cup at the hands of Wisla Cracow (Stein would later say this was 'a blessing in disguise' for they were nothing like ready for it), and early November brought one of the cruellest results in Celtic's history when sheer bad luck lost them the League Cup Final against Aberdeen.

Yet there were many fine things happening at Celtic Park as well, notably the gradual development of talented youngsters like Roy Aitken and Tommy Burns. Danny McGrain was by now an established Internationalist, and his play was often so perfect that it was said that he as worth the admission money on his own. The team had the Indian sign over Rangers beating them twice and drawing the other twice. And they also had that indefinable characteristic of being able to win against the odds. For example at Tynecastle on a dreich, typically November day, they were twice two goals down, yet recovered to win 4-3! On March 26th, they beat their emerging challengers Dundee United 2-0 at Celtic Park, and eventually finished the job by winning at Easter Road with the Hibs board once again showing their abiding envy of Celtic by refusing TV admission for recorded highlights, with even the Celtic Cine Club which did such a good job for disabled and hospitalised supporters, being excluded.

The path to the Final of the 1977 Scottish Cup was, to put it euphemistically, undistinguished. Both Airdrie and Ayr United took them to Replays, and although the Replays themselves were one sided affairs, both the first games showed weaknesses in the team's play. The Ayr United game in particular on Sunday 27th February saw Celtic well on top following a Ronnie Glavin goal but lacking the ability to kill off the plucky Honest Men. Then a moment's slackness in the Celtic defence allowed Ayr to equalize with a high proportion of the crowd already streaming out of the ground, confident the game was won, but somewhat bored with proceedings.

The Quarter Final against Queen of the South was a much more clinical and professional performance, and put Celtic into the Semi Final draw with Rangers, Hearts and Dundee. Incredibly, for the fifth time in eight seasons, Celtic found themselves pitted against Dundee at the Semi Final stage, and they had won them all! This time it was an excellent game of football with Dundee giving as good as they got. Tommy Gemmell was well into his thirties by now and played as well as ever, but the man who really caught the eye for Dundee was a red headed youngster by the name of Gordon Strachan. Goals could have come at either end, but it was Celtic's Joe Craig who broke the deadlock with ten minutes to go. Five minutes later he added another to give Celtic a slightly flattering 2-0 winning margin and put them into another Old Firm Cup Final.

This game was played at Hampden on a Wednesday night. The crowd was a disappointing 29,000 and even that was 6,000 better than the other Semi Final of the previous week between Rangers and Hearts. Now, even allowing for the folly of playing Semi Finals in midweek, these figures show the rut that the Scottish game was in at that time and are significant in the debate that was to come about sponsorship and television.

It is important to realise that the drop in attendances (a severe one in the case of some clubs) did not represent any decline in interest in the game. Football remained, and in my view always will remain a number one sporting interest in Scotland, and the game was discussed as always in pubs, factories, school playgrounds and even exotic places like the fast emerging North Sea Oil rigs. What people were now beginning to rebel against were the appalling facilities at some grounds, especially Hampden Park which would remain a disgrace until the early nineties. The terracings were foul smelling, insanitary places, car parking facilities barely existed and catering services were a joke.

A few enlightened clubs, notably Aberdeen began to see the way ahead. The penny would drop at Ibrox some years later but Celtic Park and Hampden, however rich in nostalgia, were absolute shockers and little excuse is possible for those whose apathy and deliberate neglect left them in the state they were. Directors would utter rubbish about the depopulation of Glasgow, and even rig surveys which claimed to show that 'our supporters prefer to stand', but the fact was that we were in the curious position of our national game being as popular as ever, but fewer and fewer people going to watch it.

At this point, enter sponsorship. A beer firm sponsored the Scottish Cup Final pouring much needed money into the coffers. The Free Kirk and Alcoholics Anonymous were none too happy about this, but money does talk rather loudly, and talked loud enough to insist on the Cup Final of 1977 being televised live, something that had only happened previously in 1955 and 1957. Cant began to be spouted about the 'true' supporters who follow us 'week in, week out', but those of us who hated traffic jams, worried about leaving a car unguarded, objected to the state of the terraces, sat back in our armchairs and blessed the benign combination of the beer firm and the TV companies who, in allowing us to see our own Cup Final, brought us in line with the rest of the world.

Well over a million armchairs would be squirmed about in, however, all afternoon, for the tension in living rooms was every bit as great as it was for the 54,252 who braved the rain to go to Hampden and see the following teams take the field;

Celtic: Latchford, McGrain, Lynch; Stanton, McDonald, Aitken; Dalglish, Edvaldsson, Craig, Wilson, Conn.

Rangers: Kennedy, Jardine, Greig; Forsyth, Jackson, Watson; McLean, Hamilton, Parlane, MacDonald, Johnstone.

The referee was Mr Valentine of Dundee, and his name would be on everyone's lips by the end. That this was the case is partly to be explained by the fact that this game in terms of football was an absolute shocker. Sadly too it was televised, at least in highlight form, to many countries and it did not exactly show Scottish football at its best.

There were several reasons why the game did not live up to its hype. One was that Rangers, as their own fans would admit, in 1977 lacked class players. Celtic, on the other hand who did have a few (although Ronnie Glavin, arguably the best after Dalglish, was out injured), elected to play a defensive formation. (The League Cup Final against Aberdeen had been lost thanks to a cavalier, up and at'em approach which delighted the neutrals but sent the trophy up north.) Johannes Edvaldsson the likeable Icelander, for example, was told to mark Derek Johnstone for his aerial power, and there were at least four other out and out defenders in the team. There was also the subtle influence of the Premier League which meant that players had four games a year at least in which to nurse and develop personal feuds and vendettas. Added to this, it was an Old Firm Cup Final, a lot was at stake for both teams and a victory was paramount.

Celtic, who all through 1977 had won the propaganda battle against Rangers, did so again when they appeared before kick off wearing white tracksuit tops with 'League Champions' written on them, just in case Rangers had forgotten that they had finished a good nine points behind Celtic in the Premier League.

The game kicked off in the pouring rain with Celtic playing towards the Mount Florida end. The game was fast, furious and uncultured for a spell with Mr Valentine a busy man. Following an injury to Rangers goalkeeper Stewart Kennedy sustained in a collision with a post, Celtic took a corner kick. The ball bobbed about for a bit, and then Edvaldsson, joining momentarily the attack because Derek Johnstone was back defending, shot for goal and the ball struck Derek on the hand, if you support Celtic, but on the knee, if you support Rangers. Mr Valentine gave a penalty and from my view in my armchair, I was convinced that he was right. Bravely he stuck to his decision however much Rangers protested. The TV playbacks meanwhile proved nothing at all. Mr Valentine, having had no such luxuries, said it was a penalty. And say what you want about the man who would give Roy Aitken the red card in 1984, when Mr Valentine says it is a penalty, it stays a penalty!

20 minutes had gone in this Cup Final, and it was Andy Lynch who had volunteered to do the needful. Andy was a likeable character who had recently in a game against Motherwell scored two own goals, and the rest of the team had to keep the ball away from him in case he fancied a hat-trick! It was his third penalty kick of his senior career - his previous two had been for Hearts and he missed the pair of them! You would not have thought that however as he ran up, facing the massed ranks of baying Rangers fans, and slotted the ball home.

For the next 70 minutes the standard of football deteriorated from the appalling to the putrid. Celtic's defence stood firm, as did the midfield with Aitken in particular doing very well. Soon after half time, we had been compelled to desert our armchairs and pace the living room, like caged lions. Celtic in fact had several chances to go further ahead with Joe Craig being the major sinner and Paul Wilson a minor one. At the other end, Celtic dealt with everything competently with several Rangers players like Parlane and Johnstone hardly making any contribution at all.

The count down to the final whistle was on in earnest when Rangers had their only real chance.Substitute Robertson, an impressive looking 19 year old who had replaced the tiring Watson hit the bar with a header. Apart from that Celtic coped adequately with the frenetic and hysterical Ibrox pressure, and full time brought scenes of unrestrained joy as Celtic had won the Cup for the 25th time.

It was hardly a classic final. It could well be argued in fact that it was Celtic's worst. Aitken and Stanton had been booked, the Cup itself was won by a dicey penalty, but Celtic had done what they are meant to do and that is to score more goals than the opposition. Alfie Conn had thus won a Cup Winner's medal for Rangers against Celtic and for Celtic against Rangers. Pat Stanton after years of playing brilliantly for Hibs but winning next to nothing had won a League and Cup Winner's medal in his first year for Celtic. Captain Dalglish lifted the trophy and then managed to lose his medal, which he had dropped inside someone's umbrella as he was showing the Cup to a disabled supporter. He eventually got it back, but TV viewers saw Kenny in tears as he left the field, upset at his apparent loss. We did not know it then (though we might have suspected) that we would soon be in tears about Kenny. For it would be the last time we ever saw him in a green and white jersey.

—26—
RIOT!
1980

Celtic supporters were not all that happy with their team as they approached Hampden on May 10th 1980. A couple of months previously, it had seemed that their team were on the verge of great things. The month of April however had been nothing short of an unmitigated catastrophe, and Celtic supporters were quite clearly groggy and disorientated in stark contrast to the raucous battle cries of the lads in blue.

The season had started on a high note and Christmas and New Year saw Celtic flying high at the top of the table, fighting off a surprising challenge from, among others, Morton, the surprise package of the League who had indeed beaten Celtic at Cappielow in October. Under the wise and committed management of Billy McNeill, now in his second season of the job, Celtic were also through into the Quarter Finals of the European Cup bringing back memories of the truly great days of the sixties and early seventies.

Yet the team had not played uniformly well. Aberdeen seemed to exercise a bit of an Indian sign over them in these days, for the Dons had beaten them both home and away, albeit narrowly in both cases, to put them out of the League Cup, and the reaching of the European Cup Quarter Finals had been against not the most de-manding of opposition in Partizan Tirana of Albania and Dundalk of Eire. The Dundalk game in particular had been almost embar-rassingly bad, as Celtic limped fitfully to the necessary 0-0 draw in a Celtic daft town against a team who all cheerfully admitted to being Celtic fans.

Nevertheless, there were some good players on view at Celtic Park in season 1979-80. Danny McGrain and Roy Aitken were by now Internationalists with Danny well recovered from his mystery foot injury of two years ago. Manager McNeill's two signings of the previous season Davie Provan and Murdo McLeod were quite clearly Celtic class, and Tommy Burns, although occasionally annoyingly

The Celtic pre-season picture in 1980.

Back row: Frank Connor, Colin Douglas, John Weir, Alan Sneddon, Pat Bonner, Jim Casey, Peter Latchford, David Young, David Moyes, David Kenny, Jim Lumsden. Middle row: Danny Crainie, Mark Reid, Charlie Nicholas, Jim Duffy, John Halpin, Frank McGarvey, Mike Conroy, John Buckley, Willie McStay, Paul McGrath, Brian Scott. Front row: Billy McNeill (manager), Roy Aitken, David Provan, Dom Sullivan, Tom McAdam, George McClusky, Danny McGrain, Bobby Lennox, Murdo MacLeod, John Doyle, Vic Davidson, John Clark.

inclined to overdo it with the ball and slow things down, was rapidly developing. Tom McAdam at centre half, although occasionally fallible, inspired confidence, and goalkeeper Peter Latchford was clearly a favourite with the Celtic fans.

The winter was a bad one and several games were postponed, leading to a very unfortunate pile up of fixtures in that dreadful month of April, but on the eve of the trip to Madrid to play Real, things were looking very good. For one thing, they were 2-0 up on Real Madrid, for another they were points clear at the top of the Premier League with Rangers well out of it and only Aberdeen looking vaguely like challengers. In addition, there was the clear signal that the team meant business in the signing of Frank McGarvey from Liverpool for a record fee from England to Scotland.

Sadly, the team went down 3-2 on aggregate. This of course in itself was no disgrace to lose to Real Madrid, and it certainly did seem that the team had recovered from the heartbreak of it all when they beat

Rangers at Celtic Park on April 2nd with new signing Frank McGarvey scoring the only goal of the game. What happened after that is one of the Celtic horror stories. Twice they lost to Aberdeen at Celtic Park, and twice they lost in the city of Dundee, all four times being outplayed, and there is no excuse for that other than sheer bad football - careless defending, poor attacking and a general complacent attitude which in fact threw away the League in the direction of a competent, although not yet outstanding Aberdeen team, who could hardly believe their luck.

The game at Dens Park, Dundee on April 19th was a particular shocker. The Dens Parkers, now managed by Tommy Gemmell, were heading for relegation. The game was played on a hard, bare pitch (just recovering from a dreadful winter) on a sunny but windy day. Aitken scored first for Celtic, then Dundee, playing in a relaxed style for they knew they were going down anyway, proceeded to take Celtic for 5 both against and with the wind. It was an appalling performance and frankly, somewhat mystifying. We had the distinct impression that something was going on in that horrendous April, but we have never yet been told what.

All this will explain the distinctly downcast expressions of the lads in green as they came to Hampden on that lovely sunny day of the Scottish Cup Final. Why Rangers were so euphoric is harder to explain. Their season had been an absolute shocker, and winning the Scottish Cup was their only way into Europe. Aberdeen had of course now won the League, and the League Cup had gone for the first time ever to Dundee United, whose joy was shared by quite a few football fans who felt that their magnificent contribution to Scottish football over the past 20 years deserved some sort of tangible reward.

The Scottish Cup began for Celtic with Raith Rovers at Celtic Park. Celtic won 2-1 but their inability to finish off the part-timers by a bigger score was puzzling and disturbing. Then the strong going St.Mirren came to Celtic Park. The Buddies led by a single goal at half time and for long into the second half, seemed capable of resisting the Celtic pressure. In fact, Celtic were lucky to get their 88th minute equalizer from Murdo MacLeod which happened when thousands of the fans were heading homewards convinced that the Buddies were through. This game should have been a pointer to the fact that things were not all that good at Celtic Park, but the ecstasy of the Replay drowned out any Cassandra utterances.

It was really what Cup Replays should be about. A packed crowd, dangerously crammed into that tight little ground, two goals each in 90 minutes (including a disputed penalty for each side), an ordering off (McAdam of Celtic), the scoreline see sawing, the play ebbing and flowing, and eventually an extra time winner for Celtic scored by Johnny Doyle. Even then, St.Mirren were desperately unlucky not to get an equalizer. It was all breathtaking stuff, and perhaps hid the deficiencies of the team which should have been addressed before black April.

Morton came to Celtic Park for the Quarter Final three days after the First Leg victory over Real Madrid, and the team came out to a deafening roar and the supporters carried them to victory by constant singing and chanting including 'Happy Days are here again' and other hymns of glee. The team performance was little more than competent as they won 2-0, and yet again euphoria lent enchantment.

Another break came Celtic's way in the draw for the Scottish Cup Semi Finals. Celtic at Hampden got unhappy Hibs, who, in spite of having George Best, were in the middle of the worst spell in their history and heading inexorably towards relegation. Celtic beat them 5-0, not as good a result as it seemed. In the other Semi Final, Aberdeen played Rangers at Celtic Park.

Now, had the draw come out as Celtic v.Aberdeen, the Dons might well have won, for the games were played on April 12th, by which time Celtic's self destruction button had been well and truly pressed. As it was, Celtic got another break when the weaker team won, Rangers beating Aberdeen by a solitary (albeit well taken) Derek Johnstone goal. It was thus to be Tweedle Dum v. Tweedle Dee for the seventh time in 20 years in the Scottish Cup Final.

In addition to the psychological problems of having emotionally damaged their loving support, Celtic had physical ones in the suspension of two central defenders. Both Roddy MacDonald and Tom McAdam had less than perfect disciplinary records and had picked up enough points to put themselves out of the Final. Possible replacement Casey was injured, so McNeill had to put Roy Aitken in the centre of the defence in preference to midfield (Roy, throughout his career, was quite happy to fulfil both functions) and play alongside him Mike Conroy. Conroy had played quite a few times last season and this, but had yet to make any position in the team his own. He was not particularly tall for a central defender, but McNeill spent the whole week before the Final making him practise jumping, for the aerial menace of Derek Johnstone was still a potent one.

70,303 fans turned up at Hampden in lovely sunshine to see the following teams:

Celtic: Latchford, Sneddon, McGrain; Aitken, Conroy, MacLeod; Provan, Doyle, McCluskey, Burns, McGarvey
Rangers: McCloy, Jardine, Dawson; Forsyth, Jackson, Stevens; Cooper, Russell, Johnstone, Smith, MacDonald.

The game opened, as most Old Firm games do, fast and furious. By half way through the first half referee George Smith of Edinburgh had booked two men - Tom Forsyth of Rangers and Murdo MacLeod of Celtic (McGarvey of Celtic and Stevens of Rangers would eventually follow) and the game, in direct contrast to the dismal 1977 Final between the same two teams was a good one, as both teams tried to get that elusive first goal. If anything, Celtic had the better of the early exchanges with Frank McGarvey coming close on several occasions, and the discerning supporters on the King's Park terracings noted with satisfaction that Mike Conroy, playing the game of his life, was keeping the burly Derek Johnstone in check.

Half time came and went with no let up in the action or the tension either on the terracings or the nation's living rooms. One goal, it was becoming apparent, would win this Cup. Bobby Lennox, the super fast veteran, came on for the ineffective Doyle, and this immediately livened up the Celtic attack, but still the goal would not come. Rangers too had introduced their veteran in Tommy McLean, and for the last ten minutes, Celtic having shot their bolt, Rangers took command. Twice Celtic had their fair share of luck when a ball spun off Aitken's leg and out for a corner and then Latchford was in exactly the right place for a Cooper shot. The full time whistle was greeted with a certain amount of relief at the King's Park end.

For the first time in the first game of a Final, extra time of 15 minutes each way would be played. After that, there would be a Replay, for the dreaded penalty shoot-out had not yet been invented. As is often the case after 90 hectic minutes, the extra time period is a little flatter as both teams were exhausted. The first 15 minutes were uneventful other than a Celtic claim for a penalty when McCluskey seemed to be pushed inside the box. It was early in the second period that the vital breakthrough came.

It was a curious goal. Rangers defence, defending the Mount Florida goal, had just cleared a corner kick, and with their defenders rushing out, the ball broke to Danny McGrain. Danny's weakness always was that he did not have a shot. Danny was aware of this defect, but nevertheless hammered the ball in the general direction of the Rangers goal from about 35 yards, almost like Mr Micawber in 'David Copperfield' hoping that 'something might turn up'. Something in this case did, namely George McCluskey's boot which deflected the ball past the despairing McCloy.

It was such a strange goal that there was definitely a moment's silence at the far end of the ground before the rainbow of green and white appeared. The roar took yet another split second to make itself heard, and there was definitely the impression that the referee might, for some reason or another disallow this distinctly weird goal. But no! George Smith ran to the halfway line, the Rangers defenders stared at one another in disbelief and the Celtic players led by evergreen Bobby Lennox converged on the lucky George McCluskey.

For the remaining twelve minutes, Celtic shut up shop. Billy McNeill took off McGarvey the out and out attacker and brought on the midfielder Vic Davidson, they retained possession whenever they could, they did not disdain the inelegant punt up the field when necessary and Peter Latchford in goal shouted instructions and inspired confidence. In fairness, Rangers did enough to deserve a Replay, but Celtic held out and the Final whistle blew with the ball in the safe hands of Peter Latchford.

The tidal wave of emotion was unleashed, supporters jumped and cheered, back home wives were kissed for the first time in many years by middle aged husbands, and the Cup was presented for the 26th time. That should have been the end to it - a somewhat unsatisfactory goal to finish a great match to bring a bright end to an unsatisfactory season. Sadly, there was more to come.

It started with a benevolent invasion from the Celtic end to congratulate the heroes. The police were waiting outside the ground and were not there at the crucial point in sufficient strength to prevent it. Not in itself all that bad, however, until a hostile invasion from the other end began. Thus the world was treated on its TV screens to a running battle between rival gangs of thicko's which the TV commentators 'Here comes another charge!' thoroughly enjoyed in spite of the pious protestations to the contrary.

There were injuries, but the whole thing looked worse than it was. Better deployment of police would have stopped it, and all that it showed was that tribal hatred was still around. The arguments raged on for months afterwards, but nothing took away the fact that Celtic had once again won the Scottish Cup.

—27—

BACK FROM THE DEAD
1985

If one were asked to name the most romantic and spectacular of Celtic's Scottish Cup successes, that of 1985 would come very high up the list. It had fine goals, a late comeback and a triumph against the odds, and more importantly, it was a reward for the supporters who had suffered much at the 'slings and arrows of outrageous fortune' and whose spirits had been sadly buffetted by the feeling of injustice.

It is necessary to go back to summer of 1983. Following the departure of Charlie Nicholas, which was a serious blow in itself, manager McNeill left the club in a dispute over a contract. The supporters who loved big Billy were distressed and saddened by this and it was just as well that it all came to light during the close season. Otherwise Celtic Park might well have seen the sort of demonstration which would happen a decade later. Davie Hay, a transparently likeable but luckless man, took over.

1984 saw two heart rending Cup Final defeats, the League Cup to Rangers thanks to an extra time penalty and the Scottish Cup to Aberdeen in circumstances which showed how important a person a referee can be.

It would be the autumn of 1984, however, which added a new dimension to the word 'cheat' in the English language. Before the encounter with Rapid Vienna, however, there had been an anonymous flop in the League Cup in contrast to a reasonable start to the Premier League, peppered however by some odd performances. What had cheered the supporters up however was the signing in October from Watford of Scottish Internationalist Maurice Johnston whose professions of love and loyalty to the club he 'had always wanted to play for' seemed as genuine as his undoubted talent.

But then came Rapid. We, who had long memories of a Scotland v.Austria International at Hampden Park in 1963, were expecting trouble from Austrians, but nothing on this scale could have been predicted. In 1963 at Hampden, the referee had been forced to abandon the game because of the appalling behaviour of the Austrians;

on this occasion, the behaviour was just as bad, but they got away with it and won the tie.

Down 1-0 from the game in Vienna, Celtic played to their European best at Celtic Park and beat the Austrians 3-0. One Austrian was deservedly given his marching orders, but then a fool from the Jungle threw a bottle. TV evidence showed clearly that an Austrian fell before the bottle came on, but somehow or another, ignoring evidence of ambulance men and policemen, UEFA, after making a fair judgement in the first instance of fining Celtic for the bottle incident, reacted to Rapid's appeal by ordering a Replay at a ground more than 100 miles away from Glasgow. Celtic were angry, and the players were too emotionally involved to play well. Celtic went down to Old Trafford and lost the tie.

This whole affair is worth a book in itself, and the sheer injustice of it all rankles. Perhaps Celtic should have withdrawn from the tournament in protest, as many suggested from both outwith and within the club. Everyone in Great Britain from the most rabid of Rangers supporters to the most patronising of English journalists and TV commentators agreed that Celtic were hard done by. It was clear however that there could be no expectation of any sort of justice from UEFA.

A side effect of all this was the somewhat remarkable sight on May 15th 1985 in Rotterdam of a sizeable contingent of Celtic supporters cheering on a team in blue against a team in green. This was the Cup Winners' Cup Final when Everton, not a team normally beloved of the Celtic Park fans because of their (wrongly) alleged Orange tradition, gave Rapid Vienna their come-uppance to the undisguised glee of the whole of the British Isles. Three days later at the Scottish Cup Final, the Celtic end displayed at least one banner which said 'Ha! Ha! Rapid' and people like Andy Gray, Trevor Steven and Gary Stevens were, for the moment at least, much beloved of the Celtic Park faithful.

The Rapid affair and its consequences, of course, had a detrimental effect on the League Championship challenge which stuttered to a sorry halt soon after the New Year with a number of adverse results. A glimmer of a chance came our way when we beat Aberdeen at Celtic Park impressively on February 23rd, but no sooner had all the hype about strong efforts in the run-in began than Celtic dropped a point at Tannadice and on March 16th went down at home to a mediocre Hibs side with relegation problems. The Championship was effectively given to the consistent Aberdeen on that day.

But there was no lack of talent on display at Celtic Park, and questions were asked about why they could not do better. Paul McStay was quite clearly a class player and already an established Internationalist, Murdo McLeod in midfield was gritty and determined as indeed was the other signing of the 1978-9 season Davie Provan. Davie however was injury prone and seemed to tire very rapidly late on in a game. Somewhat of an enigma was Frank McGarvey. No-one could ever accuse him of lack of effort, and he could score some lovely goals, yet there was always the feeling that he lacked incisiveness and punch. Also up front was Brian McClair, someone who, we often felt, wasn't given as many opportunities to show us his class as should have been the case.

Question marks were frequently raised about the defence with its sieve like ability to leak goals. And yet, man by man, it was hard to point a finger at anyone. Danny McGrain, by now the veteran of the team, was in the mould of Alec McNair of old, reliable, unflappable and exuding of class. Tom McAdam was a fine centre half with tremendous heading ability, and although blamed by the support for loads of defeats, never really let the side down catastrophically. And behind them was Paddy Bonner, quite clearly one of the better of Celtic's goalkeepers with a particular ability to deal with high crosses.

The team, when thus examined, did not seem all that bad. In truth, they were a good side but had the misfortune to be up against a very fine Aberdeen side, deservedly rated highly in Europe. They also had the self-destructive tendency to let themselves down in big games, games that they really needed to win. It was in this respect that questions were now beginning to be asked of Davie Hay.

Davie, himself a great player of ten years earlier, often seemed to over commit the players and to allow the heart to rule the head. The disciplinary record of the team was not particularly good. At half time in the 1984 Cup Final, following the illegal goal that Aberdeen were allowed and the harsh sending off of Roy Aitken, Davie had been seen by the TV cameras to wait for referee Mr Valentine and seem to lose the place, for which display he was lucky to be so leniently treated. A calmer approach might have led him to rush into the dressing room and encourage his men to regroup for the second half and make the best out of what had been admittedly some tough luck so far.

Much of the feelings about Hay were, of course, nostalgia for McNeill. Celtic supporters don't like to go too long without a trophy, and Hay had been quoted as saying things like this was what they deserved and that he might quit if he could not produce the silver goods by the end of the season. It was clear therefore that an awful lot depended on the Scottish Cup campaign when it started in January 1985.

The first game was at Hamilton and scheduled for January 26th. The frosty weather which had taken such a grip in January put the game off until Wednesday 30th. Celtic had not played a competitive game since the fine defeat of Rangers at Ibrox on New Year's Day, and the rustiness was very evident. In addition, the thaw at Douglas Park had been a somewhat imperfect one, and the pitch was not of the best. Half time came with the Academicals 1-0 up, and a shock staring everyone in the face. McGarvey who was substitute that night was called for by the fans singing 'There's only one Frank McGarvey'. In an interesting example of fan power, the said Frank was brought on, equalized almost immediately and with time running out deprived the gallant Accies of a lucrative Celtic Park replay by scoring a fine late winner. It had however been a very close call.

The next round brought Highland Leaguers Inverness Thistle to Celtic Park. The loveable Gaels, most of them self confessed Celtic fans, were outclassed to the tune of 6-0 in which Paul McStay scored a hat-trick, and the second half was played with the carefree Jungle urging Inverness to score, booing Celtic players when they got the ball, cheering the Thistle players.

This bizarre behaviour, which some of us thought was going too far, showed that Celtic fans can laugh at themselves, but in fact it was caused by the transistor radio. The radio and its now attendant stereo headphones was telling us that Dundee were beating Rangers 1-0 across at Ibrox, and although the referee at Ibrox seemed to allow an inordinate amount of stoppage time, the feckless Rangers could not take advantage of his generosity. It was even suggested that the Invernessians might be more frequent visitors to Glasgow in future, for the Highland League might be an appropriate place for another Glasgow team.

It was the same Dundee side which faced Celtic next in two thrilling encounters. The draw at Dens Park was one of the best games ever seen between the two of them at that quaint old ground, and Celtic were decidedly fortunate to edge the Replay 2-1 at Celtic Park, aided as they were by the dubious sending off of a Dundee player. The Semi Final draw kept Celtic and Aberdeen apart, but Motherwell threw up tremendous problems for Celtic, coming very close on several occasions in the first game, particularly near the end. The Replay however was a different matter with Celtic all over them but unable to score until the 73rd minute when Roy Aitken broke the deadlock. After that the floodgates opened, however, and Maurice Johnston added another two before the end.

The other Semi Final between Dundee United and Aberdeen also went to a Replay on the same night, and we were all very happy that we would face Dundee United rather than the seemingly invincible Aberdeen, who had more or less wrapped up the Championship by that time. But Dundee United had improved tremendously since we last met them in the Scottish Cup Final in 1974. They had won the Premier League in 1983, the League Cup a couple of times, were consistently successful in Europe and had built up a reputation as a team of technically correct rather than 'flair' players. Some people called this boring; even some of their own fans agreed, but everyone had to respect their defensive record, built up as it was on the triple centre halves of Paul Hegarty, Richard Gough and Dave Narey. They had never won the Scottish Cup, but given Celtic's inconsistency and brittleness that season, must have fancied their chances.

60,346 fans (and possibly a lot more, for an exit gate was broken at the King's Park End and many supporters rushed in without paying) saw the following teams take the field on Saturday May 18th:

Celtic: Bonner, W.McStay, McGrain; Aitken, McAdam, MacLeod; Provan, P.McStay, Johnston, Burns, McGarvey.
Dundee United: McAlpine; Malpas, Beedie; Gough, Hegarty, Narey; Bannon, Milne, Kirkwood, Sturrock, Dodds.

About the first half, the less said the better. Neither team looked worthy of being in a Scottish Cup Final, but the fat was put in the fire in the 54th minute when fine work by Davie Dodds beat Aitken on the left and the ball was pushed along for Stuart Beedie to score a fine goal. Celtic were now clearly up against it, for there was no better team in Scotland than Dundee United at defending a one goal lead. They were so good at it in fact that they never considered trying to go for another which would certainly have killed Celtic.

For a long time after that goal, the game was played in an eerie silence. The Dundee United fans seemed reluctant to believe that they were actually one up against Celtic and that they could win this game at Hampden, a place where they had never done well. Celtic fans were now strangely subdued, the banners drooping and everyone in a state of stunned, introverted melancholic brooding. The pace of the game dropped and United grew in confidence.

Davie Hay on the bench must have thought this was his own private hell. He had already taken off Tommy Burns and put on Brian McClair, but to no avail. The end of his days as Celtic manager must have loomed when he suddenly decided to grasp the nettle, however unpalatable. He took off blue eyed boy Paul McStay, who, frankly was having a shocker, and put on Pierce O'Leary. This move was booed by the fans who loved Paul and who had never been at all impressed by O'Leary.

Pierce was, in any case, an out and out defender, not what Celtic required at this time. But Billy McNeill, commentating for BBC backed up Davie by saying that there are times when a manager has to be unpopular. It was then that everyone saw that Roy Aitken was to be moved up to midfield, surely the best position for such a swashbuckling footballer.

Roy took the game by the scruff of the neck and saved Celtic. Within minutes, Celtic had won a free kick which was converted spectacularly by Davie Provan. This woke the crowd up and Hampden erupted when the winner came. The Dundee United defence failed to head a ball far enough, the ball came to Roy who charged down the right, then sent across the most inch perfect cross you could ever imagine for Frank McGarvey to head home. It was almost as if this had all been planned by Providence, and it was certainly a typical Celtic victory, as if to make up to the fans the real agonies they had suffered for the last two years.

The last five minutes were long but Brian McGinlay eventually brought it to an end to unleash an enormous wave of ecstasy. Sober reflection some days later would reflect on the influence of the crowd who certainly carried Celtic through to that second goal. Sympathy was also possible for Dundee United's long suffering fans, but we were less kindly disposed towards their austere Manager and his players whose negative tactics were not what had made Scottish football great. It was however a fine Celtic victory. We really needed that one, and Celtic had now won the Cup 27 times.

—28—
HISTORY DEMANDS ....
1988

It is a pity that historians and pub know-alls will inevitably confuse the two Scottish Cup Finals of 1985 and 1988. The clubs were the same, the scoreline was the same, the pattern of scoring (i.e. Dundee United scoring first, then Celtic equalizing and scoring again) was the same, the scorer of the winning goal was called Frank who had connections with St.Mirren, and the teams were even kicking in the same direction so that Celtic's late breathtaking winners were all scored into the King's Park goal - all this will lead to a great deal of confusion. But the circumstances were remarkably and totally different.

1988 saw a superb Celtic side. It was, of course, Centenary Year, and even with a poor side, there would have been a great deal to be happy about in reviewing 100 years of Celtic history, but the circumstances of the season in a way encapsulated all that was good in the history of the club. There was romance, there was glory and above all there was some sheer good football from a Celtic team that was probably the best since the glory days of the late sixties.

The previous season had ended in disarray as Rangers' multi-million spending spree saw them to the Championship. Davie Hay was dismissed and there was only one real candidate for the job, and that was former boss Billy McNeill, who had been pining for home ever since his leaving the club in 1983. Billy was given money to spend, and he spent wisely and well.

But the season did not get off to a great start. Defeat at the hands of Borussia Dortmund (which included a somewhat shame faced and repentant Murdo MacLeod) prevented the club from making any impact on Europe. A few weeks earlier, Aberdeen at Pittodrie finished any claims for the League Cup.Perhaps these two things were in the long term best interest for the club, because it did give McNeill a chance to build things up, try out a few players and impose his will and ideas on what at the start of the season must have been a dispirited bunch of men.

Before the season began, he had bought Andy Walker, the small built Motherwell striker who was not exactly a household name outside what used to be called the steel town. In the bargain basement, he picked up Billy Stark, very much a utility player and handy man, but who had played gloriously for Aberdeen and now seemed to have reached his sell-buy date. From Sheffield Wednesday came right back Chris Morris, probably the first Cornishman to play for Celtic. In early October Frank McAvennie came from West Ham, making much of kissing the Celtic jersey as he ran out for his first game against Hibs, and then in November, Scottish football was taken aback when Aberdeen agreed to transfer Joe Miller to his beloved Celtic. The McNeill jigsaw was beginning to fit together, and when this impressive panoply of talent was added to Davie Hay's last signing centre half Mick McCarthy, the changes in personnel at Celtic Park from last season's flops were nothing short of remarkable.

Early season form, however, was nothing startling although there was an agreeable 1-0 victory over Rangers at Celtic Park. Player/manager of Rangers, Graeme Souness got himself sent off for a tackle on Billy Stark who did not even have his boot on at the time. Contrary to received wisdom in the Jungle, Scottish football fans of other clubs do not automatically hate Celtic more than they do Rangers, and it is certainly true that in season 1987-8, people were happy that someone was standing up to the mega bucks of Ibrox.

Round about October and November, however, the team began to get it together, and to play with confidence. The festive period, always crucial, saw a brilliant McStay goal at Brockville when the team were under pressure, a last minute winner at Tannadice and a fine 2-1 win over Rangers at Celtic Park on January 2nd. This is the stuff that champions are made of, and there were very few blemishes on the team between New Year and April 23ʳd when the League was eventually won in a 3-0 victory over Dundee at a crammed and ecstatic Celtic Park.

The Cup campaign was not without its interest. The first game brought Stranraer to Celtic Park, and although there was never any real danger of the brave South-Westers beating Celtic, they might have forced a draw and a humiliating replay at Stair Park. Celtic scored first through McAvennie, and then proceded to play their worst football for some time. They could not add to their lead, and gallant Stranraer fought well, earning themselves a penalty. Quite a few of the fans (the fair minded ones) were hoping that Stranraer would score, for they deserved a goal and Celtic deserved to be taught a lesson, but sadly they did not do so, and Celtic were through to a tough looking tie against Hibs at Celtic Park.

Once again in a Cup-tie at Celtic Park, Celtic played what could most charitably be described as below par and most accurately as rubbish, and so too did Hibs. What made it worse was that this was a Sunday game, televised live, and so the whole country saw Celtic's shortcomings which on that day were considerable. Dunfermline Athletic fans, however, watching the game in their living rooms, purred with pleasure at the Jungle's acclaim of their team, for the Pars had the previous day knocked Rangers out of the Cup. The replay at Easter Road was different, for it was a fine game of football with only one Billy Stark goal (scoring a rebound off the bar) separating the two teams.

Partick Thistle were swept aside in the Quarter Final, and thus Celtic were in the Semi Finals with Dundee United, Hearts and Aberdeen. Dundee United would eventually need three games to get the better of Aberdeen in an encounter that was about as exciting as a game of chess, as a supporter somewhat unkindly put it, but the Semi Final between Hearts and Celtic at Hampden Park was a thriller with excitement, last minute drama, disputed goals, refereeing controversies, the lot. Hearts have a sad habit of blowing up in important games, particularly at the mere thought of a Celtic jersey (they had done so, spectacularly, in 1986 on the final day of the League campaign) but they never caused their supporters any more pain than they did on April 9th 1988.

After an even first half, Hearts went ahead on the hour mark although it looked to all Celtic fans and not a few of the Press that Bonner had been impeded by a Hearts player, Dave McPherson in his attempt to jump for a harmless high ball sent in hopefully rather than confidently by ex-Celt Brian Whittaker. Referee Kenny Hope, however gave the goal. For a spell after that, Hearts played composed possession football, but as the minutes ticked away, Celtic's character came to the fore as Hearts began to panic and to look like a man about to get mugged. Only three minutes remained when McGhee equalized - a curious affair following goalkeeper Henry Smith's dropping of the ball and McGhee somehow managing to squeeze the ball through almost the whole Hearts team to score.

The Celtic end erupted, and those who had been uttering philosophical aphorisms about 'You can't win them all' were now wondering if they could afford to come back for the replay. The Hearts supporters visibly sagged and a Jam Tart friend of mine told me weeks later (after he could bring himself to talk to me) that his friends all around him sat down in anguish on the Mount Florida steps (Hampden being not yet all seated), expecting the inevitable.

Even the Hearts players and management shared this pessimism, for there was something leaden footed about the way that they failed to tackle Stark and McAvennie as they set up another move and crossed into the area. Smith went up with McGhee, and to be fair, it looked a foul, although no more than Hearts' goal did. But no whistle went and Andy Walker lashed the ball high into the net as the goalkeeper failed to hold the ball. Hearts were too shattered even to protest, and cruel fans would point to their sponsor Mita and say 'Aye, Mita won the Cup, but for Mark McGhee'.

All 74,000 tickets for the Scottish Cup Final on May 14th went in hours of them being put on sale as fans sensed that only Celtic with their fine sense of history could contemplate winning the Double in their Centenary season. Dundee United, on the other hand, who had now lost 4 Hampden Cup Finals (the most recent one being last year against St.Mirren), felt that their time had to come. A great deal of interest centred on their star man Kevin Gallacher, who as the media kept reminding us was the grandson of the great Patsy.

The SFA made the surprising decision to ask Prime Minister Margaret Thatcher to present the Cup. It is, of course, for a variety of historical and sociological reasons, unlikely that many supporters of either Celtic or Dundee United and vote Conservative, and in summer 1988 she was no longer popular in her own party, let alone in depressed

Celtic players celebrate winning the 1988 Scottish Cup Final.

industrial West Scotland or ailing Tayside. But say what you want about her, she does not lack courage and she came to Hampden to face nothing more than boos and a showing of red cards telling her to take an early bath on her way back to London.

Celtic were without Peter Grant, and then in the week of the Final Paddy Bonner called off without, however, the Press getting to know about it. Paddy had had intermittent injury problems throughout the season and had aggravated his hamstring, so that the door was opened for Ulsterman Allen McKnight, who was hardly a rookie for he was already an Internationalist. The teams were:

Celtic: McKnight, Morris, Rogan; Aitken, McCarthy, Whyte; Miller, McStay, McAvennie, Walker , Burns

Dundee United: Thomson, Bowman, Malpas; McInally, Hegarty, Narey; Bannon, Gallacher, Paatelainen, Ferguson, McKinlay.

Referee George Smith of Edinburgh started the game in glorious sunshine, but the football was a lot less glorious. Miller should have scored for Celtic, but mistimed his jump, and United showed a certain amount of threat, particularly from young Billy McKinlay, but the first half was spent with both teams being very cagey.

It was early in the second half that Kevin Gallacher put United ahead with a goal of which his grandfather would have been proud. Yet it was easily preventable. A poor clear out by McKnight, a break by Gallacher and Roy Aitken could not tackle him. Roy had just been booked a minute previously for a foul on Gallacher and could not risk mistiming his tackle which would have led to a red card. Kevin was therefore allowed to run in and score, although it seemed that McKnight could have come out and done a little more to prevent it. Certainly, Aitken's angry gesticulations to him in the aftermath tended to indicate that.

United were thus ahead, but this Celtic team did not give up. They brought on substitutes in Stark and McGhee, and summoning up their two great allies - their support and their history - surged forward. Fine work by the two substitutes released Rogan on the left. Rogan floated in a cross which goalkeeper Thomson should have gone for. The ball came to Frank McAvennie who headed home. 15 minutes to go and 1-1.

Normally, supporters in Cup Finals are pessimistic, apprehensive, tense and fearful as the closing stages are approached. Not this time. There was the belief, even the expectation that Celtic had to win this one. TV pictures during an injury to Mick McCarthy show an anxious

Billy McNeill and Tommy Craig, but in the background a noisy, exultant and confident support.

A series of corners were forced on the right. Time was almost up and we were bracing ourselves for extra time, when Joe Miller took a very poor one which fortuitously reached Billy Stark's feet. Billy seemed to miskick, and equally fortuitously, the ball landed at McAvennie's feet about six yards out. Frankie does not miss these easy chances, and the terracing turned green and white once again.

Full time came soon after and Celtic had won their 28th Scottish Cup. The team seemed on the brink of true greatness. It was as well that we did not know on that lovely spring evening what we now know. The world seemed at our feet as Mrs Thatcher did her first decent thing as Prime Minister by handing over the Cup to Big Roy Aitken. You know, we almost took a liking to her!

—29—

THE LAST LAUGH
1989

After the Centenary Season glory of 1987-88, it was, I suppose, inevitable that the following season would be something of a let down. We could not guess how much a let down it would be. It was not so much a let down as a drop, as subtle a drop as a drop off the Forth Bridge, and we were left yet again as the season drew to a conclusion with only the Scottish Cup to salvage any sense of pride of honour from. But it did save us, and we had the last laugh of a painful season.

The mistake of summer 1988 was sitting back, enjoying the glory, sharing in the triumphs of the Republic of Ireland in the European Nations' Cup (3 Celts played for them and the other 8 were all supporters) and attending the Glasgow Garden Festival, admiring among other things the view of Ibrox Park from the revolving glass tower. We, in fact, stood still. It is however a necessity in football to keep moving, to bring in a few new players and generally to ginger things up, otherwise your opposition, who now play you at least four times a season, will rumble you. No new players were bought apart from a luckless goalkeeper called Ian Andrews to replace Paddy Bonner who was to be operated upon for his chronic bad back. (McKnight, Bonner's deputy in the 1988 Cup Final had been allowed to go to West Ham in the summer)

The fat was in the fire in late August when Celtic went down 5-1 to Rangers at Ibrox. This defeat was astonishing (even the Rangers players were puzzled at the lack of fight in the Celtic side) but the repercussions were widespread. The all important propaganda victory had been lost, the ill starred Ian Andrews lost confidence and further defeats followed to the likes of Aberdeen, Hibs and Dundee and very soon jokes like 'What's green and slides down the table?' became common. In such circumstances, exits from the League Cup and European Cup were inevitable, for the team had lost its way so comprehensively as to be unrecognisable from the great team of six months previously.

What had gone wrong? Clearly the loss of the excellent Bonner in goal presented a great problem (Andrews was deplorably booed by a few insensitive fans as we lost a game at Celtic Park to Aberdeen in September. Even veteran Scotland and Partick Thistle man Alan Rough, Celtic to the core, was eventually, at the age of almost 37, given a game for Celtic) but there did seem to be an attitude problem with one or two heads having swollen to unmanageable proportions, and McNeill did not seem to be providing the calming influence that he used to show on the field twenty years previously.

Yet the team rallied with the return of Bonner in the month of November, including a defeat of Rangers at Celtic Park which went some way to restoring credibility and giving us hope of a typically Celtic fightback in the New Year. But they faltered again at Tannadice on a cold day the week before Christmas (the traditionalists among us were appalled at the sight of some players wearing gloves!) before collapsing yet again at Ibrox on January 3rd. This time it was only 4-1 but it was remarkably similar to the game in August at the same venue where the team held their own until half time, wilted under a Rangers onslaught and did not have the resolve to fight back late in the game. Ex-Ibrox player and manager John Greig, commentating on the radio, was appalled and puzzled at all this, almost embarrassed at the comprehensiveness of the collapse to a Rangers side who would lose to Motherwell on the following Saturday. The League challenge was over; we all knew it and the attendances slumped.

But the Scottish Cup is always the Scottish Cup as far as Celtic are concerned, and they were fortunate in getting home draws for the first two rounds against Dumbarton and then Clydebank which were won comfortably, although not perhaps as comfortably as the 2-0 and 4-1 scorelines would tend to suggest.

The Quarter Final brought Hearts to Celtic Park for a remarkable game. The crowd was large, the excitement intense and there were one or two other added ingredients as well. In the first place, McAvennie's problems had come to a head and he had asked for a transfer back to London. Celtic Park thus presented the fairly unusual spectacle of Celtic's centre forward being booed on to the park by half the crowd but cheered by the other half, who believed that as long as he was wearing the green and white, he should be supported. As far as Hearts were concerned in these days, Celtic were the anti-Christ who had inflicted upon them untold evil in 1986 and 1988, as those who travelled on the train from Edinburgh that day were made all too aware.

This was even before the game started and it was in any case a Scottish Cup Quarter Final, at the best of times no afternoon picnic. Before half time, three players had been shown the red card following the award of a softish penalty to Celtic in front of the Hearts support. Celtic were already a goal up, thanks to Mark McGhee, although Hearts claimed offside. Still smarting from that goal, a Hearts player protested excessively about the penalty, and then after the penalty was scored by Aitken, a free-for-all developed in front of the players' tunnel and one from each side (Mick McCarthy in the case of Celtic) was invited to leave the scene with several others lucky to avoid the same fate. Half time came as a relief and with jokes being made about this being good practice for the seven-a-side tournament, both teams were clearly given a talking to by their respective managers. Celtic finished the game, winning by 10 players to 9 and by 2 goals to 1.

The Semi Final against Hibs took place at Hampden on the day after the Hillsborough Disaster with the final death toll still not clear. It was a strange atmosphere for a Semi Final, but young Steve Fulton cheered us up in a brilliant first half performance which ran Hibs ragged and saw Celtic go in 3 goals up at half time, clearly not now too bothered about the loss of McAvennie to West Ham. Hibs pulled one back in the second half, but Celtic were already in the Final. Sadly, young Fulton's potential was never fully developed, at least not in a Celtic jersey.

By the time that the Final was played on May 20th 1989, Rangers were clear champions. Their progress to the Scottish Cup Final however had been none too impressive and replays had been required against Raith Rovers, Dundee United and St. Johnstone. In addition, the week before the Final they had inexplicably collapsed at home to Aberdeen on a day that should have been a carnival for them, for that was when they were given the League Trophy. And also, by that time, Celtic fans had their own reasons to be happy.

On Friday 12th May, Celtic announced the return of Maurice Johnston, who had gone to France in 1987. It was certainly a bold move by Celtic (he had scored in all five of his games for Scotland's World Cup qualifiers) and although there were apparently a few points of detail about income tax etc. to be ironed out, his return and appearance in a green and white jersey caused nothing but optimism among the support. It was a pity that he was ineligible for the Cup Final, but the certainty of his joining the club next season had to be good news.

The weather was perfect for the 72,000 capacity crowd (tickets had been snaffled up almost as soon as they were put up for sale) to see the following teams:

Celtic: Bonner, Morris, Rogan; Aitken, McCarthy, Whyte; Grant, McStay, Miller, Burns, McGhee
Rangers: Woods, Stevens, Munro; Gough, Sterland, Butcher; Drinkell, Ferguson, McCoist, Brown, Walters.

The referee was Mr Robert Valentine of Dundee, with the impeccable credentials of being somewhat notorious in the eyes of both sets of supporters from previous Cup Finals. In 1977 he had given Celtic a disputed penalty which led to the only goal of the game and upset Rangers; whereas in 1984 his popularity with the Celtic Park fans had taken a serious knock when he sent off Roy Aitken, a decision which effectively gave the Cup to Aberdeen.

The day was hot and so was the action. In Old Firm games there is never any settling-in period, the tackles are fierce and it often needs a wise referee to be able to decide what is the best action. Sometimes a red card is justified, yet the referee must know that this sort of thing

The 1989 Scottish Cup Final is over and the party begins.

can only make the situation worse, for the temperature is like a boiling pot, simmering yet likely to boil over at any moment.

There was for example a crunching tackle on Paul McStay by Mel Sterland. Poor Mel was sadly out of his depth, but that can really be no excuse for a charge that might well have left McStay badly injured. Manager McNeill was out of his dugout to protest at that one, and perhaps a red card might have been shown if it had not been an Old Firm Cup Final.

Then such are the tricks of television photography that it looked for all the world as if Peter Grant landed a punch on Mark Walters. Ian St. John, the commentator, seemed to think so as well, for he said that it was quite a nifty right hook. It was in fact brilliantly arranged. The referee was behind both players as Peter tackled Mark. The linesman was also a long way away, the players were running towards the Celtic end, and, when the tackle went in, Peter's arm swung at random to give him more impetus and happened to come into contact with the player's face. Walters made much of it, but the Celtic end to a man were convinced that it was the sheerest of accidents.

Three minutes remained of the first half when the ball went out of play on the far side of the field half-way inside the Celtic half for a throw in to Rangers. Roy Aitken, however, calmly took the throw in for Celtic as Mr Valentine was checking the time with his linesmen. Before anyone could howl any prolonged protest, Peter Grant had hoisted a high hopeful ball deep into Rangers territory. Heads went up and the ball came to Gary Stevens, who gently passed it back to his goalkeeper. But Gary had obviously not been listening to TV commentator, Jock Brown, who, at the start of the game, had clearly warned everyone that the grass was a bit long. The ball did not travel as quickly as Gary wanted or intended, and in nipped Joe Miller to score.

Rangers retaliated at once and could have scored before half time but for some quick-witted Celtic defending; and so the first half, short on football skill but long on emotional commitment and drama came to an end.

The second half was a long one, with Celtic's midfield on top but not sufficiently in charge to push forward and score another. Rangers brought on their old guard of the late Davie Cooper (and Celtic fans shared the grief of his untimely death in 1995, for he was a fine player) and manager Graeme Souness. Souness had never won a Cup medal in either Scotland or England, and frankly did not look like winning one now, for Celtic's captain Roy Aitken, revelling as always in a

Hampden Final, had the game by the scruff of the neck, and anything that did come down the middle was gobbled up by Celtic's defensive duo of Mick McCarthy and Derek Whyte.

In the last frenetic ten minutes a half chance did come to Ally McCoist over the heads of the Celtic defence, but Ally, perhaps suspecting offside, snatched at it and put it over the bar. Ally had not had the easiest of afternoons, having been on the receiving end of a few hefty challenges from 'Dirty Mick', as Mick McCarthy was affectionately named by some of the Celtic faithful, and he did give the impression that he was always expecting another one. A few minutes later, Rangers did have the ball in the net, but referee Valentine had blown for a foul on Bonner.

We had reached 90 minutes, when, with the ball at the Rangers corner flag, Peter Grant was once again involved in things and lucky not to be severely punished. However, Celtic were awarded a free kick and Cooper was booked for retaliation. From the free kick, the ball came to Aitken who bizarrely belted the ball over the bye-line towards the Celtic fans who watched this with a split second of puzzled amazement before realising that, as Roy was sprinting back to the centre line, the idea was to hold Rangers at the half way line from the goal kick.

Celtic did win the crucial ball, and seconds later, as the ball was placed harmlessly down the left, Mr Valentine signalled the end of the game and his own variegated refereeing career. Celtic had rescued their season in traditional fashion and had won the Scottish Cup for the 29th time. We would have to enjoy this one while we had it, for the Dark Ages, as bad as anything in the 1940's or the early 1960's, were about to descend. For the moment however, we had the last laugh.

—30—

HAPPY DAYS ARE HERE AGAIN
1995

Frankly, it was the clock in the top right hand corner of our screens that we were interested in. Any pretence of being football fans who were enjoying the game had long gone. We were just willing that BBC digital clock to go round faster. We knew that there had been a lot of stoppages for injuries, and that the magic figures of 90.00 would not be enough. At moments like these, what they say about your life passing in front of your eyes is true. The child of 40 years ago who had wearied of the Clyde v.Celtic game on TV and gone to play football in the street, thus missing the horror of the last minute Clyde equalizer, the teenager of 30 years previously who begged God and referee Hugh Phillips to blow for time in the Dunfermline game, the adult who neglected his one year old son in 1985 as the great fightback against Dundee United happened, and now the middle-ager who should have worried more about blood pressure and heart attacks.

The clock had passed 90.00 and Airdrie forced a corner on the right. 'There won't be too many more chances' said Jock Brown. A goal kick eventuated. The wife and teenage daughter appalled at the tension ridden expletives. 'Les Mottram has the destiny of the Scottish Cup in his hands' says Jock. The kick up field, 93.17 on the digital clock, the whistle, the euphoria, the tears, the regrets that the revered sage who had experienced all the Scottish Cup triumphs since Joe Cassidy in 1923 was no longer here to share this one.

The joy of victory was way out of proportion to the game itself and the team's performance had not been great. That was no surprise, for the last six years had not been great—in fact they had been a catalogue of disaster, involving mismanagement, and at one point virtual extinction of the great club. 1990 had seen genuine bad luck in a penalty shoot out against Aberdeen in the Scottish Cup Final and then in the autumn a narrow, unlucky defeat in the League Cup Final at the hands of Rangers and 1992's Semi Final in the rain was also creditable, but fruitless.

Apart from that, little good can be said about the early nineties, involving depression on a scale not seen since the early sixties. Appointments of managers got stranger and stranger - Billy McNeill 'too much of a supporter to be a manager' replaced by the likeable Irishman Liam Brady who naturally 'supported Celtic all his life' but who had never managed any team and the only real connection with Celtic Park was playing against us in the European Cup for Juventus. Then he gave way, along with Joe Jordan who could have done the job, to Lou Macari, a decision greeted with surprise.

But by March 1994, the guilty men, for whom little forgiveness is possible, had gone and in the summer Fergus McCann had appointed Tommy Burns as manager. This had to be a step in the right direction, for Tommy, a fine player and astute thinker about the game, had proved himself worthy at Kilmarnock. Killie cut up a bit rough about Tommy's departure, itself a tribute to him, but Tommy never said anything other than he was going to the team he supported. To the delight of the fans, he brought with him Billy Stark, a man who had performed so well in the Centenary season, and would have been an all time great if we had got him earlier.

On the playing side, however, there was hardly any great improvement. Playing at Hampden while Celtic Park was being refurbished, the team seemed able to do nothing but draw. Yet there were some good players on view - McStay was as always superb, John Collins, Tommy Boyd and others were Scottish Internationalists, Phil O'Donnell came from Motherwell, Tosh McKinlay from Hearts, and early in January 1995 there arrived from Holland, Pierre van Hooijdonk, not exactly a household name in Glasgow, but big, bustling and able, it would appear to solve the chronic goalscoring problem.

But before Christmas, the club had faced one of its biggest disasters. On November 27th, Celtic played Raith Rovers in the Coca Cola League Cup Final at Ibrox Park. This would surely be, we felt, the end of the trophy famine, for Raith had been relegated last season to the First Division and seemed to be full of a quaint mixture of has beens and unheard of youngsters. Celtic actually played some good football, but when they went ahead late in the game, a goalkeeping error let Raith equalize, and eventually the Kirkcaldy men triumphed in the cruellest of penalty shoot outs with Paul McStay, the most talented native Scotsman by some distance over a period of more than ten years, being the unlucky man who missed.

They danced in the streets of Raith that night, but wept in the Celtic heartlands. It was a result that would haunt Celtic all season, particularly in the run-up to the Scottish Cup Final when the Press never stopped reminding us that the opponents would be Airdrie, another First Division team. There was little quaint about Airdrie. They were tough, ruthless, professional and by no means the most popular team in the First Division because of their somewhat robust approach to the game. Managed by ex Rangers player and Hearts manager, Alec MacDonald, they did have something in common with Celtic, and that was that they were homeless, sharing in the 1994-5 season with Clyde at Broadwood in Cumbernauld.

It cannot be denied that Celtic had several advantages in their Scottish Cup campaign. Easy home ties against St.Mirren (a shadow of previous Buddies teams) and then Meadowbank were followed by another home tie against Kilmarnock. It was billed as a grudge match because of the boring on-going disputes about how much Celtic had to pay for poaching Burns and Stark, it took place on a Friday night, the floodlights failed and Celtic won on a somewhat lucky penalty. It would be safe to assume that on Cup Final day, Killie fans had been temporarily converted to Airdrie.

The Semi Finals threw up Hibs v. Celtic and Hearts v. Airdrie. Hearts had put out Rangers in the previous round and much was the talk of an all Edinburgh Cup Final. Such talk smacks of romanticism

Piere van Hooijdonk scores the only goal of the 1995 Scottish Cup Final.

(although it did happen 99 years previously in 1896) and both of the Capital's sides blew it. Celtic struggled in the first game against Hibs and even missed a penalty, but the second game saw Celtic turning it on and good goals by Falconer, Collins and O'Donnell brought an excellent 3-1 victory.

The Final was to be held at Hampden on the ridiculously late date of May 27th, when it could have been played a month earlier. This was all bound up with TV contracts for the worldwide audience, and it meant that we had some 6 weeks to sweat, trying not to think of Raith Rovers who incidentally in the meantime won the First Division Championship and hoping that our stay in the wilderness would soon be coming to an end. In the game which finally relegated Dundee United (Roy Aitken's Aberdeen escaped by the skin of their teeth and Hearts were equally lucky and earned the nickname the Jammy Tarts), Peter Grant, that great Celt, was badly injured and was rated as doubtful for the Cup Final.

Peter had a habit of missing Cup Finals. 1988 saw him injured, but fit enough to hug everybody at full time, and suspension had ruled him out of the Coca Cola disaster this year. Already Celtic would be without Tony Mowbray for the Final through suspension, and Peter's driving determination would be sadly missed. It would be a major effort, however, for Peter to be fit, the physio's and the medics sadly concluded. But Peter knows what it means to wear a green and white jersey, even though it involves pain, and thank heaven, the team would wear a green and white jersey on Cup Final day rather than some of the hideous concoctions we had seen this year. Equally thankfully, Peter would be wearing one.

Hampden's reconstruction was still not finished, and this meant that, unless you were a season ticket holder or had connections, your chances of getting into Hampden were virtually nil. Thus it was the BBC for most of us to take us through our agonies and ecstasies. The reassuring voice of Billy McNeill, as well as the clinically informative one of Jock Brown would also be with us. The teams on that fine early summer day were:

Celtic: Bonner, Boyd, McKinlay; Vata, McNally, Grant; McLaughlin, McStay, van Hooijdonk, Donnelly, Collins
Airdrie: Martin, Stewart, Jack; Sandison, Hay, Black; Boyle, Smith, Cooper, Harvey, Lawrence.

The referee was Mr Leslie Mottram of Wilsontown. Before the game started, Airdrie scored a major propaganda victory. As the Duchess of Kent, looking charmingly beautiful it must be said, was introduced to the Airdrie team, captain Sandison kissed her, a practice agreeably continued by the rest of the team. The referee however didn't, nor did the Celtic team, apart from veteran masseur Jimmy Steele who had been brought out as part of the official party.

At 3.00 however, the kissing and the kidding had to stop, and Celtic, playing towards the King's Park goal, stormed into their whirwind start, hoping for a quick goal. Before five minutes were up, they missed a good chance when Mark McNally headed a corner wide. Mark had had more than a few question marks at his name, but now with his hair brushed back, he was determined to prove his worth. He was disappointed at missing that chance.

But 4 minutes later Celtic were in the lead. Good work from Brian McLaughlin on the right, led to a ball coming across the penalty area. It was poorly punted up the field, only as far as Tosh McKinlay. Tosh, now playing for the team of his dreams following a varied and not always successful career with Dundee and Hearts, sent an inch perfect

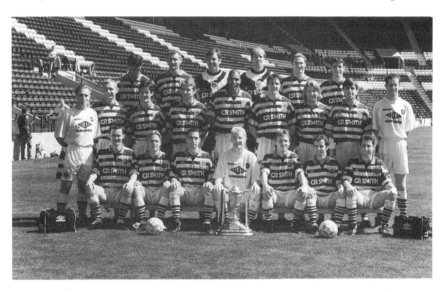

Back row: Willie Falconer, Tony Mowbray, Pat Bonner, Gordon Marshall, Stuart Gray, Phil O'Donnell. Middle row: Brian Scott, Peter Grant, Tosh McKinlay, Tom Boyd, Pierre van Hooijdonk, Malkie Mackay, Mark McNally, Rudi Vata, Billy Stark. Front row: Andy Walker, Simon Donnelly, Paul McStay, Tommy Burns (manager), Andreas Thom, Brian McLaughlin, John Collins.

ball onto the head of Pierre van Hooijdonk who immediately repaid his transfer fee by nodding home. It was a fine goal, in the Celtic tradition of McMahon, Quinn, McGrory and McNeill, and living rooms throughout the country erupted in acclaim.

Optimists now hoped that Celtic would score a barrowload, but the pessimists, for good recent historical reasons now outnumbering the optimists, noted with concern that we still had another 80 minutes to hold out. In this respect, the pessimists were correct for Celtic gradually now fell back and gave Airdrie more midfield possession than they should have. Matters were not helped when goalscorer van Hooijdonk was injured and had to go off before half time, being replaced by Willie Falconer that honest journeyman from Aberdeen.

Half time came and went, and we began to pace the floor yet again. A brilliant cross by Willie Falconer found John Collins's head, but John headed just wide. That would have given us an unbeatable lead, we felt, but that clock was just not going round fast enough. Phil O'Donnell was brought on, but the man that just kept impressing us was Peter Grant. Peter gave such a faultless and selfless display in the cause that day that the phrase 'playing for the jersey' took on a whole new significance. Shamelessly and heavily fouled by those who knew just exactly how to do it, Peter did not retaliate but kept going and played the game with one tackle on Alan Lawrence inside the penalty box coming into the brilliant category. He would thoroughly deserve his 'Man of the Match' award.

Those of us who have watched the video more than 12 times will agree that, in retrospect, Airdrie never really looked like scoring in that second half. But when you are sitting on the edge of your seat at Hampden or chewing your settee cushions at home, you cannot take such things for granted. However, the whistle came (you do actually, on the video, hear the sound of the whistle above the hubbub of the crowd) and euphoria, bedlam, rapture and ecstasy broke out.

Some booed the Airdrie lads as they climbed the rostrum for their losers' medals, others, remembering what it is like to lose a final, were more magnanimous. Paul McStay had at last won something as captain of Celtic. Was this the dawning of a new glory age? A sober reflection of the team would have to point out one or two deficiencies, but who wanted to be sober, in any sense of the word? 103 years ago, the cry had been 'Our Bhoys Have Won The Cup!' throughout the teeming humanity of Glasgow's East End. WE had now done it for the 30th time. The feelings of heartfelt relief and grateful thanks can never have been greater than on that glorious 27th of May, 1995.

SCOTTISH CUP 1888–1996
(Celtic scores first)

1888-89	01/09/88	Shettleston	h	5-1	goalscorers untraced
	22/09/88	Cowlairs	h	8-0	Dunbar 3, McCallum 2, T.Maley, Kelly, Groves
	13/10/88	Albion Rovers	h	4-1	Groves, 3 untraced
	03/11/88	St.Bernard's	a	4-1	Groves 2, McCallum, T.Maley
	08/12/88	Clyde	h	9-2	T.Maley 3, Groves 2, McCallum 2, McLaren, Coleman
	15/12/88	East Stirling	a	2-1	McCallum 2
	12/01/89	Dumbarton	a	4-1	Groves3, McCallum
	02/02/89	Third Lanark	Hampden	0-3	
	declared unofficial because of snow				
	09/02/89	Third Lanark	Hampden	1-2	McCallum
1889-90	07/09/89	Queen's Park	a	0-0	
	abandoned due to crowd encroachment				
	14/09/89	Queen's Park	a	1-2	Dowds
1890-91	06/09/90	Rangers	h	1-0	Groves
	27/09/90	Carfin Shamrock	h	2-2	Madden 2
	04/10/90	Carfin Shamrock	a	3-1	Groves, Dowds, McQuade o.g.
	18/10/90	Wishaw Thistle	a	6-2	Madden 2, Dowds, Campbell, 2 untraced
	08/11/90	Our Boys	a	3-1	Crossan 2, Coleman
	13/12/90	Royal Albert	Ibrox	2-0	Crossan, Campbell
	20/12/90	Dumbarton	a	0-3	
1891-92	28/11/91	St.Mirren	a	4-2	Madden, McMahon, W.Maley, McFarlane o.g.
	19/12/91	Kilmarnock Ath	h	3-0	Brady 2, Dowds
	23/01/92	Cowlairs	h	4-1	Brady 2, Madden, McMahon
	06/02/92	Rangers	h	5-3	Brady 2, Cunningham, McMahon, McCallum
	12/03/92	Queen's Park	Ibrox	1-0	Campbell
	declared unofficial due to crowd encroachment				

SCOTTISH CUP 1888–1996

	09/04/92	Queen's Park	Ibrox	5-1	Campbell 2, McMahon 2, untraced o.g.
1892-3	26/11/92	Linthouse	h	3-1	McMahon 2, Madden
	17/12/92	5th K.R.V.	h	7-0	Madden 5, Blessington Campbell
	02/01/93	Third Lanark	h	5-1	McMahon 3, Towie 2
	04/02/93	St.Bernard's	h	5-0	Madden 3, Blessington 2
	11/03/93	Queen's Park	Ibrox	1-2	Blessington
1893-94	25/11/93	Hurlford	h	6-0	Blessington 2, Campbell 2 McMahon, Cassidy
	16/12/93	Albion Rovers	h	7-0	Cassidy 4, Madden 2, Blessington
	13/01/94	St.Bernard's	h	8-1	McMahon 4, Madden 2, Cassidy, Maley
	03/02/94	Third Lanark	a	5-3	McMahon 3, Blessington, Cassidy
	17/02/94	Rangers	Hampden	1-3	Maley
1894-95	24/11/94	Queen's Park	h	4-1	Campbell 3, Divers
	29/12/94	Hibs	a	2-0	Campbell, Divers
	19/01/95	Dundee	a	0-1	
1895-96	18/01/96	Queen's Park	h	2-4	Blessington, Doyle
1896-97	09/01/97	Arthurlie	a	2-4	Ferguson, McIlvenny
1897-98	08/01/98	Arthurlie	a	7-0	McMahon 2, Henderson 2, Allan, Goldie, Campbell
	22/01/98	Third Lanark	a	2-3	Campbell, King
1898-99	14/01/99	6th G.R.V.	a	8-1	McMahon 3, Hodge 2, King, Divers, Campbell
	04/02/99	St.Bernard's	h	3-0	McMahon, Hodge, Campbell
	18/02/99	Queen's Park	a	4-2	untraced
		match abandoned due to bad light			
	25/02/99	Queen's Park	h	2-1	McMahon 2

	11/03/99	Port Glasgow	h	4-2	Bell 2, McMahon, Divers
	22/04/99	Rangers	Hampden	2-0	McMahon, Hodge
1899-1900	13/01/1900	Bo'ness	h	7-1	McMahon 2, Somers 2, Orr Divers, Bell
	27/01/1900	Port Glasgow	a	5-1	Campbell 3, Gilhooly 2
	17/02/1900	Kilmarnock	h	4-0	Gilhooly, Bell, McMahon, Divers
	24/02/1900	Rangers	a	2-2	Campbell, Bell
	10/03/1900	Rangers	h	4-0	McMahon 2, Hodge, Bell
	14/04/1900	Queen's Park	Ibrox	4-3	Divers 2, McMahon, Bell
1900-01	12/01/01	Rangers	h	1-0	Drummond o.g.
	09/02/01	Kilmarnock	h	6-0	Campbell 2, Divers, McOustra, McMahon, Findlay
	16/02/01	Dundee	a	1-0	Findlay
	23/03/01	St. Mirren	h	1-0	Campbell
	06/04/01	Hearts	Ibrox	3-4	McOustra, Quinn, McMahon
1901-02	11/01/02	Thornliebank	h	3-0	Livingstone 2, Campbell
	25/01/02	Arbroath	a	3-2	Campbell, Marshall, Orr
	15/02/02	Hearts	a	1-1	Quinn
	22/02/02	Hearts	h	2-1	McMahon 2
	22/03/02	St.Mirren	a	3-2	Livingstone, McDermott, Campbell
	26/04/02	Hibs	h	0-1	
1902-03	24/01/03	St.Mirren	h	0-0	
	31/01/03	St.Mirren	a	1-1	McDermott
	14/02/03	St.Mirren	h	4-0	Campbell, Murray, McMahon, Watson
	21/02/03	Port Glasgow	h	2-0	Campbell, McDermott
	28/02/03	Rangers	h	0-3	
1903-04	13/02/04	St.Bernard's	a	4-0	McMenemy 2, Orr 2
	20/02/04	Dundee	h	1-1	Hamilton
	27/02/04	Dundee	a	0-0	

	05/03/04	Dundee	h	5-0	McMenemy 2, Bennett, Quinn, Muir
	19/03/04	Third Lanark	h	2-1	Quinn, Muir
	16/04/04	Rangers	Hampden	3-2	Quinn 3
1904-05	28/01/05	Dumfries	a	2-1	Quinn, Bennett
	11/02/05	Lochgelly Utd	h	3-0	Somers, Orr (pen), Quinn
	25/02/05	Partick Thistle	h	3-0	Somers, Orr (pen), Bennett
	25/03/05	Rangers	h	0-2	
1905-06	27/01/06	Dundee	a	2-1	Somers, Henderson o.g
	10/02/06	Bo'ness	h	3-0	McMenemy, Loney, Quinn
	24/02/06	Hearts	h	1-2	McMenemy
1906-07	02/02/07	Clyde	h	2-1	Hamilton, Bennett
	09/02/07	Morton	a	0-0	
	16/02/07	Morton	h	1-1	McMenemy
	23/02/07	Morton	h	2-1	McMenemy, Hay
	09/03/07	Rangers	a	3-0	Hamilton, Hay, Somers
	30/03/07	Hibs	h	0-0	
	06/04/07	Hibs	a	0-0	
	13/04/07	Hibs	h	3-0	Somers, Quinn, McMenemy
	20/04/07	Hearts	Hampden	3-0	Somers 2, Orr (pen)
1907-08	25/01/08	Peebles Rovs	h	4-0	Kivlichan 2, Hamilton, Somers
	08/02/08	Rangers	a	2-1	Kivlichan 2
	22/02/08	Raith Rovers	a	3-0	McMenemy 2, Kivlichan
	21/03/08	Aberdeen	a	1-0	McMenemy
	18/04/08	St.Mirren	Hampden	5-1	Bennett 2, Hamilton, Somers, Quinn
1908-09	23/01/09	Leith Athletic	a	4-2	Quinn 3, Hay
	06/02/09	Port Glasgow	h	4-0	Hay 2, Quinn, Hamilton
	20/02/09	Airdrie	h	3-1	McMenemy 2, Hamilton
	20/03/09	Clyde	h	0-0	
	27/03/09	Clyde	h	2-0	Quinn, Somers
	10/04/09	Rangers	Hampden	2-2	Quinn, Munro

	17/04/09	Rangers	Hampden	1-1	Quinn
		Cup withheld due to riot			
1909-10	22/01/10	Dumbarton	a	2-1	Loney, McMenemy
	12/02/10	Third Lanark	h	3-1	Quinn 3
	19/02/10	Aberdeen	h	2-1	Quinn, McMenemy
	12/03/10	Clyde	a	1-3	Kivlichan
1910-11	28/01/11	St.Mirren	h	2-0	McMenemy, Hastie
	11/02/11	Galston	h	1-0	Quinn
	25/02/11	Clyde	h	1-0	McMenemy
	11/03/11	Aberdeen	h	1-0	Quinn
	08/04/11	Hamilton A	Ibrox	0-0	
	15/04/11	Hamilton A	Ibrox	2-0	Quinn, McAteer
1911-12	27/01/12	Dunfermline A	h	1-0	Brown
	10/02/12	East Stirling	h	3-0	Quinn 2, Travers
	24/02/12	Aberdeen	a	2-2	Quinn, McAtee
	09/03/12	Aberdeen	h	2-0	Travers 2
	30/03/12	Hearts	Ibrox	3-0	McMenemy 2, Brown
	06/04/12	Clyde	Ibrox	2-0	McMenemy, Gallagher
1912-13	08/02/13	Arbroath	h	4-0	Johnstone 2, Gallagher, Brown
	22/02/13	Peebles Rovs	h	3-0	McMenemy 2, Quinn
	08/03/13	Hearts	h	0-1	
1913-14	07/02/14	Clyde	a	0-0	
	10/02/14	Clyde	h	2-0	Gallagher 2
	21/02/14	Forfar Athletic	a	5-0	McColl 3, Dodds, McMenemy
	07/03/14	Motherwell	a	3-1	Gallagher, McColl, McAtee
	28/03/14	Third Lanark	a	2-0	McAtee, Owers
	11/04/14	Hibernian	Ibrox	0-0	
	16/04/14	Hibernian	Ibrox	4-1	McColl 2, Browning 2
1914-1919		Competition suspended because of First World War			
1919-20	07/02/20	Dundee	a	3-1	McLean, McInally, Cringan
	21/02/20	Partick Thistle	h	2-0	McInally, McStay
	06/03/20	Rangers	a	0-1	
1920-21	05/02/21	Vale of Leven	a	3-0	Cassidy 2, McLean
	19/02/21	East Fife	a	3-1	McInally 2, Gallagher

	05/03/21	Hearts	h	1-2	Gallagher
1921-22	28/01/22	Montrose	h	4-0	McFarlane 2, McInally, McLean
	11/02/22	Third Lanark	a	1-0	McLean
	25/02/22	Hamilton A	h	1-3	Dodds
1922-23	13/01/23	Lochgelly Utd	a	3-2	Cassidy 3
	27/01/23	Hurlford	h	4-0	Cassidy 4
	10/02/23	East Fife	h	2-1	Cassidy 2
	24/02/23	Raith Rovers	h	1-0	McLean
	10/02/23	Motherwell	Ibrox	2-0	Cassidy, McAtee
	31/03/23	Hibernian	Hampden	1-0	Cassidy
1923-24	26/01/24	Kilmarnock	a	0-2	
1924-25	24/01/25	Third Lanark	a	5-1	McGrory 3, Gallagher, Thomson
	07/02/25	Alloa	h	2-1	McGrory 2
	21/02/25	Solway Star	h	2-0	McGrory, Thomson
	07/03/25	St.Mirren	a	0-0	
	10/03/25	St.Mirren	h	1-1	McGrory
	16/03/25	St.Mirren	Ibrox	1-0	McGrory
	21/03/25	Rangers	Hampden	5-0	McGrory 2, McLean 2, Thomson
	11/04/25	Dundee	Hampden	2-1	McGrory, Gallagher
1925-26	23/01/26	Kilmarnock	a	5-0	Thomson 2, McLean, McInally, McGrory
	06/02/26	Hamilton A	h	4-0	Thomson, McLean, McInally, McGrory
	20/02/26	Hearts	a	4-0	McInally, McGrory, Connolly
	06/03/26	Dumbarton	h	6-1	McGrory 2, McLean 2, Thomson, W.McStay (pen}
	20/03/26	Aberdeen	Tynecastle	2-1	McGrory, McInally
	10/04/26	St.Mirren	Hampden	0-2	
1926-27	22/01/27	Q.O.S.	a	0-0	
	26/01/27	Q.O.S.	h	4-1	McGrory 2, McLean, Thomson
	05/02/27	Brechin City	a	6-3	McGrory 4, McLean, Thomson
	19/02/27	Dundee	a	4-2	McGrory, McLean, Connolly, W.McStay
	05/03/27	Bo'ness	a	5-2	McGrory 2, McLean, Thomson, McInally

	26/03/27	Falkirk	Ibrox	1-0	McLean
	16/04/27	East Fife	Hampden	3-1	McLean, Connolly, Robertson o.g.
1927-28	21/01/28	Bathgate	h	3-1	McGrory, McLean, McInally
	04/02/28	Keith	a	6-1	McGrory 3, McInally 3
	18/02/28	Alloa	h	2-0	McGrory, Connolly
	03/03/28	Motherwell	a	2-0	McGrory, Doyle
	24/03/28	Queen's Park	Ibrox	2-1	McGrory, McLean
	14/04/28	Rangers	Hampden	0-4	
1928-29	19/01/29	Arthurlie	h	5-1	McGrory 3, Connolly, J.McStay
	02/02/29	East Stirling	h	3-0	McGrory 2, J.McStay
	16/02/29	Arbroath	h	4-1	McGrory 4
	06/03/29	Motherwell	h	0-0	
	13/03/29	Motherwell	a	2-1	McGrory, Connolly
	23/03/29	Kilmarnock	Ibrox	0-1	
1929-30	18/01/30	Inverness Cal	a	6-0	McGrory 3, Wilson Connolly, Napier
	01/02/30	Arbroath	h	5-0	McGrory 2, A.Thomson, R.Thomson, Scarff
	15/02/30	St.Mirren	h	1-3	A.Thomson
1930-31	17/01/31	East Fife	a	2-1	Scarff, Napier
	04/02/31	Dundee Utd	a	3-2	Scarff 2, Napier
	14/02/31	Morton	a	4-1	McGrory 3, Napier
	28/02/31	Aberdeen	h	4-0	R.Thomson 3, McGrory
	14/03/31	Kilmarnock	Hampden	3-0	Napier. McGrory, Hughes
	11/04/31	Motherwell	Hampden	2-2	McGrory, Craig o.g.
	15/04/31	Motherwell	Hampden	4-2	McGrory 2, R.Thomson 2
1931-32	16/01/32	Falkirk	h	3-2	Napier 2, R.Thomson
	30/01/32	St.Johnstone	a	4-2	Napier 3, A.Thomson
	13/02/32	Motherwell	a	0-2	
1932-33	21/01/33	Dunfermline	a	7-1	McGrory 3, H.O'Donnell 3, R.Thomson
	04/02/33	Falkirk	h	2-0	McGrory 2
	18/02/33	Partick Thistle	h	2-1	McGrory, R.Thomson
	04/03/33	Albion Rovers	a	1-1	Napier

	08/03/33	Albion Rovers	h	3-1	Napier 2, A.Thomson
	18/03/33	Hearts	Hampden	0-0	
	22/03/33	Hearts	Hampden	2-1	McGrory, A.Thomson
	15/04/33	Motherwell	Hampden	1-0	McGrory
1933-34	20/01/34	Dalbeattie Star	a	6-0	Crum 4, F.O'Donnell 2
	03/02/33	Ayr United	a	3-2	F.O'Donnell, H.O'Donnell, McGonagle
	17/02/33	Falkirk	h	3-1	F.O'Donnell 2, McGrory
	03/03/34	St.Mirren	a	0-2	
1934-35	26/01/35	Montrose	h	4-1	F.O'Donnell 2, Paterson, Buchan
	09/02/35	Partick Thistle	h	1-1	H.O'Donnell
	13/02/35	Partick Thistle	a	3-1	H.O'Donnell 2, McGrory
	09/03/35	Aberdeen	a	1-3	McGrory
1935-36	Berwick Rangers scratched				
	08/02/36	St.Johnstone	h	1-2	Buchan
1936-37	30/01/37	Stenhousemuir	a	1-1	McGrory
	03/02/37	Stenhousemuir	h	2-0	McGrory 2
	13/02/37	Albion Rovers	a	5-2	McGrory 2, Buchan 2, Delaney
	27/02/37	East Fife	a	3-0	McGrory 2, Buchan
	17/03/37	Motherwell	h	4-4	Crum 2, Lyon, Buchan
	24/03/37	Motherwell	a	2-1	McGrory, Buchan
	03/04/37	Clyde	Ibrox	2-0	McGrory, Robb o.g.
	24/04/37	Aberdeen	Hampden	2-1	Crum, Buchan
1937-38	22/01/38	Third Lanark	a	2-1	Crum 2
	12/02/38	Nithsdale W	h	5-0	Murphy 3, Carruth 2
	05/03/38	Kilmarnock	h	1-2	MacDonald
1938-39	21/01/39	Burntisland	a	8-3	MacDonald 3, Crum 2, Watters, Murphy, Delaney
	04/02/39	Montrose	a	7-1	Crum 3, Divers 2, Delaney MacDonald
	18/02/39	Hearts	a	2-2	Delaney, MacDonald
	22/02/39	Hearts	h	2-1	Divers 2
	04/03/39	Motherwell	a	1-3	Delaney

1939-1946		Competition suspended because of Second World War			
1946-47	25/01/47	Dundee	a	1-2	McAloon
1947-48	07/02/48	Cowdenbeath	h	3-0	McPhail 2, W. Gallacher
	21/02/48	Motherwell	h	1-0	Paton
	06/03/48	Montrose	h	4-0	McPhail 2, Weir, Paton
	27/03/48	Morton	Ibrox	0-1	
1948-49	22/01/49	Dundee Utd	a	3-4	J.Gallacher 2, Tully
1949-50	28/01/50	Brechin City	a	3-0	Weir 2, McPhail
	15/02/50	Third Lanark	a	1-1	Weir
	20/02/50	Third Lanark	h	4-1	McPhail 3, Tully
	25/02/50	Aberdeen	h	0-1	
1950-51	27/01/51	East Fife	a	2-2	J.Weir, Collins
	31/01/51	East Fife	h	4-2	McPhail 2, Peacock, Collins
	10/02/51	Duns	h	4-0	J.Weir 2, Peacock, D.Weir
	24/02/51	Hearts	a	2-1	J.Weir, McPhail
	10/03/51	Aberdeen	h	3-0	McPhail 2, Tully
	31/03/51	Raith Rovers	Hampden	3-2	J.Weir, McPhail, Tully
	21/04/51	Motherwell	Hampden	1-0	McPhail
1951-52	30/01/52	Third Lanark	h	0-0	
	04/02/52	Third Lanark	a	1-2	Rollo (after extra time)
1952-53	24/01/53	Eyemouth U	a	4-0	McGrory 4
	07/02/53	Stirling Albion	a	1-1	McGrory
	11/02/53	Stirling Albion	h	3-0	McGrory 2, Peacock
	21/02/53	Falkirk	a	3-2	McGrory, Tully, Fernie
	14/03/53	Rangers	a	0-2	
1953-54	17/02/54	Falkirk	a	2-1	Fernie, Higgins
	27/02/54	Stirling Albion	a	4-3	Mochan 2, Higgins Haughney (pen)
	13/03/54	Hamilton A	a	2-1	Fernie, Haughney (pen)
	27/03/54	Motherwell	Hampden	2-2	Mochan, Fallon
	05/04/54	Motherwell	Hampden	3-1	Mochan, Fernie, Kilmarnock o.g.
	24/04/54	Aberdeen	Hampden	2-1	Fallon, Young o.g.

1954-55	05/02/55	Alloa	a	4-2	Walsh 2, Peacock, Haughney (pen)
	19/02/55	Kilmarnock	a	1-1	Smith
	23/02/55	Kilmarnock	h	1-0	Walsh
	05/03/55	Hamilton A	h	2-1	Collins, Fernie
	26/03/55	Airdrie	Hampden	2-2	Fernie, Walsh
	04/03/55	Airdrie	Hampden	2-0	McPhail 2
	23/04/55	Clyde	Hampden	1-1	Walsh
	27/04/55	Clyde	Hampden	0-1	
1955-56	04/02/56	Morton	a	2-0	Tully, Collins
	18/02/56	Ayr United	a	3-0	Collins 2, Mochan
	03/03/56	Airdrie	h	2-1	Collins, Tully
	24/03/56	Clyde	Hampden	2-1	Sharkey, Haughney (pen)
	21/04/56	Hearts	Hampden	1-3	Haughney
1956-57	02/02/57	Forres Mech	a	5-0	W. McPhail 3, Higgins, Mochan
	16/02/57	Rangers	h	4-4	W.McPhail, Higgins, Collins, Fernie
	20/02/57	Rangers	a	2-0	Higgins, Mochan
	02/03/57	St.Mirren	h	2-1	Higgins, Peacock
	23/03/57	Kilmarnock	Hampden	1-1	Higgins
	27/03/57	Kilmarnock	Hampden	1-3	Collins
1957-58	01/02/58	Airdrie	a	4-3	Byrne 2, Collins, Fernie
	15/02/58	Stirling Albion	h	7-2	Byrne 2, Smith 2, Wilson 2, Mochan
	01/03/58	Clyde	a	0-2	
	(match played at Celtic Park for safety reasons)				
1958-59	31/01/59	Albion Rovers	h	4-0	Wilson 2, Jackson, Kerr o.g
	18/02/59	Clyde	h	1-1	McVittie
	23/02/59	Clyde	a	4-3	Wilson 2, McVittie, (after extra time) Peacock
	28/02/59	Rangers	h	2-1	Divers, McVittie
	16/03/59	Stirling Albion	a	3-1	Divers, Wilson, Lochhead
	04/04/59	St.Mirren	Hampden	0-4	
1959-60	13/02/60	St.Mirren	a	1-1	Byrne
	24/02/60	St.Mirren	h	4-4	Mochan 2, Divers 2 (after extra time)

	29/02/60	St.Mirren	h	5-2	Mochan 5 (1 penalty)
	05/03/60	Elgin City	a	2-1	Divers, Smith
	12/03/60	Partick Thistle	h	2-0	Smith, Colrain
	02/04/60	Rangers	Hampden	1-1	Chalmers
	06/04/60	Rangers	Hampden	1-4	Mochan
1960-61	28/01/61	Falkirk	a	3-1	Peacock 2 (both penalties) Auld
	11/02/61	Montrose	h	6-0	Hughes 2, Chalmers 2, Byrne, McCorquodale o.g
	25/02/61	Raith Rovers	a	4-1	Hughes, Chalmers, Fernie Leigh o.g
	11/03/61	Hibernian	h	1-1	Chalmers
	15/03/61	Hibernian	a	1-0	Clark (after extra time)
	01/04/61	Airdrie	Hampden	4-0	Hughes 2, Chalmers, Fernie
	22/04/61	Dunfermline A	Hampden	0-0	
	26/04/61	Dunfermline A	Hampden	0-2	
1961-62	13/12/61	Cowdenbeath	h	5-1	Chalmers 2, Jackson, Hughes, Divers
	27/01/62	Morton	a	3-1	Carroll, Divers, Jackson
	17/02/62	Hearts	a	4-3	Divers 2, Chalmers Crerand (pen)
	10/03/62	Third Lanark	h	4-4	Chalmers 2, Hughes, F.Brogan
	14/03/62	Third Lanark	a	4-0	Hughes 2, Chalmers, Byrne
	played at Hampden for safety reasons				
	31/03/62	St.Mirren	Ibrox	1-3	Byrne
1962-63	28/01/63	Falkirk	a	2-0	Hughes, Gallagher
	06/03/63	Hearts	h	3-1	Murdoch, McNamee, Hughes
	13/03/63	Gala Fairydean	h	6-0	Murdoch 3, Hughes 2, Divers
	30/03/63	St.Mirren	a	1-0	F.Brogan
	13/04/63	Raith Rovers	Ibrox	5-2	McKay 2 (both penalties), Chalmers, Divers, F.Brogan
	04/05/63	Rangers	Hampden	1-1	Murdoch

	15/05/63	Rangers	Hampden	0-3	
1963-64	11/01/64	Eyemouth	h	3-0	Chalmers 2, Gallagher
	25/01/64	Morton	a	3-1	Hughes, Gallagher, Johnstone
	15/02/64	Airdrie	h	4-1	Chalmers, Hughes, Johnstone, Murdoch (pen)
	07/03/64	Rangers	a	0-2	
1964-65	06/02/65	St.Mirren	a	3-0	Lennox 2, Chalmers
	20/02/65	Queen's Park	a	1-0	Lennox
	06/03/65	Kilmarnock	h	3-2	Lennox, Auld, Hughes
	27/03/65	Motherwell	Hampden	2-2	Lennox, Auld (pen)
	31/03/65	Motherwell	Hampden	3-0	Lennox, Chalmers, Hughes
	24/04/65	Dunfermline	Hampden	3-2	Auld 2, McNeill
1965-66	05/02/66	Stranraer	h	4-0	Gallagher, Murdoch, Lennox, McBride
	23/02/66	Dundee	a	2-0	Chalmers, McBride
	05/03/66	Hearts	a	3-3	Chalmers, McBride, Auld
	09/03/66	Hearts	h	3-1	Chalmers, Johnstone, Murdoch
	26/03/66	Dunfermline	Ibrox	2-0	Chalmers, Auld
	23/04/66	Rangers	Hampden	0-0	
	27/04/66	Rangers	Hampden	0-1	
1966-67	28/01/67	Arbroath	h	4-0	Murdoch, Gemmell, Auld, Chalmers
	18/02/67	Elgin City	h	7-0	Lennox 3, Wallace 2, Hughes, Chalmers
	11/03/67	Queen's Park	h	5-3	Gemmell (pen), Wallace, Murdoch, Chalmers, Lennox
	01/04/67	Clyde	Hampden	0-0	
	05/04/67	Clyde	Hampden	2-0	Lennox, Auld
	29/04/67	Aberdeen	Hampden	2-0	Wallace 2
1967-68	27/01/68	Dunfermline	h	0-2	
1968-69	25/01/69	Partick Thistle	a	3-3	Hughes, Wallace, Murdoch
	29/01/69	Partick Thistle	h	8-1	Callaghan 2, Lennox, Hughes, Gemmell, Johnstone, McNeill, Wallace

	12/02/69	Clyde	a	0-0	
	24/02/69	Clyde	h	3-0	Chalmers, Hughes, Murdoch
	01/03/69	St.Johnstone	h	3-2	Chalmers, Hughes, Lennox
	22/03/69	Morton	Hampden	4-1	Chalmers, McNeill, Wallace, Johnstone
	26/04/69	Rangers	Hampden	4-0	McNeill, Lennox, Connelly, Chalmers
1969-70	24/01/70	Dunfermline	h	2-1	Hughes, Hood
	07/02/70	Dundee Utd	h	4-0	Hughes 2, Macari, Wallace
	21/02/70	Rangers	h	3-1	Lennox, Hay, Johnstone
	14/03/70	Dundee	Hampden	2-1	Lennox, Macari
	11/04/70	Aberdeen	Hampden	1-3	Lennox
1970-71	23/01/71	Q.O.S	h	5-1	Hood 2, Callaghan, Wallace, McNeill
	13/02/71	Dunfermline	h	1-1	Wallace
	17/02/71	Dunfermline	a	1-0	Hood
	06/03/71	Raith Rovers	h	7-1	Lennox 3, Gemmell (pen) Callaghan, Wallace, Davidson
	03/04/71	Airdrie	Hampden	3-3	Hood 2, Johnstone
	07/04/71	Airdrie	Hampden	2-0	Johnstone, Hood
	08/05/71	Rangers	Hampden	1-1	Lennox
	12/05/71	Rangers	Hampden	2-1	Macari, Hood (pen)
1971-72	05/02/72	Albion Rovers	h	5-0	Callaghan 2, Macari, Deans, Murdoch
	26/02/72	Dundee	h	4-0	Lennox 2, Dalglish, Deans
	18/03/72	Hearts	h	1-1	Deans
	27/03/72	Hearts	a	1-0	Macari
	12/04/72	Kilmarnock	Hampden	3-1	Deans 2, Macari
	06/05/72	Hibernian	Hampden	6-1	Deans 3, Macari 2, McNeill
1972-73	03/02/73	East Fife	h	4-1	Deans 2, Dalglish 2
	24/02/73	Motherwell	h	4-0	Deans 2, Dalglish, Lennox
	17/03/73	Aberdeen	h	0-0	
	21/03/73	Aberdeen	a	1-0	McNeill
	07/04/73	Dundee	Hampden	0-0	
	11/04/73	Dundee	Hampden	3-0	Johnstone 2, Dalglish (after extra time)

	05/05/73	Rangers	Hampden	2-3	Dalglish, Connelly (pen)
1973-74	27/01/74	Clydebank	h	6-1	Deans 3, Lennox 2, Davidson
	17/02/74	Stirling Albion	h	6-1	Hood 2, Murray 2, Dalglish Wilson
	10/03/74	Motherwell	h	2-2	Hood 2
	13/03/74	Motherwell	a	1-0	Deans
	03/04/74	Dundee	Hampden	1-0	Johnstone
	04/05/74	Dundee Utd	Hampden	3-0	Hood, Murray, Deans
1974-75	25/01/75	Hibernian	a	2-0	Deans, Murray
	15/02/75	Clydebank	h	4-1	Dalglish 2, McNamara, MacDonald
	08/03/75	Dumbarton	a	2-1	Glavin, Wilson
	02/04/75	Dundee	Hampden	1-0	Glavin
	03/05/75	Airdrie	Hampden	3-1	Wilson 2, P.McCluskey(pen)
1975-76	24/01/76	Motherwell	a	2-3	Dalglish, Lynch
1976-77	29/01/77	Airdrie	a	1-1	Doyle
	02/02/77	Airdrie	h	5-0	Craig 4, Glavin
	27/02/77	Ayr United	h	1-1	Glavin
	02/03/77	Ayr United	a	3-1	Glavin (pen), Doyle, Aitken
	13/03/77	Q.O.S.	h	5-1	Glavin 3 (2 penalties), Craig, Dalglish
	06/04/77	Dundee	Hampden	2-0	Craig 2
	07/05/77	Rangers	Hampden	1-0	Lynch (pen)
1977-78	06/02/78	Dundee	h	7-1	G.McCluskey 3, McAdam 2 Burns, MacDonald
	27/02/78	Kilmarnock	h	1-1	MacDonald
	06/03/78	Kilmarnock	a	0-1	
1978-79	31/01/79	Montrose	a	4-2	G.McCluskey 3, Lynch (pen)
	26/02/79	Berwick R	h	3-0	Lynch (pen), Burns, McDowell o.g.
	10/03/79	Aberdeen	a	1-1	Doyle
	14/03/79	Aberdeen	h	1-2	Lennox
1979-80	26/01/80	Raith Rovers	h	2-1	Lennox, Doyle
	16/02/80	St.Mirren	h	1-1	MacLeod

	20/02/80	St.Mirren	a	3-2	Doyle 2, Lennox (pen) after extra time
	08/03/80	Morton	h	2-0	Casey, McCluskey
	12/04/80	Hibernian	Hampden	5-0	Lennox, Provan, Doyle, McAdam, MacLeod
	10/05/80	Rangers	Hampden	1-0	McCluskey after extra time
1980-81	24/01/81	Berwick R	a	2-0	Nicholas, Burns
	14/02/81	Stirling Albion	h	3-0	McGarvey, McCluskey, Burns
	08/03/81	East Stirling	h	2-0	Conroy, MacLeod
	11/04/81	Dundee Utd	Hampden	0-0	
	15/04/81	Dundee Utd	Hampden	2-3	Nicholas 2 (1 penalty)
1981-82	23/01/82	Q.O.S.	h	4-0	McGarvey, McGrain, McCluskey (pen), Halpin
	13/02/82	Aberdeen	a	0-1	
1982-83	28/01/83	Clydebank	a	3-0	Nicholas 2, McCluskey
	19/02/83	Dunfermline	h	3-0	McGarvey 2, McCluskey
	12/03/83	Hearts	h	4-1	Nicholas 2, MacLeod, McGarvey
	16/04/83	Aberdeen	Hampden	0-1	
1983-84	28/01/84	Berwick R	a	4-0	McClair 2, McGarvey, Melrose
	18/02/84	East Fife	a	6-0	Burns 2, McGarvey, McClair, Colquhoun, MacLeod
	17/03/84	Motherwell	a	6-0	McClair 2, Reid, Burns McGarvey, MacLeod
	14/04/84	St.Mirren	Hampden	2-1	McClair, P.McStay
	19/05/84	Aberdeen	Hampden	1-2	P.McStay after extra time
1984-85	30/01/85	Hamilton A	a	2-1	McGarvey 2
	16/01/85	Inverness Th	h	6-0	P.McStay 3, Johnston, McGarvey, MacLeod
	09/03/85	Dundee	a	1-1	Johnston
	13/03/85	Dundee	h	2-1	McGarvey, Johnston
	13/04/85	Motherwell	Hampden	1-1	Burns
	17/04/85	Motherwell	Hampden	3-0	Johnston 2, Aitken
	18/05/85	Dundee Utd	Hampden	2-1	Provan, McGarvey
1985-86	25/01/86	St.Johnstone	h	2-0	Grant, Johnston
	15/02/86	Queen's Park	h	2-1	McClair, Aitken

	08/03/86	Hibernian	a	3-4	McClair 2 (1 pen), McGhee
1986-87	01/02/87	Aberdeen	a	2-2	McClair, McInally
	04/02/87	Aberdeen	h	0-0	after extra time
	09/02/87	Aberdeen	Dens	1-0	McClair
	21/02/87	Hearts	a	0-1	
1987-88	30/01/88	Stranraer	h	1-0	McAvennie
	21/02/88	Hibernian	h	0-0	
	24/02/88	Hibernian	a	1-0	Stark
	12/03/88	Partick Thistle	a	3-0	Walker, Burns, Stark
	09/04/88	Hearts	Hampden	2-1	McGhee, Walker
	14/05/88	Dundee Utd	Hampden	2-1	McAvennie 2
1988-89	28/01/89	Dumbarton	h	2-0	Walker, Burns
	18/02/89	Clydebank	h	4-1	Burns 2, McAvennie, Stark
	18/03/89	Hearts	h	2-1	McGhee, Aitken (pen)
	16/04/89	Hibernian	Hampden	3-1	McCarthy, McGhee, Walker
	20/05/89	Rangers	Hampden	1-0	Miller
1989-90	20/01/90	Forfar Ath	a	2-1	Morris(pen), Dziekanowski
	24/02/90	Rangers	h	1-0	Coyne
	17/03/90	Dunfermline	a	0-0	
	21/03/90	Dunfermline	h	3-0	McStay, Coyne, Miller
	14/04/90	Clydebank	Hampden	2-0	Walker 2
	12/05/90	Aberdeen	Hampden	0-0	after extra time. Aberdeen won 9-8 on penalties
1990-91	26/01/91	Forfar Ath	a	2-0	Wdowczyk, Coyne
	26/02/91	St.Mirren	h	3-0	Miller, Creaney, McWhirter o.g.
	17/03/91	Rangers	h	2-0	Creaney, Wdowczyk
	03/04/91	Motherwell	Hampden	0-0	
	09/04/91	Motherwell	Hampden	2-4	Boyd o.g., Rogan
1991-92	22/01/92	Montrose	h	6-0	Creaney 3, Coyne 3
	11/02/92	Dundee Utd	h	2-1	Creaney, Coyne
	07/03/92	Morton	h	3-0	Creaney 2, Collins
	31/03/92	Rangers	Hampden	0-1	
1992-93	09/01/93	Clyde	a	0-0	

	20/01/93	Clyde	h	1-0	Coyne
	06/02/93	Falkirk	a	0-2	
1993-94	29/01/94	Motherwell	a	0-1	
1994-95	28/01/95	St.Mirren	h	2-0	van Hooijdonk, Falconer
	18/02/95	Meadowbank	h	3-0	van Hooijdonk 2, Falconer
	10/03/95	Kilmarnock	h	1-0	Collins
	07/04/95	Hibernian	Ibrox	0-0	
	11/04/95	Hibernian	Ibrox	3-1	Falconer, Collins, O'Donnell
	27/05/95	Airdrie	Hampden	1-0	van Hooijdonk
1995-96	27/01/96	Whitehill Wel	a	3-0	van Hooijdonk 2, Donnelly
	17/02/96	Raith Rovers	h	2-0	Donnelly, Thom
	10/03/96	Dundee Utd	h	2-1	van Hooijdonk, Thom
	07/04/96	Rangers	Hampden	1-2	van Hooijdonk.